DEVELOPING SUCCESSFUL WORKER CO-OPERATIVES

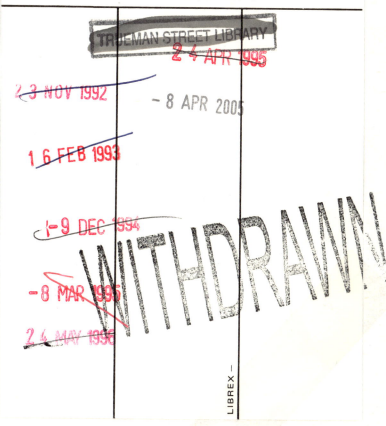

This book is to be returned on or before
the last date stamped below.

Developing Successful Worker Co-operatives

Chris Cornforth, Alan Thomas,
Jenny Lewis and Roger Spear

SAGE Publications
London • Newbury Park • Beverly Hills • New Delhi

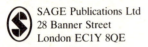
SAGE Publications Ltd
28 Banner Street
London EC1Y 8QE

SAGE Publications Inc
2111 West Hillcrest Drive
Newbury Park, California 91320

SAGE Publications Inc
275 South Beverly Drive
Beverly Hills, California 90212

SAGE Publications India Pvt Ltd
32, M-Block Market
Greater Kailash – I
New Delhi 110 048

British Library Cataloguing in Publication Data

Developing successful worker co-operatives
  1. Great Britain. Workers' cooperatives
  I. Cornforth, Chris
  334'.6'0941

ISBN 0-8039-8076-0
ISBN 0-8039-8077-9 Pbk

Library of Congress catalog card number 88-061786

Printed in Great Britain by J.W. Arrowsmith Ltd, Bristol

Contents

List of Tables and Figures   vii
Preface and Acknowledgements   ix

1   Introduction   1
Framework of the research   2
The historical development of worker co-operatives
   in the UK   10
Our research and this book   21

**2   The Worker Co-operative Sector:
     Extent, Survival and Growth**   24
The spread of worker co-operatives in the UK   24
Survival rates and growth of worker co-operatives   30
Summary   38

**3   Economic Aspects of Co-operative
     Performance**   40
Economic theories of co-operative performance   40
The performance of co-operatives in clothing, printing
   and wholefoods   48
Conclusions: financing, dependency and other factors   64

**4   Factors Affecting Co-operative Business
     Development: Sixteen Cases**   68
'Commercially marginal' co-operatives   71
'Self-developing' co-operatives   77
'Capitalised' co-operatives   83
Factors affecting co-operatives' business development   88

**5   The Costs and Benefits of Co-operative
     Working**   93
The benefits of co-operative working   97
The costs of co-operation   103
Balancing costs and benefits   107

6   Democratic Control or Degeneration?   112
The degeneration thesis   112
Avoiding constitutional degeneration: the open
   membership principle   120

The priorities of worker co-operatives: resisting
  goal degeneration   122
Resisting organisational degeneration   127
The record to date: limited gains   132

7   Co-operative Management   134
Management in simple collectives and its limitations   138
Complex collective structures   142
Leadership and initiative   146
Democratising established structures   148
New roles for managers   152
Conclusions   154

8   'For the Benefit of the Members'   155
Conflict in co-operatives   157
Promoting members' interests and handling
  conflict constructively   163
Keeping co-operative principles alive   171

**9   The Role and Impact of Co-operative Support
   Organisations**   173
Background and funding   174
Control and accountability   177
The provision of services   179
The impact on job creation   189
Strengthening the current support structure   190

**10   Building New Theory: Typology and
   Life-cycles**   193
Summary of findings in relation to theory   193
Concepts and ideas for the future   200

**11   Strengthening the Worker Co-operative
   Sector**   210
Low rate of formation – the entrepreneurial problem   211
Finance   212
Management   218
Co-operative working   220
Internal limits to growth   222
The place of co-operatives in the economy   223
Co-operative support   224
Prospects   227

References   229
Index   237

Tables and Figures

Tables

1.1 A preliminary typology of worker co-operatives   9
2.1 Estimated numbers of worker co-operatives and approximate numbers of jobs in such co-operatives, 1980–1986   25
2.2 Size distribution of worker co-operatives   26
2.3 Numbers of co-operatives and jobs in co-operatives, by sector and major sub-sector, early 1987   27
2.4 Regional distribution of co-operatives and co-operative jobs, early 1987   28
2.5 Estimated formation, numbers and failure rate of worker co-operatives each year from 1975   33
2.6 Year by year failure rate for co-operatives up to end of fifth year after start (plus comparison with all businesses)   35
2.7 Comparison of survival rates of co-operatives and businesses with different types of support   37
3.1 Average financial ratios for clothing co-operatives, 1980–3   50
3.2 Financial indicators for two selected clothing co-operatives   53
3.3 Average financial ratios for new printing co-operatives, 1979–83   55
3.4 Financial indicators for three selected printing co-operatives   57
3.5 Average financial ratios for wholefood co-operatives, 1979–84   61
3.6 Financial indicators for three selected wholefood co-operatives   63
4.1 The sixteen case studies   69
4.2 Approximate incidence of different patterns of business development in different sectors   89
5.1 Orientations to work   97

Figures

4.1 Schematic representation of main patterns of business development in different sectors   70

Preface and Acknowledgements

Research on worker co-operatives has been in progress at the Open University since 1977. In the early days there were not that many co-operatives to study. Our research focussed on the internal aspects of co-operatives, on issues such as the impact of participation on workers' attitudes and job satisfaction, and the development of democratic structures and their effect on power relations within the enterprise. We concentrated in particular on the study of larger co-operatives including both 'endowed' co-operatives and 'rescues' and were concerned to examine their relevance for other forms of industrial democracy.

As the worker co-operative sector developed so our research interests broadened. A number of very idealistic co-operatives started from scratch in the 1970s under the influence of the alternative movement. Then, with growing unemployment in the late 1970s and early 1980s came a very significant development: the promotion of co-operatives by government agencies and some local authorities as a means of job creation. This resulted in the establishment of various co-operative support organisations (CSOs), and we began research to examine the role and impact of CSOs and the factors affecting the development of worker co-operatives as businesses.

By 1983 we felt that the co-operative sector had expanded sufficiently to warrant a major research project. The main focus of the project was to examine how worker co-operatives performed, as businesses and as democratic workplaces. We also wanted to investigate what problems and barriers inhibited their development and how these might be overcome. With respect to this last point we aimed to discover what impact CSOs were having in expanding the sector and in assisting the development of individual co-operatives. We were successful in obtaining funding for this project from the Leverhulme Trust. It commenced at the beginning of 1984 and lasted for three years. This book presents the results of that research.

During the course of this work we were helped and assisted by a great many people and organisations and we would like to express our gratitude to them. First and foremost we would like to thank all those from co-operatives and local CSOs who gave up some of their valuable time to take part in the research. Thanks are due to David Hill and Susan Haberis, our editors, who played an important part in shaping the book and showed great patience as we overshot deadlines. Especial thanks to Richard Macfarlane, John Woolham, Nick Oliver and Ben Plumpton who worked as consultants to the project and prepared valuable case studies, and to David Ralley, Patrick Brown and Ian Brierley who gave us valuable support and guidance. We are also grateful to the many people who have provided insightful comments and suggestions on earlier drafts of chapters of the book, in particular Martin Honeywell, Martin Lockett, Jim Tomlinson, Jim Brown, Jenny Thornley, Janet Hannah, Keith Jefferis, Derek Pugh, Jim Curran, Rob Paton, Paul Chaplin, Peter Milford, John Berry, Martin Stott, Chloe Munro and others so numerous we are bound to forget someone! Our heartfelt thanks also go to Doreen Pendlebury, Bernie Lake, June McGowan and Jennie Moffatt, who all helped to type the manuscript – at times they must have thought it would never end. Finally we would like to acknowledge our debt to the Leverhulme Trust whose grant made our research possible.

Chris Cornforth
Alan Thomas
Jenny Lewis
Roger Spear
Walton Hall, January 1988

1
Introduction

During the last decade there has been a dramatic revival in the worker co-operative movement in Britain. After nearly seventy years of slow but steady decline, new co-operatives began to be formed again. From a low point of about thirty-five co-operatives in the early 1970s their numbers have grown steadily, passing the thousand mark in 1985. This growth has been accompanied by the formation of approximately eighty funded co-operative support organisations (CSOs). The movement has attracted a great deal of interest from the media, policy-makers and the public, who have seen in co-operatives the possibility of addressing some of the most persistent social and economic problems of our day. This positive view of the potential of worker co-operatives has been reinforced by a growing awareness of the very successful worker co-operative sectors in Italy, Catalonia and France and in particular of the Mondragon group of co-operatives in the Basque region of Spain.

Although historically worker co-operatives had their roots in the struggles of working people to overcome the exploitation that they suffered during the birth of the Industrial Revolution in Britain, increasingly they are no longer the sole preserve of the labour movement. In fact, worker co-operatives have both supporters and detractors amongst all the main political parties in Britain. However, advocates of co-operatives in each party see their potential very differently. The left sees worker co-operatives as a means of increasing workers' control over the means of production, increasing the local accountability of industry and creating new jobs in keeping with socialist values. In contrast, the right sees co-operatives as a way of making workers capitalists, bringing them into contact with the 'realities' of the market and so reducing what they see as unrealistic wage demands. The parties of the centre see co-operatives as a way of reconciling the interests of labour and capital, so reducing 'unnecessary' industrial conflict.

At a more mundane level worker co-operatives have been advocated as a potential solution to several specific problems. Co-operatives have been seen as a means of reducing the level of industrial conflict and enhancing productivity by aligning the interests of workers with those of their firm. They have been advocated as a means of creating more and better jobs and have figured quite prominently in a variety of local economic initiatives. It has also been argued that co-operatives will be more socially responsible as employers and businesses because of their control by the workforce, and because of workers' links with the local community. Clearly such significant claims require detailed examination and scrutiny.

In this book we try to avoid the over-simple views about co-operation that lie behind the divergent rhetoric of different political parties. However, we recognise the importance of the political as well as economic context in which co-operatives find themselves, and the possibility of defining success in political as well as economic or social terms. Our main aim is to examine how worker co-operatives work in practice, both as businesses and as democratic workplaces. We describe and analyse the main problems and barriers faced in developing successful worker co-operatives and consider how these might be overcome. We also evaluate some of the main policy initiatives designed to encourage co-operative development, and suggest ways in which these policies could be improved.

Before beginning this examination of the performance of worker co-operatives in Britain today we have three tasks for this introductory chapter. The first is to present the conceptual framework used to structure our research, which underlies much of the analysis presented in this book. It is particularly important to be explicit about our own assumptions in a field such as co-operation which has been the subject of analysis from a variety of academic and political perspectives. The framework is constructed by drawing upon a variety of concepts from different disciplines. Although the components of the framework are well established, we believe we have broken new ground in the way that we have combined them and applied them to study worker co-operation.

The second task is to relate briefly the background to the current wave of worker co-operatives. Worker co-operatives have a long history in Britain and it is important to understand how attitudes and relationships have developed which have helped to shape the worker co-operative movement today.

Finally we describe what research we undertook and how it combined the analysis of aggregate data with case studies of individual co-operatives. We close the chapter by explaining how the rest of the book is set out on the basis of this research.

Framework of the research

In order to locate our framework relative to the main debates concerning worker co-operatives, this section first defines a worker co-operative and then gives a brief critical overview of some of the different positions and views taken in the literature; more detailed treatments of the literature are given in appropriate chapters later in the book.

Defining a worker co-operative

There is no one definition of a worker co-operative. As we have suggested already the meaning of worker co-operation varies quite widely. However, common to most definitions is the idea of a business wholly, or substantially, owned and controlled by those who work in it and run for their mutual benefit. For our purposes a worker co-operative is a business in which the workers retain a majority control of the enterprise; control is exercised democratically on the basis of one person one vote; membership is open as far as possible to all workers; and there are limits on the returns to capital invested in the enterprise.

Open membership, democratic control and limited return on capital are three of the six internationally agreed co-operative principles that are applied by the International Co-operative Alliance to all types of co-operative. The others are equitable distribution of surplus, commitment to social and educational aims and co-operation between co-operatives. Thus, worker co-operatives can allow some external shareholding as long as workers retain formal control. As we will see later in the chapter this can be difficult to maintain without an appropriate legislative framework or constitution for the co-operative which safeguards workers' rights. The pattern of ownership can vary from purely individual shareholding on the one hand to the situation where the business as a whole is owned collectively by the workforce on the other.

In the UK the majority of the current wave of worker co-operatives are common ownership enterprises, where ownership is entirely collective apart from a nominal £1 shareholding by each member. As a result all capital has to be raised in the form of loans or built up from retained surpluses. These co-operatives exclude external shareholding. In the case of liquidation any residual assets must be given to another co-operative or to charity. Common ownership enterprises can register under the Companies Act or the Industrial and Provident Societies Act, and have limited liability.

The background theoretical and political debate

Theoretical discussion and empirical research on worker co-operatives are fragmented and often contradictory. Much of the theoretical debate on their potential has been drawn along political lines. Co-operatives have attracted both supporters and detractors from across the political spectrum.

On the left the supporters of worker co-operatives see them as a means of increasing workers' control within the enterprise, and as a step towards greater workers' control over the economy (Coates, 1976b; GLEB 1984; Taylor, 1981). Increased workers' control within the enterprise is often seen as unproblematic and guaranteed by the legal structure of co-operatives (see, for example, Bray and Falk, 1974). In contrast, the critics of co-operatives on the left emphasise that co-operatives can only be 'islands of socialism in a sea of capitalism'. They emphasise that the wider forces of capitalism will not be challenged by co-operatives, and that these forces will dictate how co-operatives behave. Consequently, rather than challenging capital, co-operatives will become capitalist (Clarke, 1979; Mandel, 1975; Webb and Webb, 1914, 1920). This debate has been conducted largely at a theoretical level, and often only a very selective use has been made of empirical findings.

As Tomlinson (1981) has argued, neither of these positions is adequate. The arguments of the critics are a form of economic determinism; while economic forces are an important constraint they do not completely determine the organisation and management of an enterprise or the goals that it pursues. On the other hand, the supporters of co-operatives do not adequately consider the organi-sational problems and external constraints on achieving democratic control. A new position is required which does not regard democracy within co-operatives as either impossible or inevitable, but instead as subject to *choice and constraint.*

This view is implicit in the work of Thornley (1981). She recognises that to survive co-operatives must operate within and to some extent constrained by the market, but that they can still represent a challenge to capital. Her book is important in broadening the terms of the debate on the left in the UK, by examining the larger worker co-operative sectors in France and Italy. Her analysis emphasises the importance of co-operatives building political alliances and secondary support organisations which can then actively mediate between co-operatives and wider market forces.

The debate concerning co-operatives on the right is less developed. The attraction lies in making workers capitalists (Bradley and Gelb, 1983), and in the ideal of 'self-help', for example workers getting together to create their own jobs. The Conservative minister Kenneth Clarke has expressed support for co-operatives as long as they do not require government support or intervention, but operate in the market and adopt efficient forms of management. However, suspicions are often aroused that co-operatives are socialist in orientation. In addition, many believe that workers will not be able to manage an enterprise successfully. These criticisms of worker co-operatives echo those of various neo-classical economists discussed on the next page.

The appeal of co-operatives to those in the middle of the political spectrum is in their potential to do away with conflict between labour and capital (Jay, 1980; Oakeshott, 1978; Young and Rigge, 1983). It is argued that, as workers will be the owners of the enterprise and benefit financially from its success, the damaging conflict of interests between workers and management will be removed, improving worker motivation and productivity. While the return on capital is limited, they also believe co-operatives will reduce the power of trade unions. Oakeshott (1978: 243) identifies the main problem with co-operatives in the past as their weak and undynamic management, although he also recognises that lack of capital and a hostile environment have been problems. He, like Thornley, looks abroad to see how these problems could be overcome and draws his main inspiration from the Mondragon co-operatives in Spain. He argues that to prosper co-operatives in Britain need a support structure like the Mondragon co-operatives and should include a meaningful element of individual ownership rather than just common ownership. However, having ruled out political alliances with the left or the right, his book gives very little indication how a Mondragon-style support structure could work in a different cultural and economic context.

The view that co-operatives will do away with conflict between labour and capital or labour and management is over-simple. Altering economic relationships within a few firms will not significantly alter the wider relations and forces within the economy as a whole. In addition, the potential for conflicts of interest within the firm will still remain, although in a different form. For example the long-term economic interests of the firm may not coincide with workers' immediate interests. However, this perspective is important in highlighting the fact that increased worker ownership and participation are likely to have important effects on the relationships between workers and managers.

Another important source of theorising about worker co-operatives and self-managed firms is within economics. Building on the work of Ward (1958), an economic theory of self-management has been developed by theorists like Vanek (1970) and Meade (1972) using the theoretical and methodological apparatus of neo-classical economics. Much of this work has been rather pessimistic about the relative efficiency of self-managed firms as compared with capitalist enterprises (Alchian and Demsetz, 1972; Furubotn and Pejovich, 1970; Jensen and Meckling, 1979). The theory is based on neo-classical assumptions such as perfect competition, and disregards both collective goals and social processes within the firms and wider social and political processes (see Lichtenstein, 1986; Mygind, 1986). We believe this means it is of limited utility for understanding the performance of a self-managed or worker co-operative sector, though it can still be a useful source of hypotheses.

Empirical research on co-operatives in the UK has been either limited in scope or restricted to the detailed analysis of a few cases. Economists such as Jones (1975, 1976, 1982) have concentrated on examining the historical performance of co-operatives established at the turn of the century. Thornley and Oakeshott have focussed on the comparative development of the worker co-operative sectors in different countries. Case studies have concentrated primarily on the organisational and business problems of a few co-operatives, particularly larger co-operatives formed from the conversion of successful firms like Scott Bader (Blum, 1968; Paton, 1978a) or to rescue failed businesses (Bradley and Gelb, 1983; Coates, 1976a; Eccles, 1981; Wajcman, 1983). There has been little research on those co-operatives formed from scratch as new businesses, and little on the economic performance of the new wave of worker co-operatives.

It was against this background that our research was framed. It was guided by a number of key assumptions and concepts, which we have made into a four-part framework, outlined below.

Wider social and economic relationships
Perhaps the most fundamental of our assumptions is that any enterprise (or individual, for that matter) is caught up in a web of social and economic relationships that go beyond the boundary of the organisation. It is not possible fully to understand the behaviour of any enterprise without taking into account these wider social and economic relationships.

This assumption permeates our analysis in a number of ways. For example, the business performance of co-operatives is considered with regard to their position in the broader economy, and more particularly within their particular economic sector. This perspective leads us to give prominence to the role of support organisations (and, potentially, the wider co-operative movement) in mediating between co-operatives and their market and institutional environment. At the individual level we consider how factors outside the workplace, such as workers' domestic situations, help to shape their attitudes towards and expectations of work in co-operatives.

Constraint and choice
As we have indicated, we are critical of the simplistic generalisations often made about co-operatives. We reject the view that democratic control will not be possible because of economic or organisational pressures. However, we recognise, unlike many advocates of co-operatives, that achieving democratic control is likely to be problematic. We adopt the position that the achievement of organisational democracy, and other goals that co-operatives may pursue, will be constrained by both environmental and organisational pressures, but that this still leaves some freedom of manoeuvre for co-operators to exercise choice over the form and goals of their organisation.

Various important constraints are analysed during the course of the book: market forces and dependency relationships; the practices of financial institutions; workers' needs and expectations; the requirements of effective management as an enterprise grows. For example, we consider how the sector in which a co-operative operates constrains its economic performance.

Unlike much neo-classical economic theory of self-managed firms we do not assume that workers' choices will be solely governed by their desire to maximise their own income. Instead we assume that workers will attempt to pursue a mixture of individual and collective objectives. As Mygind (1986) has argued, if members of co-operatives had no collective objectives then it is unlikely that they would establish a co-operative in the first place.

A dynamic approach

The third important aspect of our approach is to regard co-operatives as dynamic and changing both as businesses and as organisations (Kimberley and Miles, 1980; Lichtenstein, 1986). Our aim is to examine whether these changes follow any identifiable patterns, and to try to understand the forces and processes that give rise to them.

A starting point for our work was the classical thesis of Beatrice and Sydney Webb (1914, 1920, 1921), that worker co-operatives would either 'degenerate' or fail as businesses. This is in line with the strong tradition of pessimism in the social sciences concerning the efficiency of democratic organisations (Weber, 1968) and their susceptibility to oligarchic tendencies (Meister 1974, 1984; Michels, 1949). However, Jones (1975) has challenged the Webbs' analysis and interpretation of their results, and Batstone (1983) has questioned Meister's findings to suggest that democracy may be revived after a process of decline. In addition, other studies have suggested that under certain conditions worker co-operatives and other democratic forms of organisation can survive and maintain their democratic goals (Bernstein, 1976; Rothschild-Whitt, 1976, 1979). We adopt the position that although there are often strong pressures towards degeneration they can be resisted. In addition, pressures for regeneration can also arise, for example from new social movements sharing similar democratic goals. Our aim was to examine the pressures and problems co-operatives faced in trying to achieve their social and economic goals, and the actions that were taken to attempt to overcome them.

This dynamic perspective had important consequences for our empirical research. Where possible we examined performance at various points in time. On the economic performance of co-operatives we built up a data base using the annual returns submitted by the co-operatives to the Registrar of Friendly Societies or Companies House. Our case studies were carried out over a period of one to two years, and longer in one instance where we were able to revisit a co-operative we had already studied. In addition, we gathered information about the history of each of the cases from long-standing members and from written records.

Co-operators and co-operatives are not homogeneous
The divergent findings concerning worker co-operatives are not just a result of the different political and theoretical orientations of observers but also reflect substantive differences between co-operators and co-operatives.

Our own previous research has shown that co-operation means different things to different people. This is shaped by people's back-grounds and experiences and the social setting in which co-operatives arise. For example, a co-operative might be seen by a group of redundant workers as a way of creating their own jobs and escaping the vagaries of working for a capitalist employer. On the other hand, a group setting up a wholefood co-operative might see it as an expression of their political beliefs, for example as a means of achieving a more egalitarian society based on consumption for need rather than profit. We felt that a lack of appreciation of the different meanings that co-operatives had for people and the different goals that they pursued meant that co-operatives were often evaluated using inappropriate criteria, or that attempts to generalise research findings were ill founded. Our own approach assumes that the population of worker co-operatives is not homogeneous. During the course of the book we construct various typologies of worker co-operatives, to try to describe and hopefully explain some of their differences.

We started our research with a typology grounded in our previous analysis of a number of the 'new wave' co-operatives (Cornforth, 1983; Lockett, 1980; Paton, 1978b). This work led us to believe that the social and economic circumstances in which a co-operative was formed, and the orientation of the founder members, were very important factors in shaping how a co-operative develops. Inevitably these are not the only factors, but we felt that they gave the most useful way of categorising co-operatives available, although the typology's relevance is probably limited to the formative years of co-operatives.

Table 1.1 shows the typology in schematic form. It distinguishes three main ways in which co-operatives can be formed. Some are attempts to save all or part of a business that has failed or is failing. In other cases, a viable private business may be converted into a co-operative. Thirdly, they may be started up as new businesses from scratch.

The typology also distinguishes three dominant forms of motivation for establishing co-operatives. First, since the days of Robert Owen, co-operatives have appealed to philanthropic owners and entrepreneurs keen to reform what they perceive as injustices in the present system. 'Endowed' co-operatives, like Scott Bader (Blum, 1968), are formed when the original owners decide to hand their business over to the workforce. Although small in number, some 'endowed'

Table 1.1 *A preliminary typology of worker co-operatives*

Origin of co-operative	Dominant Motivation behind formation		
	Philanthropic	Radical/ idealistic	Job creation/ saving
Failing firm			'Rescue' and 'phoenix' co-operatives
Conversion of viable business	'Endowed' co-operatives	E.g. 'alternative' conversions	
New start	'Philanthropic new-start' co-operatives	E.g. 'alternative' co-operatives	'Job-creation' co-operatives

co-operatives are significantly larger than the majority of co-operatives in Britain. In addition, a small number of 'philanthropic new-start' co-operatives have been formed by altruistic entrepreneurs (Oakeshott, 1978; Tynan, 1980a, 1980b).

Secondly, certain groups are motivated to form co-operatives because they see co-operation as a means of pursuing their radical ideals. Perhaps the most common of these are what we have called 'alternative' co-operatives, drawing their idealism from the alternative movements of the 1960s and 1970s (Thornley, 1981). Their ideals often include a commitment to participatory democracy, equality and production for need rather than profit. However, other radical philosophies such as that espoused by the workers' control movement (Coates, 1976a) have also inspired the formation of some co-operatives. The majority of 'radical' co-operatives are 'new starts', although some have been formed as partnerships which effectively worked co-operatively and then formally converted into co-operatives.

Thirdly, people have been motivated to form co-operatives by the pragmatic desire to create or save jobs. Most of these are small 'job-creation' co-operatives started from scratch, often with the assistance of a local co-operative support organisation. Others have been formed to save jobs on the closure of all or part of a business, either as 'rescue' co-operatives where workers take over all or part of the ailing firm, or as 'phoenix' co-operatives where some workers set up a new enterprise to take on part of the old business (Coates, 1976a; Eccles, 1981; Paton, et al., 1987; Thomas and Thornley, 1988; Wajcman, 1983).

As with many typologies the boundaries between these different types of co-operative are often blurred. Not all 'job-creation/saving' co-operatives are entirely pragmatic in their orientation; they may also be inspired by radical ideals such as workers' control. 'Radical' co-operatives are often motivated by more pragmatic ideals of creating good jobs for their members. In using the typology we have had to make quite difficult judgements on which motivations dominated in a particular co-operative.

The historical development of worker co-operatives in the UK

Historical roots

Worker co-operatives, along with other forms of co-operative, have their origins in the late eighteenth and early nineteenth centuries. They were born out of the hardship and exploitation that many people suffered as the Industrial Revolution gathered momentum in Britain. The social and economic upheaval this produced led both workers and wealthy philanthropists to experiment with new forms of association and business in order to improve the conditions of working people.

Many of the early attempts to form co-operatives were motivated by people's desire to obtain unadulterated food at a reasonable price. One of the first co-operative flour mills was set up in Hull in 1765 (Thornley, 1981: 12). Essentially these were structured as consumer co-operatives, i.e. they were owned and controlled by those who consumed their produce. Attempts to form co-operatives of workers were often motivated by craftsmen trying to protect their jobs and their crafts against competition from new industrial processes. However, these were isolated endeavours not linked by any shared philosophy and did not constitute a movement.

It was the writings and activities of Robert Owen that provided the philosophy and examples which inspired the development of the co-operative movement. Owen's philosophy arose both from the need for an efficient workforce in his factories and as a response to the desperate unemployment and poverty that characterised the early nineteenth century. Owen believed that 'man's character is made for, not by, him'. He believed that the fiercely competitive capitalist environment of the time was not capable of producing a happy and moral people. Like many at the time he believed that such a capitalist system could not prevail. For Owen the solution lay in establishing small villages or communities organising their own agriculture and industry, based on principles of co-operation rather than competition. These villages would be communally owned, and labour would not be exploited but would get the full value of its product by means of the direct exchange of goods (Pollard, 1960). Owen's critique of the existing system and vision of the future found widespread support among the working class, 'because his ideas were the one coherent expression of a widespread sentiment' (Cole, 1925: 193).

A major flaw with Owen's scheme was that there was no obvious way in which such co-operative communities could be established. Owen looked to the philanthropy of the rich, but met with only limited success. Working-class co-operative associations began to look to their own resources, but even with regular subscription the means for establishing communities was beyond them. In 1827 William Bryon of Brighton proposed that co-operative associations establish their own retail stores and use the profits from trade. The idea of co-operative storekeeping was propagated widely by William King in his influential paper *The Co-operator*, started in 1828, and spread rapidly. However, the ideal of the co-operative movement was still to establish co-operative communities, and the stores were seen as a means to that end.

The trade unions, legalised in 1824, were another source of co-operative societies. As with other working-class leaders, many trade union organisers were influenced by Owenism. Co-operative societies were formed by the unemployed, or to support members during strikes, or by workers during lock-outs in order to put pressure on employers. Again a mixture of pragmatism and idealism inspired these ventures. Some were a temporary response to prevailing economic conditions; others struggled on, striving towards Owen's vision of a new society (Bonner, 1961: 26).

As with small capitalist businesses the failure rate of these early co-operative societies was quite high. Bonner (1961: 39) puts the failures down both to internal weaknesses, such as poor management and occasional dishonesty, and to external causes, including paradoxically the social movements of the time:

> The struggle for the Reform Bill, the agitation for factory legislation, the revolt against the new poor law, and the Chartist movement, with their exciting mass demonstrations, great expectations, and the sense of those taking part of being involved in matters of great moment and of making history, must have made the little co-operative store or productive society appear humdrum and rather inconsequential affairs.

As we will see later in this book, Bonner's analysis has some parallels today. The fortunes of the new wave of worker co-operatives are also affected both by changing economic and social circumstances and by internal problems such as lack of skills and experience in business management.

Owen attempted to unite the idealistic co-operative societies and the new militant trade unions. In 1833 a meeting of trade unions and co-operative societies decided to form the Grand National Moral Union of Useful and Productive Classes, which led to the formation of the Grand National Consolidated Trade Union in 1834. This was an amalgamation of existing unions and co-operative societies. Its membership expanded rapidly, but it was short lived. From the start the union was under pressure. It faced hostility from government and employers. Its financial base was weakened by the need to support members on strike or locked out by employers. In addition, the union suffered from internal conflicts between Owen and other leaders over whether social change could be brought about through reform or class warfare. The collapse of the Grand National Trade Union brought down or weakened many trade unions and co-operative societies, and the co-operative movement fragmented (Pollard, 1960: 88).

Although some of the initial fervour may have waned, interest in Owen's vision of co-operation lived on. During the 1840s various 'redemptionist societies', led by the Leeds Society, continued to gather funds to establish co-operative communities which emphasised the need 'to retain for the worker the whole produce of labour in order to end poverty and raise the working class morally and intellectually' (Pollard, 1960: 91). Two other initiatives were also started in the 1840s which were to have a profound impact on the direction and leadership of the co-operative movement during the remainder of the century. First, in 1844 a group of weavers in Rochdale launched a co-operative society which, due to its commercial success, became the model for consumer co-operation throughout the world. Second, in 1848 a group of middle-class lawyers and clerics formed the Christian Socialists, who campaigned to change society through the establishment of co-operative workshops.

The Rochdale Equitable Pioneers' Society started with the aim of establishing a co-operative community and emancipating labour from capitalist exploitation. Their co-operative store was to be the first step in this process. However, over time, the leadership became more and more involved in the operation and expansion of the successful society and diverted from the original ideals. An important factor in this process was the early decision by the Pioneers to pay a dividend on purchases. Although this was probably only a pragmatic device to attract custom to the stores it represented a major break with Owenism. The surplus from trading was no longer entirely for community funds, but a proportion was given back to individuals for their own benefit. This resulted in attracting members interested in immediate economic benefits who did not necessarily share the society's original ideals.

Such developments were part of a more general trend within the co-operative and labour movements during the 1840s and 1850s (Pollard, 1960). As economic conditions gradually improved and the Factory Acts restrained some of the worst excesses of exploitation, many working-class organisations became more oriented to accepting the capitalist system and improving the workers' lot within it rather than replacing it.

This conflict between the original ideals of the movement and the pragmatism of many newer members was also evident in the Rochdale Society's attempt to establish co-operative workshops. Inspired by their original ideals, in 1854 they set up a cotton mill, the Rochdale Co-operative Manufacturing Society, as a joint stock company with shareholding open to workers and outside members. Workers were paid a dividend and had some say in the direction of the enterprise. The business was successful, and in 1859 a decision was made to build a new mill. New external shareholders were attracted in order to raise capital. The new members objected to the bonus for workers, and the latter's influence diminished. By 1862 the co-operative had been transformed into a capitalist firm owned and controlled by external shareholders (Bonner, 1961).

The Rochdale Co-operative Manufacturing Society provides an early example of what became known as the 'degeneration' of producer co-operatives into capitalist enterprises. This phenomenon, and whether or not it is inevitable, is an important theme throughout this book.

The Christian Socialists were social reformers, again dedicated to overcoming the poverty and unemployment of the working classes, though their solutions were more limited than Owen's vision. Inspired by the *Associations d'Ouvriers* established after the revolution in France, they advocated setting up 'self-governing' workshops, which would be owned and controlled by the workers who worked in them. A number of workshops ('philanthropic new-start' co-operatives in the terms of our typology) were established between 1850 and 1852, usually at the initiative of, and funded by, their Christian Socialist promoters. Most were short lived, and illustrate the problems, still relevant today, of trying to form co-operatives 'top-down'.

The workshops suffered a number of internal problems. Workers were not carefully selected, and there was no training in co-operative principles. In addition, many members were not used to the factory system and the discipline it imposed. The managers were chosen by the promoters rather than the workforce. As a result there was poor discipline and frequent quarrelling between managers and workers. The workers also lacked knowledge of the commercial and administrative aspects of running a business.

External circumstances and pressures worked against these co-operative workshops as well. They suffered from discrimination by suppliers who refused normal trade credit. They also had difficulty in establishing a market, partly because of subsequent downturns in the economy and partly because the workers did not have access to many of the customary channels through which business was conducted.

The Christian Socialists had more success and influence in other areas. Most notably they sponsored the Industrial and Provident Societies Act which was passed in 1852 and, for the first time, gave co-operatives a specific legal framework within which to operate. A number of Christian Socialists, most notably E.V. Neale, became active in the co-operative movement, and eventually Neale became the first general secretary of the Co-operative Union. Neale advocated that the immediate objective of the co-operative movement should be to establish producer co-operatives backed by the successful consumer co-operative stores which would also provide their market. He believed that it was through the spread of producer co-operatives that workers could escape the exploitation of capital.

Unfortunately by comparison with consumer co-operatives, there was no clear model for producer co-operatives, and in particular no clear agreement on the role of workers. Many producer co-operatives based their model of membership on the community. In such circumstances it was unclear who should be the prime beneficiary of the co-operative, and without safeguards for workers' interests it was possible for external shareholders to dominate, as at Rochdale. Where consumer societies and trade unions sponsored producer co-operatives they often retained control in order to safeguard their investments. This has parallels with at least one modern rescue co-operative (Uglow, 1985).

Other protagonists viewed co-operation primarily as a new means of distributing profits to consumers and producers rather than capitalists (Milford, 1986: 127). As a result a producer co-operative was seen simply as an enterprise in which workers shared in the profits. Even some capitalist companies that started profit-sharing schemes were hailed as examples of producer co-operation. As with some employee share ownership schemes today, these schemes were largely inspired by the need to gain greater productivity and commitment from labour. However, they generally gave few if any rights to workers to influence the control of the enterprise. As economic circumstances changed many profit-sharing schemes were abandoned.

The model of self-governing workshops, although including a strong element of paternalistic guidance, most clearly embodied principles of workers' control. However, associations of workers alone had difficulties raising capital. The failure of the Christian Socialist workshops also tended to discredit the idea. In addition, the model did not recognise or formalise the links with the consumer co-operative movement that Neale and his followers envisaged.

By the 1860s and 1870s many consumer co-operative societies were very successful. Many of their leaders decided to invest their surplus capital to further co-operative production. Investments were made in a range of industries including engineering, coal-mining and textiles, and over two hundred co-operatives were formed (Thornley, 1981: 22). Without constitutions that established and safeguarded the rights of workers, many became dominated by outside interests such as consumer societies, trade unions or other external shareholders. In common with other new enterprises many of these societies also failed. Some suffered from poor management and internal disputes. Others were established too hastily in highly risky businesses, and many were hit by the downturn of trade during the Great Depression (Bonner, 1961: 113). In consequence a number of consumer co-operative societies, including the Co-operative Wholesale Society, established in 1863, lost money in the failure of productive societies.

During the last quarter of the nineteenth century there was a vigorous debate among the activists and leaders of the co-operative movement about how production should be organised. A number of societies, led by the successful and economically powerful Co-operative Wholesale Society (CWS), were keen to develop their own factories. They argued that attempts to establish producer co-operatives had ended in failure, and were not in the wider interests of consumers. The wider membership were largely apathetic towards these debates and member participation in meetings was often low. As Milford (1986: 130) notes: 'Consumer co-operation had become an institution of Victorian Society, functionally useful, but no longer an expression of a mass social movement seeking change.'

Gradually the CWS moved more and more into setting up its own factories. At first it was forced by advocates of producer co-operation to adopt a form of profit sharing in these factories, but this was abandoned twelve years later. By 1880 the number of productive societies had dwindled to fifteen. In reaction to this defeat Neale and others helped to establish the Co-operative Productive Federation (CPF) in 1882 to promote and assist producer co-operatives. 'It marked an acceptance of the failure to win the whole movement to their cause' (Milford, 1986: 130).

Nevertheless the formation of the CPF marked the beginning of a relatively successful and dynamic phase for producer co-operatives. In the ten years following the formation of the CPF the number of producer co-operatives trebled. Many were concentrated in the East Midlands in the footwear, hosiery and clothing industries, which were undergoing industrial change (Bonner, 1961: 115). Many were 'job-creation' or 'rescue' co-operatives formed out of strikes and lock-outs, often with union backing. These societies were often economically successful (Jones, 1976), and some survive to this day.

It is interesting to ask why these societies succeeded while many other types of producer co-operative had failed. A number of factors stand out. First, for the first time a clear model was developed, based on a partnership between consumers and producers. Workers had the right to become shareholders, share in the profits and take part in management. The other major shareholders were consumer co-operative societies, and occasionally trade unions. Producer co-operatives of this type became known as co-operative co-partnerships. Secondly, the co-operative societies provided much of the capital for these enterprises and a market for their products. They also had a say in management, which according to some observers helped to reinforce managerial authority and led to greater internal stability.

Although economically successful, co-partnerships stopped being formed in any quantity after 1914, and their numbers gradually declined. They faced continued hostility from the CWS. But perhaps more importantly they lost the ideological battle within the co-operative and labour movements. The attack against them was led by the Fabian Society and in particular Beatrice Potter, who later married Sydney Webb.

Beatrice and Sydney Webb (1914, 1920, 1921) gave a 'theoretical basis and justification for consumer co-operation' (Bonner, 1961: 136), while attacking the concept of producer co-operatives. They argued that the consumer interest was a universal interest, and that consumer co-operatives would do away with profit-making at the public expense. In contrast, they believed that producer co-operatives benefited only those who worked in them. They would compete with each other or combine to impose price and quality on the consumer. In addition, the Webbs concluded from their empirical studies that producer co-operatives would either fail or degenerate into capitalist firms. They pointed to past failures, highlighting weaknesses such as lack of capital, poor markets, inadequate skills and poor management (Thornley, 1981: 27) and those co-operatives that had become dominated by external shareholders or a minority of workers.

After that, political attitudes on the left towards producer or worker co-operatives were largely negative. Municipal enterprises and nationalisation began to dominate the thinking of the Labour Party and the trade unions in their pursuit of social ownership. A more decentralised vision of socialism was briefly revived with the rise of guild socialism (Cole, 1944: 284-292). Again this movement arose out of social and economic dislocations, this time produced by the end of the First World War. Guild socialism aimed to transfer industry and services to public ownership but with control delegated to guilds, including all workers. Industry was to be run to meet community need rather than profit. In 1920 a National Building Guild was formed encouraging the formation of building guilds. These guilds took the form of producer co-operatives (as the government of the day did not support public ownership). However, they did not admit profit sharing. The guilds were supported by trade unions and the CWS. They built for local authorities on contract and were favoured by the form of government subsidy at the time which made private contracts expensive. However, with a change in the system of subsidy the guilds collapsed.

Without ideological or practical support, producer co-operatives almost completely stopped being formed. They 'quite literally disappeared from the agendas of reformers, trade unionists and working people' (Bate and Carter, 1986: 59). Abell (1983) has associated the decline of worker co-operation with the lack of entrepreneurs attracted to the co-operative option, rather than with any inherent weakness in the way co-operatives perform. Indeed, many of the co-partnerships continued to perform well throughout the century (Jones, 1976). Some had a long period of successful trading but were unable to respond to the big market changes of the 1950s and 1960s with no strong movement to protect them (Bennett, 1984). By the time the 'new wave' of worker co-operation began in the 1970s, less than thirty co-partnerships remained, and most of these have now ceased trading.

The 'new wave' of worker co-operatives
As with the formation of co-operatives during the nineteenth and early twentieth centuries, the recent re-emergence of worker co-operatives in Britain can be linked to various economic, social and cultural dislocations of the capitalist system. This 'new wave' of worker co-operatives can be partly traced back to the activities of Ernest Bader in the 1950s, but since then two historical factors have been of crucial importance. The first was the development of a radical alternative culture during the 1960s with its critique of big business, bureaucracy and representative democracy. The second was the economic crisis of the 1970s and 1980s, which produced factory closures, mass redundancies and unemployment on a scale unparalleled since the 1930s.

Ernest Bader was a Quaker who converted his successful chemical business into the Scott Bader Commonwealth, a business owned in common by the workforce. In 1958 he founded an organisation called Democratic Integration in Industry (Demintry) to promote common ownership enterprises. Initially effort was directed at persuading others voluntarily to convert their businesses into common ownerships. This strategy met with very limited success, and Demintry had only five member organisations in 1971. About this time Demintry changed its name to the Industrial Common Ownership Movement (ICOM) and became more active in trying to promote new co-operatives, based on common ownership, and to secure wider support for co-operative development. However, it was not until the mid-1970s that the number of co-operatives really began to grow.

In 1976 the Labour government backed a Private Member's Bill, supported by ICOM, which became the Industrial Common Ownership Act. This gave legal recognition to common ownership enterprises and allocated £250,000 to provide finance for promotional bodies and to fund a small co-operative loan fund run by Industrial Common Ownership Finance (ICOF). Perhaps just as significantly, ICOM published that year a set of model rules which made it easier to register a business as a common ownership co-operative.

A large part of the initial impetus for forming new co-operatives came from the alternative movement. Many young people, influenced by the hippy and youth cultures of the 1960s, were concerned by what they saw as the damaging social and ecological consequences of modern industry and commerce, and by the hierarchical and authoritarian nature of many organisations. Some became involved in various collective or communal activities as a way of putting their beliefs into practice. Over time some of these activities were turned into businesses. There was a need for a legal form of enterprise that reflected these alternative values, and the ICOM model rules, with their embodiment of collective ownership, appealed to many. As a consequence many of the co-operatives set up in the mid- and late 1970s were in businesses where the product or service also embodied radical ideals: for example, wholesaling or retailing wholefoods, community printers and radical bookshops. These co-operatives brought new ideals into the co-operative movement with their commitment to non-hierarchical forms of working and to producing for social need. They have also provided an important source of able personnel to staff the local co-operative support organisations that began to be established in the late 1970s. However, like the founders of ICOM they had few links with the main political parties or the labour movement.

These developments gained little publicity. It was what came to be known as the 'Benn' co-operatives (Coates, 1976a; Eccles, 1981) that brought worker co-operatives into the public eye. These three co-operatives were formed out of failed private businesses where the workforce, led by their shop stewards, actively tried to resist closure. They occurred in 1974–5 during the height of a wave of worker 'sit-ins' protesting against business closures. Tony Benn, the Secretary of State for Industry in the Labour government of the time, offered these co-operatives financial support. However, the co-operatives were hastily established with inadequate planning and little or no provision for training in co-operative principles or practice, and were all under-capitalised. One failed quickly, but the other two survived for a number of years. Given the difficult circumstances of their formation, and their inadequate financing, it is unfair to label these efforts as complete failures; however, this was the main view expressed in the media. The effect, as happened during the last century, was to create an image that co-operatives were organisations of last resort and prone to failure.

Probably the most important development in the continuing revival of the worker co-operative sector has been the formation of local co-operative support organisations (CSOs). Originally these came from the efforts of small groups of local activists, radical professionals and politicians, influenced by the alternative movement and by other moves towards decentralised, grass-roots activity. CSOs can be seen partly as vehicles for promoting the ideals of co-operation, often specifically those of common ownership, and partly as one of a number of fragmented, pragmatic responses to increasing unemployment.

The first two CSOs were formed in Scotland and West Glamorgan in 1976 and 1978 respectively. By autumn 1986 approximately 100 of these organisations existed, and about 80 had obtained money to employ full-time development workers (CDA, 1986). Most of them are independent local co-operative development agencies (CDAs), but a small number are regionally rather than locally based, and a minority have been established as part of the local authority. The average size of those able to employ staff is just over three full-time equivalent posts. The majority of funding for CSOs has come from Labour-controlled councils or from central government grants aimed at rejuvenating urban areas which also require local government support.

As we will see in Chapters 2 and 9, the development of local CSOs has had a profound effect on the development of worker co-operatives. These agencies have directed resources to enabling the unemployed and disadvantaged to form 'job-creation' co-operatives, and have also assisted 'rescue' and 'phoenix' co-operatives, though in smaller numbers. Many of these co-operatives are in service sectors such as retailing, repair work and cleaning; others are in the low-capital areas of manufacturing such as the clothing industry. This is due partly to the limited financial resources that unemployed workers have to invest in their businesses, and to the limited financial resources available to CSOs for investing in co-operatives. In addition, the workers' skills are frequently in these areas. Most of these co-operatives are very small, the average size of a 'new start' being about four workers.

In the meantime, in 1978 the Labour government had passed a Bill, with all-party support, which established a small national Co-operative Development Agency (CDA). The proposal had been supported by all the different branches of the co-operative movement, although there were important differences over the role such an agency should have. Originally it was intended that the CDA should support all the different co-operative sectors, including housing co-operatives, credit unions and so on. In practice it decided to concentrate on what it called industrial and service co-operatives, which in the main meant worker co-operatives and to a lesser extent community co-operatives.

The board of the CDA and its first director were all appointed by the Secretary of State for Industry. The first director was formerly an under secretary in the Department of Industry with responsibility for small businesses, who had reached retiring age. He appointed a staff with little or no experience of the co-operative movement. ICOM had no representation on the CDA's board. The CDA was far removed both physically and in terms of experience from the majority of worker co-operatives in the UK.

In order to try to create what it saw as a respectable image for co-operatives the CDA tried to distance itself from 'rescues' like the Benn co-operatives, and put its initial efforts into trying to persuade people into converting their businesses into co-operatives. This met with little success.

Later under a new director, a senior manager seconded from the private sector and appointed by the Conservative government, the CDA has tried to promote co-operatives as another form of small business. During this phase it has been more successful. Most importantly it has promoted the spread of local CSOs, often obtaining support for new CSOs in non-Labour-controlled authorities, and to some extent has provided local support for co-operative development in areas without CSOs. It has also developed new model rules for co-operatives, published a regular directory of co-operatives and CSOs and liaised with government over legislation that will affect co-operatives.

However, relationships between the CDA and other sections of the worker co-operative movement have not always been good. Some of its actions have been controversial: for example, the promotion of co-operatives that allow external shareholding, and the encouragement of co-operatives in cases of privatisation. In particular, many have been disturbed by the lack of accountability of the CDA to the co-operative movement, particularly since democratic control is one of the basic co-operative principles. Despite these problems the CDA has demonstrated that there is a role for a national organisation to liaise with central government, to help co-ordinate statistics on the co-operative sector, to promote co-operative legislation and to help promote support for local CSOs.

As with the co-partnership model of the 1890s, ICOM's model of common ownership has been an important facilitating and unifying factor in the new wave of worker co-operatives. Local CSOs, sometimes staffed with ex-activists from alternative co-operatives, have usually promoted ICOM model rules. Independent local agencies have operated an informal network for several years, and this has recently formalised itself into a third national organisation, the National Network of Local Co-operative Development Agencies (NNLCDA). The network and ICOM between them form the idealistic wing of the new movement, for example pushing forward equal opportunities and opposing any links between co-operatives and privatisation.

On the other hand, in the most recent years the movement has also broadened, with a variety of new ideas in response to the unremitting depth of the unemployment problem. Large agencies cover the whole of Wales and Scotland respectively, the Wales Co-operative Centre being sponsored by the Wales TUC. In London, the West Midlands and elsewhere, Labour local authorities made co-operatives part of their economic development strategies at a regional level, and certain aspects of this have survived the demise of the Greater London Council and the metropolitan counties. Very recently there has been a trend towards the setting up of more very small local CSOs in shire county areas. Both ICOM and the national CDA have produced a variety of model rules for worker, community and secondary co-operatives. There have also been a number of new schemes for increasing investment in co-operatives.

Our research and this book

The research on which this book is based was conducted between January 1984 and December 1986. Our empirical work has been in three parts. Early on we surveyed local CSOs and later we did more detailed studies of two local CSOs and of one of the regional initiatives, the co-operative development work of the Greater London Enterprise Board under the GLC's London Industrial Strategy.

Second, we collected and analysed statistical data on the formation and survival of co-operatives, concentrating on the ten years since the Industrial Common Ownership Act, and more detailed financial data on co-operatives in printing, clothing manufacture and wholefoods. The latter data are most complete for the period 1978–83, so they miss the most recently formed co-operatives.

Finally, we conducted sixteen case studies of co-operatives, examining their development both as business and as democratic workplaces. Almost all our case studies were common ownership enterprises, though one remains an informal partnership and another has its own special company structure. Two were 'alternative conversions'; four were 'rescues' or 'phoenixes'; the rest 'new starts'. The more long-standing, and hence those whose performance can best be evaluated, started before CSO assistance was widely available; a few of our case studies are more recent and had such assistance.

Plan of the book
The book examines three different aspects of the performance of worker co-operatives: how they perform as businesses, as places to work and as co-operative organisations. In addition we look at the organisation and work of local CSOs and other support structures for co-operatives, and at the development of the new worker co-operative movement.

Chapters 2, 3 and 4 examine the business performance of worker co-operatives. Chapter 2 provides a statistical overview of the co-operative sector, including the distribution of co-operatives by industry, location, size and type. Most importantly it examines the survival and life-spans of co-operatives and compares them with other small businesses. In Chapter 3 we present a more detailed analysis of the performance of co-operatives in three industrial sectors: printing, clothing manufacture and wholefoods. Chapter 4 goes on to identify three common patterns of business development for co-operatives, which are used to present our case studies. By the end of Chapter 4 we have used statistical and case-study data to identify important internal and external factors that affect the successful business development of worker co-operatives.

Chapter 5 considers what co-operatives are like as workplaces. It analyses co-operators' expectations and experiences of key areas of working life in co-operatives, and how they are influenced by factors such as their past experience of work, their domestic circumstances and the other alternatives open to them. Special consideration is given to the rewards and difficulties of being an activist or leader in co-operatives. The chapter concludes by summarising the main costs and benefits of working in a co-operative.

Chapters 6 to 8 examine how our case studies performed as co-operatives and the problems they faced developing democratic forms of management and organisation, and make some suggestions for how these problems may be addressed. In Chapter 6 we draw upon labour process theory and the sociology of organisations to provide contrasting explanations of the process of degeneration, and subject them to critical review. An analysis of case studies suggests that co-operatives can enable workers to gain more control over work, but this is limited by important constraints. Chapter 7 discusses the new methods of democratic management being evolved in co-operatives, and a number of problems that have emerged. Chapter 8 suggests that democratic management alone is not enough to promote members' interests and maintain a commitment to co-operative principles. It considers what else can be done to keep alive the spirit of co-operation.

Chapter 9 examines the system of local and occasionally regional support that has evolved in the UK to promote and develop the worker co-operative sector. The chapter concludes by analysing the strengths and weaknesses of this decentralized system of support, and outlines some of the areas in which the system needs to be strengthened if these weaknesses are to be overcome.

Finally, in Chapters 10 and 11 we present some implications of our findings for theory and practice respectively.

2
The Worker Co-operative Sector:
Extent, Survival and Growth

Worker co-operatives may embody a number of ideals, but unless they can compete as businesses in what is essentially a capitalist world they will remain an insignificant force. Most of this book is based on case studies of particular co-operatives. But, before looking at those examples, let us see how significant and successful the co-operative sector is becoming overall, in business terms.

Even staying in the strict confines of business performance, there are several ways of attempting to measure how well co-operatives are performing. First, there is the extent and spread of worker co-operatives. We would not have been studying co-operatives, or writing this book, but for their great resurgence in numbers over the last ten years. But we need to know how co-operatives are spreading in more detail. How many jobs? In which parts of the country? Which are the favoured business sectors for co-operatives? Co-operatives are said to be small: how small? And is this changing? We introduced in Chapter 1 the idea of different types of co-operative: which of these is most responsible for the growth in numbers? We devote the first half of this chapter to answering these questions.

Second, how well do individual co-operatives perform? Do they do better than small businesses? If you form a co-operative, are you likely still to be in business in four years' time? In the second half of this chapter we present figures for the survival rate and growth of co-operatives and where possible compare them with small businesses. Clearly, these are very crude measures of success. Even in economic terms there is a whole range of measures of performance – and we shall see in Chapter 3 how co-operatives fare in terms of various specific measures of wealth creation, efficiency and so on. For the moment, by restricting attention to simple measures, we have been able to survey all UK worker co-operatives registered or starting trading since 1970. This is the first time comprehensive figures for their survival rate have been computed.

The spread of worker co-operatives in the UK

In Chapter 1 we saw what a period elapsed between the last surge of activity in the promotion of worker co-operatives and the recent wave – or series of waves – of new co-operatives. Table 2.1 shows how the number of co-operatives trading has varied since 1880. Some of the 'co-partnerships' set up in the 1890s failed quickly, but many survived through two world wars, although their numbers declined especially during the 1950s and 1960s. Their survivors were joined, first by Scott Bader and the few other 'endowed' co-operatives following their example, then by the alternativists of the 1970s and most recently by increasing numbers of 'job-creation' and 'rescue' co-operatives.

Table 2.1 *Estimated numbers of worker co-operatives and approximate numbers of jobs in such co-operatives, 1880–1986*

	Old (pre-1945) co-operatives (mainly co-partnerships)		'New wave' co-operatives		All co-operatives	
	No. of co-ops	No. of jobs	No. of co-ops	No. of jobs	No. of co-ops	No. of jobs
1880	15[1]	n/a			15	n/a
1914	73[1]	n/a			73	n/a
1923	44[1]	5,200[1]			44	5,200
1939	40[1]	8,000[1]			40	8,000
1948	46[1]	6,600[1]			46	6,600
1958	41[1]	4,900[1]	3[2]	500[3]	44	5,400
1968	30[2]	3,400[1]	8[2]	600[3]	38	4,000
1975	23[2]	2,200[3]	48[2]	1,000[3]	71	3,200
1980	19[2]	1,400[3]	260[2]	2,500[3]	279	3,900
1982	18[2]	1,300[3]	402[2]	3,700[3]	420	5,000
1984	15[2]	1,000[3]	718[2]	6,500[3]	733	7,500
1986 (end)	10[2]	600[2]	1,224[2]	7,900[3]	1,234	8,500

Sources:
[1]PA Management Consultants, 1985; but *ICOM Newsletter* March/April 1980 gives figures of 109 co-operatives in 1905 and 89 in 1945 – the latter in particular seems much too high
[2]London ICOM Worker Co-operative Database, modified (see text)
[3]Own approximation, using estimates from a variety of sources sometimes contradictory

The number of co-operatives has rocketed over the last ten years, but the rate of formation is no longer increasing and has levelled off since 1984 at just over 300 per year. The number of jobs in co-operatives has grown less fast, from a low point of around 3,000 jobs in about 70 co-operatives in 1975 to the equivalent of between 7,500 and 9,500 full-time jobs in over 1,200 co-operatives by the end of 1986. This is for two reasons: first, the old co-partnerships (and the 'Benn co-operatives' of the mid-1970s) gave rise to several failures of large co-operatives; second, the average size of the new starts is small and is possibly getting

Table 2.2 *Size distribution of worker co-operatives*

No. of employees (full-time equivalents)	Worker co-operatives in this size range early 1987[1]			(Previous estimate of % of co-operatives in each size range, mid-1985)
	No.	%	Full-time equivalents[2]	
1–4	522	59	1,438	(54)
5–9	239	27	1,560	(30)
10–19	89	10	1,174	(10)
20–49	28	3	827	(4)
50 plus	13	1	1,695	(2)

[1] For the 1987 figures about 350 co-operatives where number of jobs is entered as zero or unknown are excluded from this table (for 1985, about 150 co-operatives are similarly excluded). Fuller information would give a higher total number of jobs but probably an even greater proportion of very small co-operatives than indicated by this table
[2] One part-time job counted as half a full-time equivalent

Source: London ICOM Worker Co-operative Database

even smaller. In fact, co-operatives in general are very small, with mean size about 7 full-time equivalents and a median size of only 4. Table 2.2 gives more detail and shows the increase in the smallest co-operatives over the last year or so. However, some co-operatives do become established and grow in numbers later, and growth is one aspect of co-operative performance we look at in the second half of this chapter.

It is worth noting, however, that all co-operatives are groups, usually with more than one employee; by comparison, in the world of small business, two out of three people working for themselves do so alone, and 'most small enterprise owners opt for a "steady-state" business', i.e. shunning growth (Curran, 1986).

In terms of major business sectors, there are virtually no worker co-operatives in agriculture and fishing and relatively few in building. There is a greater proportion of co-operatives in manufacturing than of small businesses. However, the largest number of co-operatives, as with small businesses, is in services.

It is more revealing to look at the distribution of co-operatives into specific sub-sectors, as in Table 2.3. The figure of 27 per cent of co-operatives being manufacturing co-operatives hides the fact that these are concentrated in printing, clothing manufacture – particularly the cut, make and trim (CMT) part of the sewing industry – and engineering. Similarly, the proportion of co-operatives in retailing is very close to the figure for small businesses, but the co-operatives are overwhelmingly in wholefoods and book retailing. Many of the service sector co-operatives are in catering, cleaning or media of some

Table 2.3 *Numbers of co-operatives and jobs in co-operatives, by sector and major sub-sector, early 1987*

	No. of co-operatives[1]	Jobs in co-operatives – measured in full-time equivalents[2]	% of co-operatives in this sector (and % of businesses in the sector, end 1985)[3]
Fishing, forestry and agriculture	18	78	2 (13)
Building and construction	77	301	7 (15)
[General building]	[44]	[218]	
Manufacturing, engineering, production (incl. mining, metals, energy, water supply)	307	2,762	27 (10)
[Clothing, footwear, furnishings	[70]	[803]	
[Printing and publishing]	[115]	[564]	
Retail	168	763	15 (18)
[Retail – books, etc.]	[31]	[133]	
[Retail – food etc.]	[89]	[428]	
Transport	22	177	2 (4)
Wholesale	28	198	2 (8)
[Wholesale – food, etc.]	[19]	[176]	
Other services	501	2,168	45 (32)
[Restaurants, catering]	[73]	[212]	
[Entertainments, cultural, media]	[178]	[720]	
[Computing, business services]	[48]	[136]	
Classification not known	137	244	
Total	1,258	6,691	

[1] Figures include all co-operatives still trading. If the 10 co-operatives started before 1945 are excluded, the total jobs reduces to 6,083; the main sub-sector affected is clothing, etc., where only 66 of the 70 co-operatives, with only 376 jobs, started since 1945

[2] Co-operatives with numbers of jobs unknown are included as though they had no jobs; hence correct number of full-time equivalents must be higher than given here

[3] Percentage of co-operatives in each sector calculated ignoring those with classification not known

Source: London ICOM Worker Co-operative Database. Final column based on VAT registrations, from *British Business*, 31 July 1987.

kind. Although there are some co-operatives in high technology and professional services such as software consulting or language schools, there are a number of service areas such as hotels, estate agents or accountancy where traditional small partnerships are important, with virtually no co-operatives at all.

In Chapter 3 we will be looking more closely at some of the sectors of small business where co-operatives are concentrated. For the moment, let us simply note that these are often characterised either by easy market entry in terms of capital and skill requirements (e.g. CMT), or by easy identification between the job and some kind of political or social commitment (e.g. printing), or both (e.g. wholefood retailing). Also important are declining industries where there are few alternatives for people with particular skills (e.g. engineering). However, for the very newest co-operatives, this concentration into particular sub-sectors, while continuing, may be becoming less marked. With continuing high unemployment and more activity from local CSOs a wider range of people appear to be starting co-operatives. In addition, activists and agencies committed to co-operativism are setting out to overcome the difficulties for co-operatives of raising finance so that they can enter a wider variety of businesses.

Table 2.4   *Regional distribution of co-operatives and co-operative jobs, early 1987*

	No. of co-operatives	Jobs in co-operatives (full-time equivalents)	% of co-operatives in this region	% of businesses in this region (end 1985)
London	401	1,896	32	33
South-East	52	444	4	(London and South-East)
East Anglia	46	120	4	4
South-West	52	267	4	10
West Midlands	94	321	8	9
East Midlands	94	1,480	8	7
Yorkshire and Humberside	127	530	10	8
North-West	126	418	10	9
North	79	297	6	4
Wales	92	363	7	5
Scotland	81	480	6	8
Northern Ireland	7	37	1	3
Region not known	7	32		
Total	1,258	6,685		

Notes as Table 2.3
Source: London ICOM Worker Co-operative Database. Final column based on VAT registrations from *British Business*, 31 July 1987

Worker co-operatives have been spreading in all parts of the country, but not quite evenly. The greatest concentration is in London, with 32 per cent of all co-operatives currently trading, whereas the South-West and the rest of the South-East have relatively few co-operatives (see Table 2.4). Within each region, it is urban areas with relatively high unemployment rates that have on the whole spawned most co-operatives.

Co-operative formation tends to be further concentrated in certain localities within the urban or metropolitan areas; for example, in London 65 per cent of new co-operative start-ups have been in only seven boroughs. These are mostly the localities with the longest-established local CDAs, reinforcing Taylor's (1983) finding that areas with local CDAs have more co-operatives set up than other areas, or than before they had CDAs. It may also be that the influence of these local CDAs is part of the trend towards smaller co-operative start-ups. It will be interesting to see if the recent spread of local support for co-operatives to cover much more of the country leads to a more widespread increase in co-operative start-ups, not so concentrated in areas of high unemployment.

It is harder to get a picture of the relative numerical strength of each of the types of co-operative start-up suggested in Chapter 1. Table 1.1 presented a preliminary typology of worker co-operatives on a matrix with two dimensions: the origins of a co-operative; and the dominant motivation behind its formation. The second of these is obviously not readily amenable to quantitative measurement. Records and statistics will not clearly distinguish, for example, 'alternative' from 'job-creation' co-operatives, particularly since co-operative members more often than not hold simultaneously a number of different, even conflicting, motivations.

As for the origins of co-operatives, we believe that we have a reasonably accurate record of co-operatives formed from failing businesses. We are less sure of the figures on conversions. The earlier conversions, following Scott Bader, were endowments of ordinary small businesses by philanthropic owners, and these are easy to identify. However, more recently there have been conversions from community projects of various kinds and from partnerships with an existing co-operative or alternativist orientation, and these are less clear-cut. (Two of our case studies are of this type, and another remains, fourteen years after starting to trade, an unincorporated partnership that might appear to be a new conversion if it took on an incorporated co-operative constitution.)

We estimate that sixty-seven of the co-operatives trading at the end of 1986, i.e. between 5 per cent and 6 per cent, were 'rescues' or 'phoenixes'. We do not have such a figure for conversions, though in our survey of local CSOs we estimated that 3 per cent of the co-operatives they deal with are conversions, as against 6.5 per cent that are rescues or phoenixes (Cornforth and Lewis, 1985). This means that approximately 90 per cent of worker co-operatives are new starts. However, rescues and phoenixes, though much smaller than the three well-known Benn co-operatives, are substantially larger on average than new starts.

Survival rates and growth of worker co-operatives

Co-operative activists often claim that co-operatives out-perform small businesses without saying where their evidence comes from. For example, in the special issue of *The New Co-operator*, ICOM's newsletter, put out in summer 1986 to mark the tenth anniversary of the Industrial Common Ownership Act, we read that the co-operative sector 'has already proved its worth over and over again in cost effectiveness and durability, with a staying power demonstrably better than that of small businesses in the private sector'.

This tendency to make claims without clear evidence goes for statements on small business performance too, but these usually say the chances of failure are high. Scott (1982) quotes seven examples, including a BBC TV programme *Can We Make Jobs?* of 6 August 1980, which stated categorically: 'Three-quarters of new businesses don't survive the first two years'. Scott himself made a study based on all Scottish companies registered in 1969. He found that over 60 per cent traded for more than five years, and most of these for the whole eight-year period of his study. Twenty-three per cent never traded, and only 16 per cent began trading and then failed within five years. In fact, the largest percentage of liquidations was only 6 per cent of the total trading in any year.

Scott's study was of a sample of businesses, and they were registered companies, thus excluding many small businesses which are sole traders or unregistered partnerships. Several other studies based on regional or other limited samples have given varied results. The two most authoritative sources of estimates of business failure rates both use large-scale databases.

First, studies at the Department of Trade and Industry (DTI) based on VAT returns for the UK as a whole show a higher failure rate than found by Scott, of 9 to 12 per cent of total 'stock' per year (DTI, 1987b; Ganguly, 1983). (Ganguly (1983) gives slightly lower failure rates, but we have recalculated so as to make the definition of the total 'stock' of businesses consistent with our calculations for co-operatives.) These same studies also show that the early life of a small business, especially the first 30 months and particularly the period from 6 to 18 months, is the most risky (Ganguly and Bannock, 1985). The failure rate varies little from year to year or from region to region, in line with Birch's (1979) findings for the USA. Long term, the chance of survival seems to settle at around 40-45 per cent of businesses continuing for ten years or more.

The other set of large-scale studies is based on the files of the credit-rating organization Dun & Bradstreet, and gives broadly similar results, with a similar estimate of the chances of survival over ten years (Stewart and Gallagher, 1985). However, the figures arrived at for the failure rate of the smallest firms (those employing between 1 and 19 people) are somewhat lower than those derived from VAT registrations, and this failure rate has apparently fallen, from an average of 7.3 per cent for 1971–81 to 6.3 per cent in 1981–82 and 4 per cent in 1982–83. Gallagher and Stewart (1986) explain this by suggesting that, although insolvency rates among small firms have increased during the recession, the number of owner-managers ceasing to trade for other reasons, such as switching to a new business, has fallen, perhaps because the lack of alternatives causes them to hang on to their present position at all costs. One should note, however, that Dun & Bradstreet's files produce a database which, though very large, is still only a sample. In particular, it underestimates the numbers of very small firms, and of those smallest firms, the more stable and longer-lived are more likely to get a credit rating, so that the figures arrived at may be unreliable and probably underestimate the failure rate in this 1–19 size range. Gallagher and Stewart (1986: 896) themselves agree that 'the better figure is no doubt that found by Ganguly'.

These two sets of large-scale data-base studies, particularly the one based on VAT returns, give us the main points of comparison against which to judge the survival rates of co-operatives. Their sources of data have both been criticised as not entirely representative of small businesses in various ways, of which the discussion above gives an example (see e.g. Storey and Johnson, 1986). However, the results have been derived with considerable caution and have a lot in common. If we also note that take-overs of successful companies form a fair proportion of deregistrations and liquidations, and that many are formed with no intention of trading long term, the actual failure rate of VAT-registered small businesses must be lower than the 9 to 12 per cent quoted above. Co-operatives will have to have a very low failure rate to have 'demonstrably better' staying power.

It is quite difficult to work out reliable figures for co-operatives' survival rates. First, what is a start-up? Just like small businesses, some co-operatives register but never really trade. Second, what is a failure? Again, like small businesses, some successful co-operatives are 'taken over'. Alternatively, they may cease to be co-operatives but continue trading as private businesses; they may merge with other co-operatives; their members may leave and form new co-operatives or companies; or they may simply disband voluntarily.

There are other measurement problems because of co-operatives forming such a new, fast-growing sector. We can hardly measure how many co-operatives fail within ten years when less than 100 of the new co-operatives were registered by 1976. If we just look at how many co-operatives cease trading each year, the figure may look surprisingly high because there are always such a lot of new co-operatives, and, like small businesses, they are most vulnerable early on. And, biggest problem of all, it is hard to get complete information on older, failed co-operatives – but if these are left out, then the survival rates appear better than they are.

For our estimates of survival and failure rates, we started with the London ICOM Worker Co-operative Database, updated as far as possible with information from ICOM, the national CDA, various local CSOs and others. We added information on 'dead' co-operatives from the same sources but were left with a certain amount of incomplete data, e.g. co-operatives known to have ceased trading but at an unknown date. If we did not know the year of start of trading we assumed registration date was start date. Then we had to decide which co-operatives to include in our analysis. We took those that began trading or registered from 1946 onwards, though there were very few startups before 1970, and most of our calculations take that year as the starting-point. Our data are updated to the end of 1986, and information on 1987 is ignored, but the figures for 1986 itself should be treated with particular caution, since full information may not yet have been obtained. We also deleted community co-operatives, actors' agencies, 'instant muscle' schemes, etc. in an effort to get a list of worker co-operatives only. Then we checked carefully to avoid double-counting and eliminated alternative trading names, subsidiaries, etc. Finally we estimated the dates of 'birth' and/or 'death' for co-operatives with incomplete information. We did this by checking whether they were listed as 'live' in any of the national directories (CDA 1980, 1982, 1984, 1986) and then allocating co-operatives' births or deaths to possible years in the same proportion as those on which we had full information.

Several calculations were done altogether. First, we should note that in our revised dataset there have been 1,896 worker co-operatives registered from 1946 to 1986, of which 1,224 were estimated to be still trading at the end of 1986, an overall survival rate of 65 per cent. This cannot really be compared with figures for small businesses, since the rate of formation of the latter is fairly constant, whereas the majority of co-operative start-ups are in the more recent years. Nevertheless, to try to get some sort of correspondence, we estimated that 1,750 of the above co-operatives began trading since the beginning of 1978, of which 1,154 were still trading at the end of 1986, a survival rate of 66 per cent, whereas only 60 per cent of VAT registrations from 1974 inclusive were still registered at the end of 1982, a similar time-span.

Column 7 of Table 2.5 shows the failure rate each year from 1975 as a percentage of the 'stock' of co-operatives trading in that year. The figure used for total 'stock' is the number of co-operatives

Table 2.5   *Estimated formation, numbers and failure rate of worker co-operatives each year from 1975*

	No. of new co-ops that year[1]	% still trading at end of 1986 (with comparable figure for all businesses)	Adjusted 'stock' of co-ops that year	No. of co-ops ceasing to trade	Failures as % of 'stock' (with % failure rate of all businesses)	
1975	11	55%		73	2	3%	(11%)
1976	29	52%		91	1	1%	(11%)
1977	39	44%		124	0	0%	(12%)
1978	82	40%	(34%)	185	5	3%	(12%)
1979	63	49%	(40%)	252	5	2%	(9%)
1980	92	50%	(44%)	325	16	5%	(10%)
1981	94	46%	(49%)	402	29	7%	(9%)[2]
1982	199	42%	(51%)	519	52	10%	(10%)
1983	270	49%	(63%)	702	104	15%	(10%)
1984	325	68%	(73%)	895	143	16%	(10%)
1985	308	84%	(86%)	1,069	120	11%	(11%)
1986	317	97%	(97%)	1,261	186	15%	(10%)

[1] Figures for VAT registrations are constantly updated; above table gives slight readjustment between 1979 and 1980

[2] Estimate of 1981 failure rate for businesses may be affected by civil servants' industrial action

Sources: Estimated dates of 'births' and 'deaths' of co-operatives based on London ICOM Worker Co-operative Database as explained in the text. 'Stock' of co-operatives is number of co-operatives live at start of year plus half the number starting that year

Figures for businesses based on VAT registrations and deregistrations, *British Business*, 12 August 1983, 3 April 1987 and 31 July 1987. Figure for 'stock' of businesses is not that used in the *British Business* reports but an adjusted figure: number of businesses registered for VAT at start of year plus half the number of new VAT registrations during the year

trading at the beginning of the year plus half the number starting to trade during the year. You can see that the failure rate has fluctuated but generally got worse over the years, particularly in 1983, 1984 and 1986 with failure rates of around 15 per cent. This compares somewhat unfavourably with the rates for all businesses of 9 per cent to 12 per cent based on VAT deregistrations, but this difference can probably be explained by the high proportion of co-operatives still in their first two or three most vulnerable years.

Table 2.5 also shows, in column 3, the percentage of co-operatives started in each year still trading at the end of 1986. From 1986 back to 1982 the survival rates get worse, as one might expect given the chance of failure compounding for any one co-operative as each year goes by. Particularly for co-operatives starting in 1982 or 1983, the survival rates are somewhat worse than the rates given in column 4 for all businesses. However, the survival rate of co-operatives registered in 1981 or earlier is about the same or greater than the figure for 1982, implying that those co-operatives established earlier survive better. Almost half of co-operatives from 1979 have survived 7½ years, the same proportion as those from 1983 that have survived just 3½ years. Although the numbers of early co-operatives were small, the 'staying power' of those established before 1982 was certainly better than that of conventional businesses.

Table 2.6 looks at how many years co-operatives survive from their start. Unfortunately, to see, for example, how many co-operatives survive 8 years we would be restricted to co-operatives starting 1978 or earlier, and the numbers involved are unreliably small, so we have done this calculation only up to 5 years. For co-operatives starting 1981 or earlier, the failure rate is only 35 per cent for 4 (or more like 4½) years, which compares well with the rate for small businesses of about 40 per cent failure after 4 years. However, more recent co-operatives, as we have already seen, have a much worse failure rate, and in the lower part of Table 2.6 we can see this quite clearly. This is probably because more 'weaker' co-operatives have started more recently, rather than that the years from 1982 on have been more difficult for all co-operatives, though the latter may also be true to some extent. However, there is also an indication that the worst years in this respect were 1982 and 1983, and that co-operatives starting in 1984 and 1985 are surviving almost exactly as well as other businesses – though we must treat this finding with caution, because the data on recent failures may still be incomplete.

Let us look closer at Table 2.6 and the pattern over 1, 2, and up to 5 years. For the earlier co-operatives at least, it seems to indicate that in the second year co-operatives are more vulnerable than before or after. When we remember that the first 'year' in fact averages about eighteen months, it becomes clearer still that the tendency is for co-operatives not to fail quickly but then to become just as likely to fail as small businesses (see also Cornforth and Lewis, 1985). It seems that while the peak period of risk is similar in both cases (see DTI, 1987a, for an analysis of business life-span), for co-operatives it may be a little later. This may reflect unwillingness to give up an idea when that would involve questions of group responsibility and commitment; or simply the more ready availability of practical assistance and advice in the early stages of a co-operative's life.

In order to get some idea of whether survival chances are affected by factors such as which sector or region a co-operative is in, we have used

Table 2.6   *Year by year failure rate for co-operatives up to end of fifth year after start (plus comparison with all businesses)*

	Total number starting	Co-operatives ceasing trading:				
		By end of year after start year	By end of 2nd year after start	By end of 3rd year after start	By end of 4th year after start	By end of 5th year after start
Co-operatives starting 1975–81	410	31 [8%]	72 [18%]	108 [26%]	144 [35%]	170 [42%]
Co-operatives starting 1982–3	469	103 [22%]	177 [38%]	233 [50%]		
Co-operatives starting in 1984	325	58 [18%]	103 [32%]			
Co-operatives starting in 1985	308	49 [16%]				
(VAT registrations for 1974–9)	(478,000)	(19%)	(32%)	(42%)	(49%)	(54%)

Sources: as Table 2.5

a single figure for survival rate, namely the proportion of co-operatives formed since 1946 surviving to the end of 1986. As noted above, for all co-operatives this rate is 65 per cent, though this single figure has little meaning since it combines a larger proportion of recently formed co-operatives with smaller numbers of older co-operatives that seem to survive better. However, on the whole we can use the variation in this figure as an indication of variations between sectors or regions.

Let us look first at the variation in survival rates between major sectors. For example, for small businesses, the retail sector has the second worst survival rate, perhaps because take-overs as opposed to closures are particularly common. However, worker co-operatives in the retail sector, particularly wholefood shops (83 per cent), have one of the highest survival rates. By contrast, building co-operatives survive much less well than the average, whereas building firms in general come out a little above average. The same is true for co-operatives in production, though there the survival rate is pulled down particularly by a low rate (58 per cent) for co-operatives in clothing manufacture. Overall, it is intriguing to note that the sectors where ordinary businesses survive best tend to be those where there are most co-operative failures, and vice versa. Part of the explanation probably lies with the particular sub-sectors into which co-operatives are concentrated. However, this does suggest that some of the factors behind the survival of co-operatives may be different from the factors governing whether small businesses survive.

As for regional distribution of survival rates, our data show little variation for co-operatives in the different major regions of the UK. Leaving aside Northern Ireland, East Anglia, the South-East and the South-West, all of which have few co-operatives anyway, the rate varies only from 63 per cent for London and for the West Midlands up to 72 per cent for Scotland, and these do not correspond particularly to regions with the lowest and highest survival rates of businesses generally.

It is difficult to estimate reliably the survival rate for rescues and phoenix co-operatives, because of their small numbers. On our figures, 67 of the 87 known post-war co-operative rescues were still trading at the end of 1986, a survival rate of 77 per cent. If this figure is accurate, it shows that rescues survive somewhat better than other co-operatives, which is perhaps surprising, given the difficult circumstances inevitably surrounding the rescue attempt.

We also made some crude comparisons, in terms of survival rates, between co-operatives and small businesses receiving different kinds of assistance. Table 2.7 shows a collection of results from different sources. Clearly, the different methodologies used in each study and the different times at which they were carried out make the comparison at best only indicative. However, whereas co-operatives survive about as well as businesses in general, it seems that businesses started on the Enterprise Allowance Scheme survive less well and the clients of enterprise agencies, except for the smallest firms, survive better. We suggest there may be two factors at work here. First of all, local CSOs, like the Enterprise Allowance Scheme, succeed in spreading the option of starting a co-operative, or other business, to a very wide range of people, including many groups disadvantaged in the labour market in various ways. Without continuing support, a higher failure rate would be expected, as with the figures for the Enterprise Allowance Scheme. However, local CSOs do offer intensive support, which can offset the first factor and bring the survival rate back up again. Note that the years in which co-operatives' failure rate got worse correspond with the period when local CSOs were spreading rapidly; now that they and their methods for in-depth co-operative development (see Chapter 9) are established, the survival rate is improving again. Enterprise agencies, by contrast, deal mainly with those defining themselves as entrepreneurs in the traditional sense; further, their clients are likely to be those sufficiently well organised to seek advice. In these circumstances, even though the support offered is not so intensive as

Table 2.7   *Comparison of survival rates of co-operatives and businesses with different types of support*

Type of business/support	Proportion surviving 3 years
All VAT-registered businesses (registered 1974–82)	63%
Worker co-operatives (starts 1975–83)	66%
Worker co-operatives (starts 1982–3 only)	56%
Enterprise Allowance Scheme businesses (starts from 1983)	53%
Enterprise agency clients (1987 survey)	85%
Enterprise agency clients (less than £20,000 turnover)	69%

Sources: rows 1–3 as Table 2.5; row 4, *Employment Gazette*, August 1985 and October 1986, Labour Research, January 1987; rows 5–6, Business in the Community survey, 1987

that provided by local CSOs, it is not surprising that enterprise agencies achieve a high survival rate for their clients.

Finally, we wanted to look at the growth in jobs of those co-operatives that survive and develop, by comparison with the frequency of job loss through business failure. We looked at co-operatives registering or starting to trade in the two years 1979 and 1980, and attempted to find how many workers there were in 1980, 1982, 1984 and 1986 in each co-operative. Unfortunately the data available are quite incomplete and may be inaccurate. In particular, the number of workers given for a co-operative's first year is probably often overestimated, since the co-operative may have registered with a greater number of members than could ever be realistically supported as workers. Again, different sources vary in the care with which they differentiate full- and part-time jobs. After leaving out the most uncertain data and those co-operatives starting too late in 1980 to have 1980 job figures available, we were left with data for only 73 of the 155 co-operatives starting in those two years.

As expected (see Table 2.5 above), slightly more than half of these had failed by 1986. Of the 524 jobs represented by these 73 co-operatives in 1980, 334 were lost again by 1986 through 41 of these co-operatives ceasing to trade within those six years, including several of the larger ones. However, of the co-operatives that survived six years, 20 grew in terms of jobs against 6 shedding jobs, with 6 retaining the same number, a net gain of 28 jobs. On this evidence, while those co-operatives that survive do not remain entirely static, their job gains or losses tend to be quite marginal, with a few notable exceptions. Some co-operatives may have started over-ambitious and been forced to cut back. Others have grown fairly dramatically, but these are few in number. Storey et al. (1987) point out for small manufacturing businesses that it is a tiny proportion that experience dramatic growth in jobs. Although the growth of even the most successful co-operatives is on a smaller scale, the same general finding appears to hold for co-operatives.

Summary

We can summarize the main findings of this statistical overview of worker co-operatives in the UK as follows:

1. Worker co-operatives have grown rapidly in number over the last te years, though the rate of growth has levelled off since 1984. They have not grown so rapidly in jobs, due to a few large failures of older co-operatives and the decrease in the average size of start-ups.
2. The mean size of a co-operative is about 7 workers and the median only 4. This does not vary much from region to region, except for the influence of a few large co-operatives.
3. Co-operatives are distributed between major sectors and between regions roughly in the same proportions as small businesses, except that there are very few co-operatives in agriculture, or in East Anglia, the South-West and the South-East outside London, and the number of co-operatives in manufacturing and production is somewhat above what would be expected for small business generally.
4. However, within sectors and regions, co-operatives are concentrated in particular sub-sectors such as CMT, printing, catering, wholefoods and bookshops, and in urban areas of high unemployment and areas covered by CSOs.
5. About 6 per cent of co-operatives are rescues or phoenixes. These tend to be of larger than average size, and are even more concentrated in terms of sector, into mainly CMT and engineering, with some printing and others of various kinds.
6. It is not true that co-operatives have much better survival rates than small businesses. In fact, small businesses survive pretty well – only 9 to 12 per cent of the total stock of businesses fail each year. Co-operatives have performed similarly or slightly worse, but the difference is probably accounted for by the fact that so many co-operatives are new and hence more prone to failure.
7. Like small businesses, co-operatives appear most likely to fail within the first three years. For co-operatives the peak vulnerability is between 18 and 30 months after the start.

8. In the more recent years of our data (particularly 1983 and 1984) the failure rate for co-operatives has got worse. However, in 1985 and 1986 the survival rate appears to be improving again.

9. Contrary to the trend for small businesses, retail co-operatives appear to survive particularly well, whereas co-operatives in building and in manufacturing fail more frequently than would be expected for small businesses in those sectors. Similarly, though there is little significant variation in survival rates for co-operatives in different regions, what variation there is certainly does not follow the expected regional pattern for businesses in general.

10. Rescue and phoenix co-operatives fail less frequently than others, despite their difficult starting circumstances.

11. Co-operatives survive much better than businesses on the Enterprise Allowance Scheme, but not so well as the average client of an enterprise agency. We suggest that local CSOs' success in promoting co-operation widely to all sections of the population might have tended to push the failure rate up. However, with a more difficult task than enterprise agencies in terms of the range of clients, CSOs still manage to assist co-operatives to achieve a survival rate comparable to ordinary small businesses.

12. In terms of jobs, those co-operatives that survive tend to remain fairly static, with the few notable exceptions, as with conventional small businesses, of a very small number of co-operatives growing rapidly.

Altogether, this means it is reasonable for co-operative activists to be proud of the recent record of co-operatives, but not to overstate it. It is also clear that the surge in the number of co-operatives is not just a facet of the increased interest in small business; one must look elsewhere for the reasons for their spread, and their relative success. One aspect warranting detailed attention is the concentration of co-operatives of different types into particular sub-sectors, and the way the survival rates in those particular sectors vary in a different way from the survival rates of small businesses. Hence in the next couple of chapters in order to look at business performance of co-operatives in more detail we will concentrate on identifying different patterns of performance among co-operatives in contrasting sectors.

3
Economic Aspects of Co-operative Performance

In this chapter we look further at the business performance of co-operatives and how this is affected by various economic factors. We go beyond the simple questions of survival and growth in numbers, addressed in the last chapter, to the use of various business indicators. Do those co-operatives that do survive perform as well or better than conventional small businesses? Co-operatives, like conventional firms, are in the business of wealth creation and have to use their labour efficiently in order to compete in the market.

We argue that the most appropriate ways of measuring efficient wealth creation by co-operatives do not necessarily use the same indicators as those evolved for measuring the performance of capitalist firms. A co-operative is owned and controlled by those who work in it, on an equal basis, rather than by those who put money into it. As with a conventional business, we may question the extent to which the legal or constitutional position is reflected in practice – for example, in both cases those in management positions may wield effective control rather than the legal owners – but the fact remains that co-operatives are based on essentially different principles from conventional capitalist firms, as witness the co-operative slogan: 'Labour hires Capital, rather than Capital hiring Labour.'

Economic theories of co-operative performance

The best developed school of economic thought on the performance of worker co-operatives was stimulated by the experiences of Yugoslavia since 1948, and is epitomised by the work of Jaroslav Vanek. Following articles by Ward (1958) and others, the seminal work in this school is Vanek's (1970) *General Theory of Labour-Managed Market Economies*. The Ward–Vanek model applies the method of neo-classical economics to an economy composed of labour-managed firms related via a market mechanism. Although its original application was thus to a labour-managed economy, theoretical results from this model have been taken to apply to worker co-operatives in a capitalist market.

Whereas, in orthodox neo-classical theory, the firm is seen as acting to maximise return on capital employed, i.e. profitability, in the Ward–Vanek model the labour-managed firm, or co-operative, acts to maximise the income of each worker-owner. Since, in the neo-classical model of the capitalist economy, the market mechanism ensures optimal efficiency in each individual firm, the question was asked whether labour-managed firms would match this level of efficiency. Vanek (1971, 1975) concluded that they would not, and that the reason was the combination of their different objective (maximising income per worker rather than profitability) with a difference in the source of finance. He compared the case of a co-operative financed entirely through collective saving or retained surplus with that of a capitalist firm financed by external borrowing. Under these circumstances, Vanek argued, a co-operative would tend to under-invest, under-produce and under-employ compared to a capitalist firm, and he considered his arguments to be 'so powerful in explaining the shortcomings of ... conventional forms of producer co-operatives ... that they offer an ample explanation of the comparative failure of these forms' (1975: 446).

Before going any further, it is worth explaining why this complete contrast in the way the two forms of business are supposedly financed makes sense at the theoretical level – and also why in reality they may not be so different. A capitalist firm, in the neo-classical model, is an entity in itself, distinct from those who may invest in it, including those who set it up. Capital invested in the firm will move elsewhere if it can get a better rate of return, so it is reasonable to assume that all its capital behaves like external funds that have to be paid the going rate of interest – otherwise these funds cannot be retained in the firm.

Of course, in practice there is a big distinction between the owner's (or owners') 'equity' and interest-bearing loans – or external debt. If there is any surplus after the revenue from sales has been used to meet all costs, including interest payments and wages, then this surplus is profit that belongs to the owner(s). The owner(s) may take out some of the profit, but otherwise it goes to increase the equity. Total capital employed is always comprised of equity and external debt. The former carries control, bears risk and conveys a kind of identity with the organisation in perhaps a psychological as well as a financial sense, whereas the latter simply gains interest. Financial analysts calculate the 'debt-equity ratio' or 'gearing', and conventional wisdom is that this ratio should not be too high. If it is, the owners will be loading the risk of too large a business on to too small an amount of their own funds. In contrast to this, in Vanek's analysis a capitalist firm is characterised as financed entirely by external debts.

A worker co-operative, on the other hand, is not distinct from, but is comprised of, its owners, i.e. those who work in it. In the pure version of Vanek's theory, the co-operative can only be capitalised from members' contributions or by collective savings from retained surplus. To the members of a co-operative, wages are not a cost but are their reward – they are in business to earn income for themselves. From what remains when other costs are met out of revenue, but before paying themselves anything (i.e. from value added – see below), they must decide to take a certain amount as wages or income, and retain the rest in the business. This retained surplus is owned 'in common', and members do not benefit individually in terms of an increased personal financial stake whenever surplus is retained for reinvestment.

In practice, as with the capitalist firm, things are not so simple as Vanek's model suggests, even with common ownerships. Although retained surplus held in common and used for reinvestment is certainly one important basis on which such co-operatives might become capitalised, they may also benefit from 'soft' loans from their members and from friends and supportive institutions or specialist loan funds, as well as commercial loans. Other types of co-operative may in addition offer 'equity participation' – a share in ownership on a financial basis – so that individual workers might have capital stakes in their co-operative as well as loans bearing interest; and outside institutions might also invest on an equity basis as well as giving loans (see Chapter 11).

'Equity participation' is regarded by many as contrary to basic co-operative principles, even if only a minority stake is held by the workers as individuals and outsiders all together and the 'common ownership' held by workers collectively has overall control. However, there are three pragmatic arguments in its favour. There is the possibility of better access to different sources of capital, and the fact that capital invested as equity need not carry interest or require regular repayments. Finally, if individual members have capital stakes, allowing them to benefit personally from the increased worth of the co-operative should it be successful, then this may improve their long-term commitment.

In Vanek's model, not only is there no equity participation, but a co-operative has no external (or internal) loan finance either. Co-operators, supposedly wishing to maximise their own incomes, have to decide how much surplus to keep in their business, i.e. how much to reinvest in the future of their jobs, and how much to take now. Particularly since they might leave and have nothing to show for what they had agreed to reinvest, Vanek argues that they would tend to vote themselves too high a wage or bonus and 'under-invest' in the co-operative. Similarly, faced with an increase in demand, rather than risk their own capital, expand and take on more workers, they would prefer to share the benefits among themselves, perhaps by raising prices – they would 'under-employ' and 'under-produce'.

Vanek concludes that co-operatives can avoid this inefficiency only by resorting to external finance, and that they should pay a price for capital which 'reflects its scarcity'. He argues that the effects of a hostile capitalist environment are able to explain 'only a part, and perhaps only a small part, of the difficulties of the co-operatives' (1975: 453). However, he still thinks that the conventional banking system is unlikely to finance co-operatives satisfactorily, so that a secondary support structure is necessary, among whose functions would be the supervision (but not control) of the capital market (1975: 35).

Vanek's work has been developed and criticised in various ways (for a survey see Defourny, 1982). Among more recent critics Stephen (1984) has demonstrated some of the inconsistencies in Vanek's arguments and claims that shortage of funds (of whatever type) is a more likely source of problems for co-operatives than restrictions on the type of financing (1984: 96).

There are several other criticisms to be made of Vanek's approach. As we began to see above, small firms and co-operatives are actually not all that different in type of financing, and in fact they both report similar problems in obtaining finance. They both are mainly financed by external loans, from friendly sources and from commercial sources such as banks. Also, small business owners may feel similar restraints towards the risky use of their own retained surpluses as those hypothesised for co-operators. Until they begin to grow substantially, which, as noted in Chapter 2, occurs only for a minority, small businesses do not rely on external equity any more than most co-operatives.

Note, too, that neo-classical economics tends to look for equilibrium models, and Vanek's typification of a co-operative bears no relation to its history but assumes it is well established. However, we need to understand the way co-operatives are set up, develop and possibly fail, particularly since the UK co-operative movement today consists largely of co-operatives recently started up. Lichtenstein (1986) gives some useful pointers towards a life-cycle model of 'alternative organisations', arguing that the static neo-classical model is 'overburdened'.

Finally, it seems odd to premise a theory about collective organisations on the idea of maximising individual incomes (Mygind, 1986). We discuss orientations to work in Chapter 5 below. There we argue that 'instrumental' motivations and the requirement for material rewards cannot be ignored, but they are certainly not the only basis on which most co-operatives operate. Indeed, co-operatives incorporate such a range of idealistic and other motivations among their members that the idea of maximising one variable, however defined, seems unlikely to give rise to a good model of co-operatives' behaviour.

Where Vanek's work has been most important is in promoting the ideas of self-management and co-operation and in pointing out the importance of secondary support organisations. In the context of this chapter our attention is focussed on whether the type and source of financing, rather than just the availability and quantity of financing, affect how well co-operatives perform.

However, our approach differs from that of the neo-classical economists. We expect co-operatives of different types to behave differently and regard their success or failure as a developing process rather than as something determined at one time. In this chapter we look for distinctive patterns of business performance, particularly for a co-operative's first few years.

We expect *both* external *and* internal constraints to affect co-operatives' chances of success or failure. In this chapter we concentrate on economic constraints, including the effect of different market sectors as well as the internal factors of type and amount of financing discussed above. Thus, our approach requires a way of analysing the performance of a co-operative in relation to the particular industry of which it is a part. For this we use ideas derived from Marxist labour process theory; in particular, the analysis of small businesses' position in the labour process.

Co-operatives as small businesses but with a difference
One can think of the capitalist labour process as extending throughout the whole economy, or whole sectors of it, and the individual small business taking on certain tasks within what then appears as an economy-wide division of labour. Nichols (1980) looks at this in terms of 'levels of control', and we take a similar approach. Thus in Chapter 6 we see how the individual small business or co-operative has a relatively high degree of control over its own labour power, and to some extent over product/market choices and the physical means of production or technology, but only the largest enterprises have any substantial degree of control over investment and overall resource allocation.

On the whole, small firms always tend to be dependent on large firms, or on markets dominated by large firms, and to contain only the lowest levels of control within them. However, the degree and type of dependency vary markedly from sector to sector. Different typologies of dependency for small business have been developed by Averitt (1968) and by Shutt and Whittington (1987). Following the latter fairly closely, we can suggest three main categories of small business, namely: (a) those directly dependent on particular large businesses, for example via sub-contracting; (b) those in a more differentiated, competitive market and hence to some extent more independent, but with no possibility of control over market conditions as a whole; (c) those which by innovation or by restricted market loyalty have a particular niche in which, despite their small size, they can exercise some localised market control and thus also enjoy some limited independence.

Although small businesses of all types could be found within the same business sector, in general a particular sector will tend to have small firms mainly of one type. Thus, the clothing industry, being dominated by giant retailers and a smaller number of large manufacturers, has many small firms of the first, ultra-dependent, type, especially cut, make and trim (CMT) firms. The printing industry, on the other hand, has a substantial sector of independent small firms producing specialist, almost tailor-made products for a highly differentiated market. The third category of small business would be epitomised by specialist science-based companies.

As Rainnie (1985a: 163) comments, co-operatives too 'have to survive in a world that is not of their own making ... a world dominated by large capital, and must therefore fit into one or other of the categories ... devised for all small businesses'. We chose to analyse the performance of co-operatives in three sectors – one for each category. Clothing and printing fitted the first two respectively. These were important areas for the co-partnerships of the late nineteenth century, and market conditions played a large part in their decline in the 1950s and 1960s (Bennett, 1984). Once again, substantial numbers of co-operatives are being formed in these two sectors. For an example of the third category, we turned to wholefoods, where market innovation has allowed co-operatives to occupy a special niche.

However, to characterise these sectors from the point of view of co-operatives, we need to include other factors as well as those immediately important for small businesses. What tradition of labour organisation is there in a particular sector? What potential is there for identification with the job, or the product? Are there possibilities for protecting oneself against the market?

We go on to decide which business indicators are appropriate for measuring efficient wealth creation in co-operatives, and then give a little more detail on each of the three sectors before looking at the performance of co-operatives in that sector.

Measuring wealth creation in co-operatives
As noted above, in the most general terms 'wealth creation' is an objective that co-operatives have in common with conventional businesses. But those businesses would use 'profitability' as a measure of how efficiently wealth was being created, and this is not suitable for co-operatives.

This is not to say that co-operatives should not be 'profitable', in the loose sense of requiring to make a surplus to survive. However, 'profitability' is used in the stricter sense of return on capital employed. This means a ratio, such as *operating profit* : *net assets* (or the ratio of some other definition of profit to some other definition of capital employed). Once a definition of profitability is agreed on, the notion of *maximising* profitability can be used to decide if a proposed new development is worthwhile, to judge which of several lines of business is performing best or to see how a firm's performance varies from year to year.

There are three ways in which this approach is not appropriate for co-operatives, and thus three changes are to be made. First, we use *value added* rather than *profit*. Value added is what remains when all material and overhead costs have been deducted from sales income, and the division of value added into wages and profit is determined quite differently in a co-operative from in a capitalist company. To emphasize how greater profit cannot be used to indicate better performance in a co-operative, consider a group of co-operators meeting to decide whether to increase their wages. If they do, profits will be reduced, but this does not mean poorer performance!

At a pragmatic level, value added accounting is becoming acceptable to the accountancy profession. Marris (1984) gives an accountant's argument for its use for co-operatives, stating that 'Value added is the true contribution of the business to its worker members.' Value added is also increasingly used by conventional firms, though the practice of presenting value added accounts to employees has been criticised as a means by which management further manipulates the workforce (e.g. Hird, 1983). Value added presents a 'picture of a unity of interests in the financial performance of a given business organisation, whereas in fact there exists a basic conflict of interests' (Burchall et al., 1985: 17). This conflict of interests is not done away with in co-operatives, but is in principle open to the workers to resolve democratically.

It may also be argued on an ideological level that co-operatives are an attempt to move away from the exploitation of labour by capital. Even though, in practice, managers of capitalist firms may not necessarily act as though they are profit-maximisers (see e.g. Cyert and March, 1963; Mintzberg, 1973), profit has a key role in the ideological maintenance of the capitalist system. Jefferis and Thomas (1987) give a fuller argument, on this level too, in favour of using value added rather than profit.

Our second change is to measure return *to labour* rather than return to capital. From the above, it is clear that we regard value added as appropriate for measuring the quantity accruing to labour (rather than simply looking at incomes, as in Vanek's model discussed above). What is not so clear is how to represent labour so that we arrive at a useful ratio. Value added *per worker* is the most obvious choice (or per full-time equivalent). However, this has the practical difficulty of measuring part-time work accurately, as well as some more basic problems to do with comparability between sectors and between levels of skill and technology.

Profitability as a measure for individual firms' performance fits perfectly with the requirement of capital for a return wherever it is invested. These are two sides of the same coin in the capitalist system. This means profitability can be used in principle to compare any firm's performance with that of any other firm. In theory this type of measurement is a basis for resource allocation. Unfortunately, even in a hypothetical labour-managed economy, *value added per worker* cannot fulfil such a universal function, though it has a universal meaning as a measure of labour productivity.

Normally, a co-operative with higher levels of technology, a more highly capitalized co-operative or one with higher-skill levels would score higher on this measure. However, this could not be used as a simple basis for reallocating labour to the more 'efficient' co-operatives. First, labour is not homogeneous, unlike capital, and to improve skills requires training and other inputs. Secondly, again unlike capital, labour is not so readily mobile; and, thirdly, 'labour' means individuals who have their own motivations and make their own choices.

This leads us on to our third change. The idea of maximising is replaced by measuring a set of related variables. *Value added per head* and *average gross wage* are two of these, and the relationship between these two, wages as a percentage of value added, is also important. We also use some material measures of efficiency such as the ratios *value added*: turnover and *value added* : *net assets*, and a measure of degree of capitalisation – *net assets* : *per head* – as well as some other financial ratios such as *liquidity* and *external loans* : *net assets*. (This last has a similar function to the conventional gearing ratio, but separates *external* loans from all internal sources together. The latter, including loans from members, collective savings and retained surplus, are all regarded as forms of 'own capital' for co-operatives. By contrast, in conventional analysis internal loans would be classed with external loans and both contribute to high gearing.)

We do not expect to be able to make comparisons between co-operatives with different levels of skill or technology. However, within particular sectors (or, better still, specific sub-sectors) we can make comparisons between different co-operatives and between co-operatives and the average for conventional firms, and see changes or trends appearing over time.

The performance of co-operatives in clothing, printing and wholefoods

The three sub-sectors we have chosen to look at in detail are all well represented among the new worker-co-operatives. They are all examples of the tendency noted in Chapter 2 for co-operatives to be concentrated in certain sub-sectors. From Table 2.3 we see that 23 per cent of all production co-operatives are in clothing, footwear and furnishings, and 37 per cent are in printing and publishing, while 53 per cent of retail co-operatives and 68 per cent of wholesale co-operatives are in food, mostly wholefoods. (Note that we are including footwear along with clothing. A few of the new co-operatives are in footwear, along with several of the surviving co-partnerships.) As for survival rates, clothing co-operatives fare somewhat worse than co-operatives in general, whereas co-operative printers are about average and wholefoods retailers in particular have a much better survival rate.

In what follows, we use more detailed financial data on co-operatives in each sub-sector to calculate performance ratios for each co-operative and averages for each sub-sector. We have used all available data from annual returns to the Registrar of Friendly Societies and Companies House. However, this means the latest year for which we have data for a reasonable proportion of co-operatives is 1984, and the data approach completeness only for 1983 and earlier years. Given that the number of new co-operatives continues to increase, it is not surprising that our data are based on quite a small proportion of the co-operatives currently trading, and are inevitably biased towards relatively older co-operatives – and, of course, towards survivors. Nevertheless, we believe the data are sufficient to give some useful results.

Clothing and clothing co-operatives

The British textile and clothing industry has been transformed since the Second World War. Its three main elements – textiles, clothing manufacture and retailing – have been affected differently. Textile manufacturing has become much more concentrated into large-scale units operated by multinational companies that can switch production easily from one country to another. In the last fifteen years half the jobs in the UK in textiles and clothing have been lost, and by 1986 four major groupings accounted for more than half the employment in the textile industry. Similarly, over half the retail sales in the United Kingdom are accounted for by large multiple retailers (Rainnie, 1984); in other words, retailing, like textiles, has become dominated by a small number of large firms.

However, in the clothing manufacturing sector, most firms are still small and technologically backward, with sewing-machines each operated by one person. The large retail chains exercise considerable power over the many small manufacturing firms that supply them. Either they involve themselves very closely and control all aspects of the manufacturer's work, or they adopt an 'arms length' approach, which gives rise to a vast subcontracting network, with orders being split and passed on, production deadlines shortening and profit margins reducing along the way. The most exploited are those at the end of the chain, either homeworkers or small CMT firms. These make up finished goods without holding stock, using materials and patterns provided by customers. For these, the market combines the worst of both types of relationship. They get small, unpredictable runs to tight deadlines, and are probably still closely dependent on only one or two customers.

According to WMCC (1983), there is great scope for improving productivity in clothing firms by simple improvements in management and better use of existing resources. In practice, though, small clothing firms compete by low wages in a relatively labour-intensive industry. Many firms pay at least some of their workers less than the already low basic rate (which was only £1.70 per hour in 1986). However, a minority of small firms are craft or design based and have been able to succeed by moving up-market.

Trade union organisation is mostly very weak in small clothing firms. Rainnie (1985b: 213) argues that 'apparent industrial relations harmony, in this case, can be explained by a mixture of the isolation of shop stewards from the union, the weakness of the union, the resulting weakness of workplace trade unionism and the general position of women at work and the role of the family'.

Most clothing co-operatives have been rescues or job-creation co-operatives. There is not a lot of scope for politicisation of the product, or for positive identification of the job of sewing-machinist with wider social goals. However, despite all the drawbacks CMT does offer cheap market entry, although the craft and business skills of design, cutting, marketing, etc. needed for the successful upmarket type of small clothing firm noted above are not widespread.

Table 3.1 shows the average performance of those new clothing co-operatives for which we have data, 1980–83. We have made some comparisons with figures for clothing firms in general from *Business Monitor*, and for 1982 with those co-partnerships still trading. However, we should note that we are not really comparing like with like, since the co-operatives tend to be new, small and restricted mainly to CMT, whereas the co-partnerships are larger, and the *Business Monitor* figures include all types of clothing firm. Let us look briefly at each ratio in turn.

Table 3.1 *Average financial ratios for clothing co-operatives, 1980–3*

	No. of co-ops included in data	Total no. of co-ops registered/trading that year	Value added per head (£)	Average gross wage (£)	Wages as % of value added	Value added as % of turnover	Net assets per head (£)	Value added: net assets	Liquidity	External loans as % of net assets
1980	5	5	1,394 (4,545)[1]	2,386 (2,741)	171% (67%)	47% (42%)	899	1.55	0.89	129%
1981	8	9	1,946 (5,094)	2,061 (3,039)	106% (66%)	53% (42%)	861	2.26	1.20	80%
1982	11	15	2,008 (5,740;7,572F)	2,262 (3,334;4,511F 3,233P)	113% (65%)	53% (42%; 46%F)	424	4.74	1.00	176%
[1982 CPFs]	[5]	[5]	[4,793]	[4,846]	[101%]	[38%]	[5,917]	[0.81]	[1.96]	n/a
1983	8	25	3,250 (6,242)	3,066 (3,453P)	94% (64%)	54%	427	7.62	1.08	79%

[1] Figures in round brackets are for all UK clothing establishments. Those with an F are for all UK footwear establishments P=production workers only. *Source: Business Monitor.*
[2] Figures in square brackets (1982 only) are for clothing and footwear co-partnerships

Value added per head. This ratio is a measure of productivity of labour or wealth creation, and is basic to our approach. For the co-partnerships, it is close to the overall industry figure, though not keeping pace with the annual increase in the industry at large. However, as expected perhaps, the average value of this ratio is extremely low for the new co-operatives. Apart from the limitations of CMT, co-operatives formed with a heavy training or retraining element are likely to have low productivity initially; some part-time jobs may be counted wrongly as full-time, and any increase will be masked each year by more new entries with low productivities. Under-utilisation due to poor sales initially will also give a low figure. Value added per head does increase from less than a third to over half the industry figure between 1980 and 1983. Unless it continues to increase, new co-operatives in this sector will remain only marginally viable.

Average gross wage As with the previous figure, this is distorted, both for the co-operatives and in *Business Monitor*, by differences in the ways part-time employment is counted. The figures for the co-partnerships include bonuses and payments to provident funds, etc., which may account for their being above the industry average. The new co-operatives, on the other hand, show figures which, though increasing, are below what is already a very low industry average wage. Note, however, that new co-operatives entering with deliberately low wages for a time will keep the average wage for all co-operatives down.

Wages as percentage of value added This measure relates to the last two and shows how much of the wealth created is taken as wages, the remainder being available for reinvestment (or to go to outside causes, to meet tax requirements or, in a conventional business, a dividend on equity invested). A figure above 100 per cent indicates a loss, which would have to come from accumulated reserves, from previous or increased borrowings, or from a subsidy. Vanek's argument, above, would lead us to expect co-operators to take more in wages than is given in conventional firms. This ratio is certainly higher, even in the co-partnerships, and this is in relation to a lower labour productivity. They seem to be drawing on reserves to keep wages up and perhaps not reinvesting enough to improve productivity. However, the new co-operatives' high values for this ratio relate to low wages. The picture is of very low initial productivity (or perhaps poor sales), partly compensated for by low wages but partly by outside wage subsidy, by losses out of initial investment or by new external loans.

Value added as percentage of turnover Different sub-sectors with different relations to the market will give very different values for this ratio. CMT firms, not carrying stocks, can have very high figures, whereas footwear co-partnerships or craft-based clothing firms would have lower figures. Having said that, variations indicate better or worse margins, caused by changes either in material efficiency or in relative prices obtained. The figures indicate that the new co-operatives are working to a healthy enough margin, though as averages they may hide a good deal.

Net assets per head   As a measure of capital employed, the very low values for new clothing co-operatives show both how easy entry to this market is - or, at least, entry to the least profitable CMT part of the market – and how extremely under-capitalised these co-operatives are. And the net assets per head are getting less! This is perhaps the biggest contrast with the co-partnerships.

Value added : net assets   Halfway to being a measure of return on capital, increases in this ratio might indicate greater efficiency. However, caution is needed in interpreting the high and increasing figures for new co-operatives. As WMCC (1983) commented on profitability in the clothing industry, because there is such a low level of assets employed, there is a misleadingly high rate of return.

Liquidity   This measure gives an indication of how safe a firm is from becoming insolvent. A value of around 0.8 to 1.0 would be regarded as reasonable. The new co-operatives have average figures in this range, while the co-partnerships have higher figures, indicating the healthy reserves several of them still have. Of course, particular co-operatives could well have much lower liquidity ratios.

External loans as percentage of net assets   The high figures are analogous to a high gearing ratio for conventional firms. However, net assets figures here are so small that individual large loans will cause great fluctuation even in the average. It is worth noting that some loans are immediately going to finance losses (otherwise these figures could not be above 100 per cent), but loans still keep coming. (The co-partnerships have no external loans at all; their financing is partly by members' shares, partly by internal loans and partly from reserves.)

Variations in performance   Several references have been made to the possibility of averages hiding large variations. In 1982, for example, the eleven new clothing co-operatives for which we have data had *value added per head* figures ranging from –£20 and £62 to £2,308 and £4,035, though not one of them reached the industry average. Table 3.2 gives two contrasting examples for which we have three or four years' data.

Table 3.2 *Financial indicators for two selected clothing co-operatives*

	No. employed	Turnover (£)	Value added (£)	Net assets (£)	Value added per head (£)	Average gross wage (£)	Wages as % of value added	Value added as % of turnover	Net assets per head (£)	Value added : net assets	Liquidity	External loans as % of net assets
Happy Hands (started 1980)												
1981	3	9,624	275	1,989	917	980	107%	29%	663	1.38	1.22	0
1982	8	15,531	7,241	648	905	1,355	150%	47%	81	11.17	0.65	n/a
1983	11	31,790	23,171	(−2321)	2,106	2,211	105%	73%	n/a	n/a	0.16	n/a
Wilshaw Rainwear (started 1981)												
1981[1]	24	55,712	42,585	7,576[2]	3,549	3,344	94%	76%	314	11.24	1.31	33%
1982	27	134,761	108,945	7,722[2]	4,035	3,833	95%	81%	286	14.11	1.01	32%
1983	39	135,163	112,339	8,103[2]	2,880	3,062	106%	83%	208	13.86	0.98	42%
1984	35	146,592	129,098	6,728[2]	3,689	3,764	102%	88%	192	19.19	1.00	26%

[1] Six months only; turnover and value added figures doubled in calculations to give comparable ratios to other years
[2] All these figures understated because this co-operative obtained fixed assets very cheaply from previous firm's liquidator

The first of these, Happy Hands, to some extent fits the average picture painted above of a marginal, under-capitalised new clothing co-operative with low productivity increasing somewhat, wages not quite so low relatively speaking, and hence making a loss in its initial years. The increase in *value added as percentage of turnover* is in fact a change from craft-based production to CMT, the latter being more feasible with virtually no capital. Reducing liquidity and negative net assets could have meant impending business failure, but in fact this co-operative continues to survive and is one of our case studies.

Wilshaw Rainwear is a phoenix co-operative that seems to have been able to continue in a fairly stable condition after the previous firm's failure. It is not so badly capitalised as appears from the figures, having been able to acquire machinery, etc. very cheaply during the take-over. Wages have fluctuated a little, approximately around the industry average, but value added has only been just high enough for this, leaving virtually nothing for reinvestment, not unlike the picture for the co-partnerships. Wilshaw has a small amount of external loan finance, but is mostly financed internally, by members' loans and the undervalued fixed assets, which act rather like the undervalued property held in reserves by certain co-partnerships.

Printing and printing co-operatives
The structure of the printing industry is quite different from that in clothing and textiles. Large publishing houses and newspaper publishers tend to have in-house printing facilities, but can also put out work to medium-size or small firms. However, the industry is not dominated by a chain of subcontracting relationships linked to a few large firms, the reason being the large amount of business conducted at a fairly local level, directly for customers and to their individual specification. The market is highly differentiated and allows for large numbers of small firms. Two-thirds of printing firms employ less than fifty people, so this is one sector where the typical size of a worker co-operative is not unlike that of a conventional firm.

The printing industry overall in the UK is not in such severe decline as clothing and textiles, though particular traditional centres like London are hard hit. There is nothing like the same degree of import penetration, though large publishers do place orders in South-East Asia to some extent. However, whereas we noted that clothing manufacturing technology has not advanced enormously, printing has been transformed by new technology. This has been most notable in newspapers and the large publishing houses, but affects all parts of the industry quite deeply. It is not cheap to enter the market as a general jobbing printer and keep up to date, though there are some specialist areas such as typesetting where entry is easier.

Table 3.3   *Average financial ratios for new printing co-operatives, 1979–83*

	No. of co-ops included in data	Total no. of co-ops registered/ trading that year	Value added per head (£)	Average gross wage (£)	Wages as % of value added	Value added as % of turnover	Net assets per head (£)	Value added : net assets	Liquidity	External loans as % of assets
1979	13	24	4,405	3,676 (5,261)[1]	89%	50%	3,797 (8,824)	1.16	1.89	41%
1980	16	29	5,288	4,717 (6,364)	94%	50%	4,196 (8,573)	1.26	2.03	43%
1981	20	32	6,105	5,376 (7,248)	93%	47%	3,745 (9,117)	1.63	1.39	36%
1982	22	40	6,299 (13,314) (12,441s)[2]	5,164 (8,041) (6,784p)[3]	87% (59%)	45%	3,103 (9,861)	2.03	1.30	53%
1983	17	44	5,957 (14,424) (13,276s)	4,648 (7,433p)	82% (61%)	40%	4,348	1.37	1.03	24%

[1] Figures in brackets are for all UK printing establishments
[2] s = small firms with less than 100 employees
[3] p = production workers only

Traditionally, printing is an industry in which the workforce, particularly male craft workers, has exercised considerable control over the labour process. There is a high degree of politicisation and unionisation, even in small firms. Cockburn (1983), in her critical analysis of print unions, points out that these are societies of craftsmen that predate capitalism itself, and argues that they are an example of a skilled male élite using various means to perpetuate its dominant position. Besides strict adherence to a system of apprenticeships, craft status and differentials, print unions operate 'call books' by which their unemployed members should be offered jobs in strict rotation.

Printing co-operatives have if anything an even higher degree of unionisation (Harris, 1985). The controls exerted by the unions are a strong pressure to unionise, and in addition co-operators often feel political solidarity towards unions. The differentiated nature of the market, mentioned above, allows them to specialise in work for left-wing, feminist, black or community groups, and for trade unions also. However, some printing co-operatives have strong commitments to equal opportunities and to demystifying the trade, and this conflicts with the male domination and craft basis of the unions.

Table 3.3 shows the average financial ratios for those new printing co-operatives for which we have data, 1979–83. The stronger position of small firms in the printing sector and of their workforces is reflected in their higher labour productivity, greater capitalisation and higher wages. However, relative to these higher levels, the worker co-operatives on average are proportionately about as far below conventional firms as they are in clothing. As in clothing, *value added per head* for printing co-operatives is on average about half or less than half the industry average, and *average gross wage* is well below the industry average but above half of it. *Net Assets per head* is similarly about half the figure for the industry as a whole, or less.

The change in the average performance over the five-year period is not so striking as for new clothing co-operatives, probably because several were well established before 1979, so the effect of very new co-operatives, though present, does not dominate the figures. If anything, average performance has declined slightly. It is worth noting that a lower figure for *value added as percentage of turnover* could indicate a policy of cheap pricing to particular groups the co-operative wishes to support. However, the figure for *wages as percentage of value added*, though higher than that for all printing establishments, is consistently below 100 per cent, indicating that printing co-operatives, with their relatively low wages, are able at least to find some surplus to reinvest. They do, as shown by the last column in the table, rely much less on external loans than do clothing co-operatives, and their liquidity has also been high, if anything unnecessarily so, though the 1983 figure

Table 3.4 *Financial indicators for three selected printing co-operatives*

	No. employed (f/t equiv.)	Turnover (£)	Value added (£)	Net assets (£)	Value added per head (£)	Average gross wage (£)	Wages as % of value added	Value added as % of turnover	Net assets per head (£)	Value added : net assets	Liquidity	External loans as % of net assets
Amazon Press (started 1977)												
1980	1.5	8,381	1,316	1,739	878	1,262	144%	16%	1,160	0.75	n/a	n/a
1981	1.5	10,646	1,774	2,807	1,182	804	68%	17%	1,872	0.63	1.09	53%
1982	2	11,076	663	2,501	332	760	229%	6%	1,250	0.26	1.85	60%
1983	2	18,525	4,216	1,213	2,108	2,196	104%	23%	606	3.47	0.61	124%
1984	2	26,932	2,535	2,621	1,267	2,037	161%	9%	1,310	0.96	0.67	251%
TPC (started 1979)												
1980	3	33,367	9,776	8,344	3,259	1,883	58%	29%	2,781	1.17	1.66	39%
1981	4	70,877	17,572	10,257	4,393	2,270	52%	25%	2,564	1.71	1.26	16%
1982	5	54,009	15,111	9,755	3,022	2,364	78%	28%	1,951	1.55	1.39	4%
1983	5	55,456	16,179	10,643	3,235	2,404	74%	29%	2,129	1.51	1.65	8%
1984	5	84,604	23,651	10,380	4,730	4,371	92%	28%	2,076	2.27	1.49	8%
Lithosphere (started 1980)												
1980	8	90,286	50,228	57,529	6,278	4,381	70%	56%	7,191	0.87	2.84	65%
1981	8	131,799	60,219	50,885	7,527	7,534	100%	46%	6,360	1.18	1.38	73%
1982	10	250,345	113,656	52,665	11,366	8,611	76%	45%	5,266	2.16	1.45	43%
1983	10	411,915	219,851	164,866	20,857	10,815	52%	53%	16,487	1.26	0.68	9%
1984	21	535,364	399,094	396,586	19.004	9,106	47%	75%	18,885	1.00	3.23	51%

is lower. The general picture is of greater stability and self-reliance than in the case of clothing co-operatives, though at a relatively low average level of productivity, wages and capitalisation.

These average figures again hide a great variety of individual patterns. The variation in productivity is even greater than for clothing co-operatives. *Value added per head* in 1983 ranged from four co-operatives with figures below £2,000 to five above £6,000 of which one was well over the industry average at £20,938. There are certainly a number of printing co-operatives with extremely low productivity and wages, which may be kept going by a combination of external subsidy and political commitment from the members. Table 3.4 gives three contrasting patterns of development for different printing co-operatives over a number of years. The first is an example of such a politically committed but commercially marginal co-operative. The second has built itself up from a somewhat marginal position into a more commercially successful operation. Again, this is one of our case-study co-operatives, and we know that this change has continued successfully. In fact, several printing co-operatives have started as low-paid, low-productivity community-oriented presses and developed themselves as businesses later, prodded partly by the need to pay union rates in order to work with the labour movement. We know of only one phoenix printing co-operative with a stable performance like that of Wilshaw in clothing, so instead have chosen for our third example the most commercially successful printing co-operative. Lithosphere appears to have combined the advantage of a reasonably well-capitalised start (as a conversion from the internal print department of a national charity) with an internal dynamic of growth and development.

So the apparently stable averages hide a big split among printing co-operatives, between a number of co-operatives with continuing very low productivity and wages and a number that are developing themselves as businesses to varying degrees. The appearance is that, on average, wages and productivity for co-operatives in this sector are as far below the industry average as is the case for clothing co-operatives. However, it may still be that the constraints are less fierce and that marginal printing co-operatives have a more realistic choice. They can choose to keep prices artificially low; to subsidise work for organisations within particular social and political movements; to promote equal opportunities, flexible working, skill-sharing, etc.; and to put up with low productivity, low value of sales and hence low wages. But they can also choose to move out of this position to a greater commercial orientation.

Wholefoods and wholefood co-operatives

We chose wholefoods, both wholesale and retail, as the third sub-sector in which to look at worker co-operatives' business performance for several reasons. First, wholefood co-operatives have an important place in the new co-operative movement, being numerically significant from the mid-1970s and to some extent epitomising the alternativist strand of the movement. Secondly, in terms of our three types of relationship of small firms with the market, they have been, initially at least, examples of the third, most independent, innovative type. Thirdly, there is strong potential for political commitment to the product. Healthy eating and collective working often go together in a vision of an alternative lifestyle. Finally, many wholefood co-operatives are relatively long-lived and are surviving well in a time when their market position is no longer such a clear-cut 'niche', so that their performance may give clues as to what to expect from well-established co-operatives in general.

Wholefoods are still not distinguished as a category by standard sources such as *Business Monitor*, and CAG (1986a: 3) preface their report by noting that 'the health and wholefood business is the least researched part of the UK food business'. Their definition of wholefoods is 'pure, unadulterated foods, most of which are unprocessed. Those that are processed have undergone minimal change and contain no additives or preservatives. The few that have undergone considerable transformation (e.g. the soy products) are based entirely on natural ingredients.' They report that the UK turnover in all health food and wholefood items increased from £30 million in 1973 to £220 million in 1983, of which just over half (£121 million) was spent directly in specialist health and wholefood shops (CAG 1986a: 3).

This is in a context where food production, processing and distribution in general are increasingly concentrated in the hands of large national and multinational companies. The promotion of wholefoods was a reaction against these trends in the food industry. However, concern with health and nutrition and the acceptance of the importance of a low-fat, high-fibre diet have only recently become widespread. The conventional food industry used to regard wholefoods as an eccentric and marginal niche, and paid it little attention, except for Booker McConnell, the UK multinational, which owns both the nationwide chain of 160 Holland & Barrett shops and the wholesale operation Brewhurst. The latter, with sales of approximately £35 million in 1983, is the largest distributor of health and wholefoods in UK. However, large bakers and certain supermarket chains have recently entered the wholefoods area in a big way. Booker themselves have established Realfare, a marketing and supply 'membership group' supplied through

Brewhurst, with membership in 1983 of 680 shops, including a few co-operatives.

There are a number of independent wholesalers, both general and specialist, and a significant number of these are co-operatives. By 1983 the co-operative wholefood wholesalers had a joint turnover of some £10 million, or 5 per cent of the total market, and would collectively rank as the third biggest wholesaler in UK (excluding supermarket chains as direct purchasers).

Previously, the co-operative wholefoods wholesalers had enjoyed a fairly cosy relationship with the co-operative retailers they supplied. Some, such as Suma (see Chapter 4), were initially set up with the support of loose federations of co-operative wholefood shops. More recently, the main co-operative wholesalers themselves have maintained an implicit agreement not to compete with each other geographically. But the market has now become much more open and less segmented. Particularly in the case of retailers, the wholefood co-operatives have either to innovate and specialise further, or face a more competitive future, in which they may become more like small print firms in their dependency relationships.

The jobs offered by wholefood co-operatives are mainly shop, catering or warehouse work. These are on the whole low-paid in conventional industry, and not areas of high unionisation or politicisation. The main union is the Union of Shop, Distributive and Allied Workers (USDAW), which in fact has close historical links with the established co-operative movement, but no particular connection with alternative politics. USDAW faces the general difficulties of trying to organise a fragmented workforce, many of whom are part-time, seasonal or short-term workers, in an industry where, despite increased concentration of ownership, workplaces are fairly small and scattered, and many jobs are becoming more routinised and alienating.

Table 3.5 gives the average values of our selected financial ratios for those wholefood co-operatives for which we have data, 1979–84. A number of these co-operatives had been trading for a few years before 1979, and some as partnerships with a collectivist orientation from the early 1970s, before converting to a co-operative legal form after the publication of ICOM's model rules in 1976. This, together with the larger numbers of co-operatives involved, gives the figures in Table 3.5 more stability than the corresponding figures for printing, and even more than for clothing.

Value added per head and *average gross wage* have both increased considerably over the six years for wholefoods co-operatives, to a greater extent than for printing or clothing. The increase in *average gross wage* is much more marked than for the other sub-sectors and, given that this is generally a low-wage area, puts average wages

Table 3.5 *Average financial ratios for new wholefood co-operatives, 1979–84*

	No. of co-ops included in data	Total no. of co-ops registered/ trading that year	Value added per head (£)	Average gross wage (£)	Wages as % of value added	Value added as % of turnover (£)	Value added : net assets	Net assets per head (£)	Liquidity	External loans as % of assets
1979	28	34	2,064	1,960	95%	13%	1.30	1,586	1.78	35%
1980	35	46	2,505	2,304	92%	14%	1.39	1,805	1.57	44%
1981	41	53	3,097	2,911	94%	13%	1.26	2,455	1.35	39%
1982	42	58	3,582	3,259	91%	12%	1.34	2,681	1.31	37%
1983	43	69	3,672	3,488	95%	11%	1.31	2,808	1.14	37%
1984	32	80	4,775	4,154	87%	11%	1.37	3,483	1.08	35%

in wholefood co-operatives quite close to industry averages. The proportion of value added retained rather than paid out as wages is consistently higher than for printing co-operatives, though not as high as the profit levels recorded in conventional firms. This may help to explain the rise in *net assets per head*, despite the low figures, particularly in earlier years, for *external loans as percentage of net assets*. In other words, the wholefood co-operative sector has been strengthening itself through building up collectively owned reserves.

The figures for *value added as percentage of turnover* are much lower than for clothing or printing, simply reflecting the much greater turnover in retailing or wholesaling. In fact, wholesaling can expect to generate an even lower figure than retailing. If there were more co-operative wholefood caterers or manufacturers, these average figures would be higher.

Finally, note that the *liquidity* figures, like those for printing co-operatives, have moved down to what is still a reasonable level – just! - from perhaps an unnecessarily high one.

As with printing and clothing, the average figures hide a variety of individual patterns. However, looking at the single indicator *value added per head* in one year, 1983, does not give a clear split into some co-operatives with high and others with low productivity. Discounting co-operatives with very low figures for special reasons (e.g. being very new, about to go out of business, etc.), more than half cluster round the average, with values between £2,500 and £5,000. This probably reflects the fairly large number of relatively long-lived wholefood co-operatives, which may have reached fairly stable positions over a number of years.

Again we have chosen three examples to illustrate the different patterns (Table 3.6). The second and third of these are two of our case studies. The first, Honeysuckle, is perhaps typical of the many wholefood retail collectives started with no external support, which have had to become rather more competitive but whose figures for *wages, value added per head* and *net assets per head*, despite considerable increases, remain quite low. The second, Wholegrain Foods, was running for six or seven years before our figures begin. Performance has been fairly stable around the industry average, *wages* and *value added per head* increasing only slightly faster than inflation. (The big rise in *net assets per head* and fall in *value added : net assets* does not show reduced efficiency; it reflects big increases in fixed assets, mainly property. Wholefood shops are perhaps more likely to own their premises – or long leases on them – making ratios involving net assets hard to interpret.) Finally, Suma also traded for some years before 1979, but has managed fairly consistently to return a higher *value added per head* figure which has made possible both increases in

Table 3.6 *Financial indicators for three selected wholefood co-operatives*

	No. employed (f/t equiv.)	Turnover (£)	Value added (£)	Net assets (£)	Value added per head (£)	Average gross wage (£)	Wages as % of value added	Value added as % of turnover	Net assets per head (£)	Value added : net assets	Liquidity	External loans as % of net assets
Honeysuckle (started 1977)												
1979	5	52,092	6,217	6,120	1,243	1,064	86%	12%	1,224	1.02	1.68	0%
1980	5	71,275	7,191	2,681	1,198	1,463	122%	10%	536	2.68	1.14	0%
1981	5	64,742	13,678	3,933	2,736	1,968	72%	21%	787	3.48	1.51	0%
1982	4	59,919	11,023	3,374	2,756	2,134	77%	18%	844	3.27	1.02	0%
1983	4	66,274	12,581	4,261	3,153	2,452	78%	19%	1,066	2.95	1.28	0%
1984	4	75,768	14,326	5,724	3,581	2,956	83%	19%	1,431	2.50	1.20	28%
Wholegrain Foods (started 1971)												
1979	14	256,486	60,181	10,343	4,299	3,463	81%	23%	739	6.82	1.14	29%
1980	14	273,176	71,091	40,732	5,078	4,473	88%	26%	2,909	1.75	1.37	76%
1981	12	363,389	73,921	91,725	6,160	4,774	78%	20%	7,644	0.81	1.39	42%
1982	12	448,448	90,180	143,795	7,515	5,199	69%	20%	11,983	0.63	1.47	51%
1983	19	570,792	104,687	251,260	5,510	3,852	70%	18%	13,224	0.42	1.09	34%
1984	20	853,591	139,129	280,223	6,956	5,324	77%	16%	14,011	0.50	1.01	44%
Suma (started 1974)												
1979	10	930,689	65,699	67,782	6,570	3,391	52%	7%	6,778	0.97	1.55	33%
1980	10	1,237,778	115,554	156,062	11,642	4,638	40%	9%	15,606	0.75	1.60	30%
1981	14	1,596,985	156,956	232,884	11,211	5,593	53%	10%	16,635	0.67	1.66	24%
1982	17	2,056,908	171,154	215,943	10,068	6,538	65%	8%	12,703	0.79	1.53	22%
1983	27	2,772,514	213,591	258,133	7,911	6,618	84%	8%	9,560	0.83	1.30	24%
1984	27	3,122,138	312,435	272,188	11,572	8,452	83%	10%	10,081	1.15	1.25	18%

wage levels and retention of large amounts of surplus. Reinvestment in the business, financed increasingly from retained surplus, has been steady, and growth in numbers as well as turnover possible.

Suma is a wholesaler, and, as noted above, the idea of some degree of control over a specialised market niche continues to apply much better to wholefood wholesalers than to retailers. Both are now in a more competitive market, but retailers much more so. It seems to be hard for retail wholefood co-operatives to maintain over long periods the high degree of commercial marginality that some community or political printers have maintained. Many have improved their efficiency, wage levels, etc. considerably, though one might still call them marginal. Some of the more long-lived wholefoods co-operatives have developed themselves in their first few years to a degree that they have a stable position at or above the industry average for wages and productivity. A few, like Suma, have continued to develop beyond this point.

Conclusions: financing, dependency and other factors

We set out in this chapter to find out, in economic terms, how co-operatives perform compared to small businesses. We noted Vanek's argument that, because of their ownership structure and the way they are financed, worker co-operatives will be less efficient than capitalist enterprises. We also gave our own view that external factors such as a co-operative's dependent position within the capitalist labour process will constrain its performance, although this will be just as true for small businesses, and internal factors such as the type of financing could still be important. We have now looked at the economic performance of co-operatives in three sectors: clothing and footwear, printing and wholefoods. Can we say which argument is better?

On the two main criteria of labour productivity (*value added per head*) and wages (*average gross wage*), clothing and footwear co-partnerships perform reasonably well, showing that the co-operative form is not intrinsically inferior. However, both the new clothing and the printing co-operatives perform on average well below the respective industry averages. It seems that this is for different reasons in the two cases.

The new clothing co-operatives are extremely poorly capitalised (*net assets per head* about one-tenth the figure for the co-partnerships) and are in fact mainly confined to the CMT part of the market. The low performance seems to be an average of several young, marginal, CMT co-operatives establishing themselves by means of 'sweat equity' (i.e. workers' underpaid efforts partly compensating for lack of capital), with very low wages and productivity in the early years, and some phoenix co-operatives with performance figures nearer to the industry norm.

The printing co-operatives are less poorly capitalised, but their wage levels, though higher than those in clothing co-operatives, are lower in relation to what is a fairly highly paid industry. However, the averages here hide a much bigger variation. The most successful printing co-operative performs well above the industry average, and several printing co-operatives have become quite commercially successful. Others have extremely low figures for productivity and wages, and it seems these are maintained by political motivation.

Finally, wholefood co-operatives, particularly wholesalers, generally perform well in relation to the low wages in retailing and the distributive trades generally. A few of them are marginal, but the majority have stable figures near the industry average, and several not only pay good wages and show increases in productivity but have grown substantially in terms of numbers employed.

Let us look at Vanek's argument on financing in relation to our findings here. Note that he characterised worker co-operatives as financed internally, by contributions from members and by retained surpluses, and argued that this would lead them to under-invest, under-produce and under-employ relative to capitalist firms. However, we have just seen that many of the co-operatives that are performing best in relation to other small firms, in wholefoods and in the printing sector, are growing and developing mostly on the basis of such internal finance.

Thus, Vanek's argument, which would suggest that external loan financing is the most useful type, is not borne out by this evidence. Note, however, that most of our figures are on the start-up period, whereas Vanek's model assumes well-established, ongoing co-operatives.

Over-reliance on external loans is the equivalent of high gearing. To some extent at least, this type of financing can act as a burden to be repaid; some co-operatives use their early surpluses (created by 'sweat equity') to replace loan capital with internal, collective reserves. Hence, as they develop, their asset base can become very stretched. Other co-operatives can use their retained surpluses as a kind of equity to lever in external loans and build up capital. Both these processes can occur, and it is not at all clear that the *type* of financing is a factor that *determines* the likelihood of, say, development and growth rather than continued marginality. However, overall *lack* of finance may be one factor that restricts co-operatives to the more dependent positions in the market. We mentioned above the argument that there is a need for the co-operative movement to develop new financial structures allowing equity participation, since reliance on external loans seems to limit the amount of finance that can be obtained, and strict adherence to one financial structure may be too inflexible. However, we also noted that equity participation is considered by many to contravene basic co-operative principles. So far, there are very few new co-operatives with equity participation, and we have no evidence on their performance.

How co-operatives are financed can vary at different stages in their development. Although co-operatives starting up, particularly clothing co-operatives, often relied heavily on external loans, the established co-operatives we studied approximated more to Vanek's model of collective financing from retained surpluses. There is the possibility, at least, that, once capitalised (however that occurs), some co-operatives may indeed 'under-produce' and 'under-employ' – in other words, stagnate or decline in the way Vanek postulates. However, there is also in some cases a clear dynamic to continued development. It is not yet clear to what extent the type of financing affects this.

As for our argument on dependency, the evidence, though inconclusive, tends to show a clearer effect than that of financing. We noted that, in all three sectors studied, average figures hid large variations. There are several distinct patterns of performance. In some sub-sectors such as CMT, many small firms are so heavily dependent that clothing co-operatives of this type are simply internalising a degree of exploitation that exists for workers in other clothing firms or for outworkers. In other sectors, such as printing, small firms have more independence, though in a competitive market. Thus printing co-operatives have a realistic degree of choice, so that if they suffer collective exploitation it is self-imposed in the name of some political or other wider aim. Other printing co-operatives have found it possible to develop commercially – the constraints are not too heavy. Wholefoods gave us an example of the most independent type of small firm in one of the least constrained sectors. Wholefoods co-operatives are often as successful as other small firms, or more so.

However, this leaves aside altogether what is a success or a failure. A marginal co-operative may cease trading when support fades but may have provided an excellent service for many years, whereas members of a co-operative that takes on more commercial goals may feel they have lost their early idealism. Much of the rest of this book is concerned with non-economic aspects of co-operative performance. First, though, the next chapter describes the detailed case studies we made in terms of patterns derived from the data in this chapter on business performance. It begins to explain why some co-operatives are able to develop, within the constraints of finance and dependency, more than others. Subsequent chapters then use the case studies in their discussions of motivation and commitment, co-operative management and so on.

4

Factors Affecting Co-operative Business Development: Sixteen Cases

In this chapter we combine two tasks. First, we present the sixteen case studies on which much of this book is based (see Table 4.1 for a summary of their main characteristics). Then we use evidence from these case studies to continue the discussion of the various factors affecting co-operative business development.

We present our case studies in three groups, according to broadly differing patterns of business development. These patterns are roughly derived from the variations in economic performance during the early years of a co-operative that we found in Chapter 3.

We suggest that in business terms there are two main types of co-operative start-up. The first type we call 'shoestring'. Such co-operatives have very little capital and depend heavily on the commitment of their members, including 'sweat equity'.

This type of start-up gives rise to two main patterns. First, there are co-operatives that continue with low levels of productivity, capitalisation, etc., in some cases for many years. We call these *commercially marginal*, and Happy Hands and Amazon Press (Tables 3.2, 3.4) are clear examples. They may be supported by continuing outside subsidy as well as by continuing low wages. This 'self-exploitation' is not in principle different from what small business owners do, but it may work differently because it extends to all workers and might be better termed, as suggested by Macfarlane (1987a), 'collective exploitation'.

The second main pattern occurs when co-operatives that start on a shoestring develop later. The 'sweat equity' may turn into capital held in collectively owned reserves; external loans may also help capitalisation on the basis of demonstrated or expected success. Wages and labour productivity both approach or exceed average levels for the industry. We call such co-operatives '*self-developers*'. TPC is an example (see Table 3.4); Suma and Wholegrain were self-developers before the period of the data in Table 3.6.

The other type of start-up is based more on financial investment and not so exclusively on members' unaided commitment. Co-operatives of this type can include rescues where assets have been acquired cheaply so that the investment is subsidised. (This does not apply to all rescues and phoenixes however – some of the latter are very

Table 4.1 *The sixteen case studies*

	Sector	Start-up type, orientation	Dates	No. of Workers	Structure
Commercially marginal co-operatives					
Happy Hands	Clothing (CMT)	New start, job creation	1980–	22	Collective (+co-ordinator)
Oakleaf Books	Bookshop	New start, alternative	1979–85	3–4	Simple collective
The Bean Shop	Wholefood shop	New start, alternative	1971–	3–4	Simple collective
WICC[1]	Wholefood catering	New start, job creation	1984–	3–4	Collective (+co-ordinator)
The Cycle Co-op[1]	Bicycle shop	New start, job creation	1984–	4–6	Simple collective
La Fontaine	Restaurant	New start, job creation	1984–6	2–3	Simple collective
FDC[1]	Clothing (design)	New start, job creation	1984–6	3–4	Simple collective
Self-developing co-operatives					
Suma	Wholefood wholesaling	New start, alternative	1974–	35	Complex collective
Wholegrain Foods[1]	Wholefoods (variety)	New start, alternative	1971–	20	Complex collective
Lake	Language school	Phoenix, alternative	1978–	6–8	Collective (+co-ordinator)
Recycles	Bicycle shop	New start, alternative	1977–	5–6	Simple collective
TPC[1]	Printers	New start, alternative	1979–	10	Collective
Capitalised co-operatives					
Red Dragon Stores	Supermarket	Rescue, job saving	1984–6	4–5	Collective (+manager)
Union Pheonix[1]	Engineers	Phoenix, job saving	1984–	15	Dual control structure
The Engineering Co-op[1]	Engineers	Rescue, job saving	1983–	12	Dual control structure
The Clothing Co-op	Clothing (CMT)	Pheonix, job saving	1983–86	6–26	Dual control structure

[1] The names of these co-operatives are fictitious in order to preserve confidentiality.

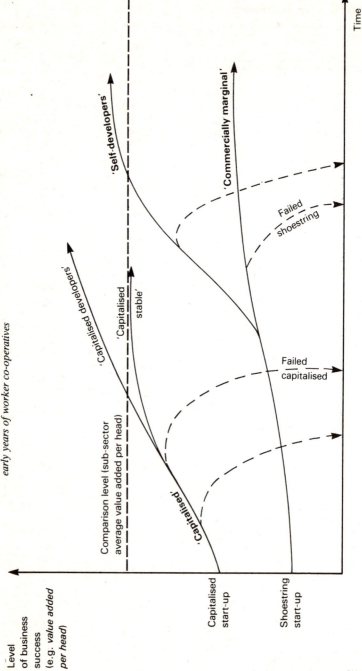

Figure 4.1   *Schematic representation of main patterns of business development for early years of worker co-operatives*

much 'shoestring' affairs.) We call this type *'capitalised'*, though this is very much a relative term, and such co-operatives are still often short of capital. In principle, conversions and new starts might equally be 'capitalised' from the start, for example when effort has gone into raising funds for an ambitious new venture. So far, there are few examples of this, and we have not studied any cases in depth, but they could well be more important in the future.

Several patterns can arise from a capitalised start-up. For example, some co-operatives, like Wilshaw Rainwear (see Table 3.2), quickly achieve, and then maintain, wage and productivity levels close to the average for the industry they are in, and this might be termed a 'stable' pattern. Others, despite their reasonably good level of capitalisation, may become marginal or fail quickly. In yet other cases, there may be a pattern where a capitalised start-up is followed by development and growth taking the various indicators quickly well above the industry average. We could call such co-operatives 'capitalised developers' but we know of few candidates for inclusion in such a category. The printers, Lithosphere (see Table 3.4), may be one such.

In what follows, we treat 'capitalised' co-operatives as one group, since there are not yet enough examples to distinguish these possible patterns very clearly.

Figure 4.1 shows the various patterns schematically. The vertical axis is a composite indication of business performance, which could include *value added per head*, *average gross wage*, etc., and the horizontal axis represents the first years (say, five or six) of a co-operative. Each of our three groups ('commercially marginal', 'self-developers' and 'capitalised') is represented by a family of curves, and each includes possible business failure.

'Commercially marginal' co-operatives

As pointed out above, 'shoestring' co-operatives may continue to trade for a number of years, or they may cease trading if their external or internal support is no longer forthcoming. We have called these 'commercially marginal', but one should not be too hasty in labelling such co-operatives as failures. A marginal co-operative may provide an excellent service before ceasing to trade as a result of changes outside its control, such as the loss of a regular subsidy due to political or policy changes. Or a co-operative paying low wages may nevertheless provide its workers with a better deal than they can get elsewhere. Let us introduce some examples.

Oakleaf Books

Oakleaf Books (see Plumpton, 1988) traded for nearly seven years as a radical bookseller. The initial working capital came partly from an external grant, partly as small loans from supporters and partly as 'sweat equity' when the full-time workers took no wage. The co-operative made a very small net trading profit during the first year. Wages when paid were very low.

During 1979 a new large shopping centre was being completed nearby. The lease on a tiny shop unit was negotiated in a rather out-of-the-way specialist arcade, all they could afford or were likely to be allowed as a radical shop. Unfortunately the city-centre shop made a critical loss, and after a year the co-operative decided to close it. By this time turnover at the main shop had built up but was still far too low for financial viability. Despite considerable efforts, shop sales only remained stable over the remaining years, with increased competition from a city-centre bookshop which began to stock more radical publications.

In order to try to boost turnover Oakleaf began to supply institutional customers such as libraries. Turnover on these sales nearly doubled from 1980 to 1983, but slumped dramatically in 1984 with the cuts in educational budgets. This was really the beginning of the end for the shop.

In 1984 a loan was taken out against the security of Oakleaf's building to finance the trading loss. However, the situation did not improve in 1985. The workers did not want to make further losses which would have jeopardised the loans made to them by their supporters, so they decided to go into voluntary liquidation and pay off all their creditors.

Oakleaf's basic problem was their inability to increase turnover to a point where they could operate without subsidy. This was probably largely due to their poor location. Had they set up in the city-centre, their prospects might have been better, although they would have had to compromise more on their choice of stock.

It is pertinent to ask how Oakleaf managed to survive so long. The first relevant factor was the financial and moral support from supporters. Second came the various external grants it managed to obtain. Third, and most important, was the commitment and dedication of the shop workers, who tolerated low wages and poor working conditions (£40 per week in 1985). Undoubtedly the workers' political commitment was important in maintaining their commitment to the shop. Also it is possible, as Rothschild-Whitt (1976) observed elsewhere, that the poor conditions actually reinforced the workers' solidarity and commitment at least in the short term. The founders left after a few years, allowing other committed people to join. As one said: 'Paradoxically, I think this led to a greater degree of solidarity amongst us, but this commitment could not be maintained for ever.'

Although Oakleaf did not become a viable business, it did succeed for nearly seven years in achieving its social objectives of promoting and selling literature supporting radical social change, and becoming an information centre and focus for local cultural and political activities.

Happy Hands[1]

Happy Hands is a women's clothing co-operative in South Wales. Two of the founders met on a course in sewing-machining at the local Skills Centre in 1979 and heard about co-operatives from another woman on the course. There was certainly no chance of part-time work locally for women with children, so with five others they set about creating work for themselves. With help from the local CDA, they prepared a business plan based on making soft toys and party-plan selling, and got a £2,500 loan from ICOF which enabled them to start trading in 1980.

Now, after two changes of premises and several changes of product line, Happy Hands employs about 22 women (down from a high of 28) on CMT work. Even within that they are restricted to the least profitable making-up work, lacking the skills to do cutting or the resources to include trimming and pressing. However, their reputation for quality is good, and they have a fairly regular supply of work. Although the job content is fairly standard for the industry, there is a little more flexibility and mobility than usual, with about half the workforce competent on all machines, and minor co-ordinating tasks delegated to certain members on top of their machining jobs.

Happy Hands' most important success is in achieving its aim of providing part-time employment, with flexible hours of work and holidays, for women with young children. They run two overlapping time shifts during school holidays, and keep to a basic 25-hour week. But the wage level has remained very low – in 1985, £35 per week, i.e. £1.40 per hour against a local rate of £1.70 for machinists. However, wages would have to more than double before the gain would offset tax and loss in benefits such as Family Income Supplement. Clearly it is not worth paying even the paltry rate of £1.70 if jobs are to be kept part-time.

It is important to realise that working at Happy Hands is for many women actually materially beneficial compared to other possibilities. It is not that non-financial aspects, such as freedom from supervision and a good working atmosphere, attract women despite the low wages. Many could not afford to stay if they could do better for themselves or their families elsewhere. But part-time jobs are not available. By working part-time flexible hours, they can save on child-care, and transport to and from work is arranged. These things mean money savings, and together with retaining social security benefits due to low wages and staying below the tax threshold, they make it possible for a woman working 25 hours at £1.40 at Happy Hands to have more money in her pocket (and more time with her family) than if she worked 40 hours at £1.70.

Over the years the co-operative has consciously kept wages down and built up reserves, ploughing back its surplus into paying back its ICOF loan and owning its machines outright. They have tried to move into more profitable lines of work but had to revert to CMT. Conditions are not even secure from week to week, with defaults from customers causing occasional weeks with no pay at all.

It is extremely difficult for such firms to break out of marginality. To move to manufacturing and marketing one's own designs means simultaneous quantum jumps in skills, investment, risk, the complexity of management functions and working capital needs. Nevertheless the co-operative is still looking for ways to develop the business, as it continues towards the end of its sixth year.

Other 'commercially marginal' co-operatives
The Bean Shop (see Woolham, 1987) is typical of small marginal wholefood shops. A collective of three to four people, trading since 1971 as an unincorporated partnership, and partially dependent on voluntary labour, it has also provided a centre for community and political activities over the years. More recently it has provided stable though low-paid employment for its partners.

The Cycle Co-op is a bicycle shop started by a small group from an unemployed workers centre. It began seriously under-capitalised, relying primarily on a £1,000 grant and £5,000 overdraft. Initially the six members worked for nothing. During its second year the co-operative experienced a major cash flow crisis when the workers, inexperienced and untrained in stock control, book-keeping and financial management, and unaware of seasonal fluctuations in their trade, expanded their stock without fully considering the consequences. Eventually some founder members left the co-operative, and it continues to survive as a marginal business.

West Indian Catering Co-operative (WICC) was formed in 1984 by a group of unemployed people providing an ethnic catering service. The idea came from one woman who became the effective manager of the co-operative. The original business plan, which the local CDA helped to formulate, won a prize in a national competition, which provided some start-up capital and places on a training course. WICC began trading on an informal basis and only started keeping proper financial records a year later. During the first eighteen months no wages were paid, at least formally, and members remained on benefits. Eventually WICC registered as a co-operative, obtained a loan from a sympathetic local authority and started to pay wages.

Member turnover in WICC has been quite high; only one founder remains. Members want to make the business a success, but have a much less clear commitment to and understanding of co-operative principles. WICC runs rather like a family business and became a co-operative at least partly because advice and support were readily available from the local CDA and the local authority.

The co-operative has a good product, although its service is erratic. Before its demise, the GLC, directly and indirectly, was its main customer. Since then, it may not have a sufficient market, and its future is highly uncertain.

Fabric Design Co-operative (FDC) had three founders with experience in the fabric trade. Their motivation was twofold: to escape exploitatively low fees for designers and to contribute to improving the economic position of ethnic minorities by creating an ethnic business. Their original idea was to produce small batches of fabric to their own designs, to be printed as ordered by a subcontractor.

The co-operative approached their local authority, which was keen to promote ethnic businesses, for support. The council offered a £1,000 setting-up grant and a loan guarantee scheme. Their officer drastically revised the co-operative's business plan, increasing the projected turnover fourfold, and advised them to print their own materials in a council-owned factory unit. Unfortunately this business plan was flawed: it was not based on adequate market research, and seriously underestimated working capital. The members lacked the experience to realise this. Their problems were exacerbated by protracted negotiations for the bank loan and loan guarantee, which effectively left the co-operative without working capital for nine months. It never recovered from this poor start and incurred heavy losses in the first eighteen months of trading. A subsequent study revealed that the business would have needed at least £45,000 injected to have a reasonable chance of surviving. However, the members remained unable to provide a realistic market plan, and after two years the business drifted into compulsory liquidation.

La Fontaine's three members previously worked in a local hotel. A change in management, which they felt was profit- rather than customer-orientated and demanded more unpaid overtime, led them to start their own restaurant business, assisted by the local CDA. Member loans and a small overdraft all went to equip and stock their rather large premises.

Trade still had not built up to a viable level after a year. Based on their hotel experience with 'captive' customers their business plan grossly overestimated what they could sell. Overheads were very high, particularly as they paid a very high rent as short-term sub-tenants, and the bank consistently refused them a loan to buy the lease. Wages reduced from £70 to £20 a week or less. One member left. The other two remained determined to succeed but were forced to close, although they hoped to start another co-operative catering venture, and one became active on the local CDA's management committee.

Discussion
Broadly speaking co-operatives that start on a shoestring and remain marginal can be divided up into two categories. There are those like Oakleaf Books and The Bean Shop, set up for political and social reasons. Commercial factors were of secondary importance in their formation, so for example both set up in areas where it turned out they could not develop an adequate market to break out of marginality. In a few cases alternative co-operatives actively refuse to adopt certain practices associated with managerialism, and this can lead to inefficiency. Most often, as at both The Bean Shop and Oakleaf, political orientation affects commercial viability even when businesses are run efficiently, for example in terms of the limited range of stock they were prepared to sell. In addition The Bean Shop deliberately tried to keep its prices very low so that it could make wholefoods available to the poorer sections of the community. As time went on both co-operatives had to adopt a more commercial orientation in order to survive, though in Oakleaf's case with the market moving against small radical booksellers this was not enough.

Given their poor business performance, how can this type of commercially marginal co-operative survive for so long? Perhaps the most important factor is the commitment that comes from their political beliefs and the solidarity that is created through collective working and surviving hardship together. They are reinforced in their commitment by outside supporters and sympathisers. External support has also been important materially. It is difficult for members of marginal co-operatives to sustain poor pay and working conditions indefinitely, particularly as workers get older and their financial commitments increase, although some co-operatives have been able to survive by recruiting new committed workers to replace those who move on.

Other marginal co-operatives are set up either by the unemployed to create their own jobs, or by workers wanting to create their own business to escape from what they feel are exploitative conditions in their existing jobs. These co-operatives often become trapped in highly dependent sectors such as CMT where profitability and wage levels are low. However, some, like Happy Hands, are able to continue because they manage to meet the needs of their members better than other alternatives.

In our examples, the development of this type of business was hampered by lack of start-up capital and, as in many conventional small businesses, by lack of business skills and experience. At FDC these problems were compounded by poor advice from a local authority adviser. WICC also suffered from poor work discipline and the demise of one of its major customers. At The Cycle Co-op the main problems were lack of financial management information and very poor stock control, plus overstaffing. The main weaknesses at La Fontaine were poor market research and inadequate marketing. If under-capitalised co-operatives such as these are to survive in the longer term, sweat equity alone will not be enough to save them. They must be able to learn quickly and develop or acquire the skills that they lack.

'Self-developing' co-operatives

We defined 'self-developing' co-operatives as those which begin operation at low levels of capitalisation and value added per head, but unlike the 'commercially marginal' co-operatives manage to improve their business performance. They are able to reinvest retained surpluses and/or bring in new loans, and over time become well established and capitalised. Such co-operatives can then offer their members wages and conditions that compare well with other small businesses, and continue to provide a good-quality service to their customers.

Recycles

Recycles (see Oliver, 1987) began trading in 1977, after the three founder members, all active in the bike community in Edinburgh, decided to pool their talents and meagre resources to make a living out of repairing bicycles. They raised about £1,500 in loans and obtained premises in a derelict council-owned shop. After fitting, only £300 was left for stock. The founders had no formal training in bicycle repair work, and little experience of running a business. The first eighteen months were a hard, day-to-day struggle. Lack of stock reduced sales levels and efficiency. Wages were the equivalent of the dole, for a six-day week.

One of the members returned to the dole to look for more profitable ideas. Bicycle hiring looked like a promising venture because of the tourist trade. Further finance was raised through a personal bank loan, and from friends of the founders, plus £1,000 from ICOF, the application being supported by the Scottish Co-operative Development Commitee (SCDC).

The cycle hire and repair businesses operated more or less autonomously during 1978. The hire business, in new premises obtained from a friend, began to make money. Aware that business would decline in the winter, one of the founders decided to start stocking new cycles for sale over the Christmas period. This was done largely without consulting the members in the repair shop. Unfortunately the bike trade was poor that Christmas, and the co-operative had a lot of unsold stock. This precipitated a chronic cash-flow crisis. Recycles called in SCDC and with their help secured a further loan from ICOF to pay off their creditors. However, the incident soured relations between two of the founders, and one left.

After this came a phase of increased business awareness and formalisation of procedures. With advice from SCDC, the co-operative began to acquire and practise financial management skills. During 1979 the business expanded and developed, and wages increased to £50 a week. They leased an adjacent shop and then in the summer of 1980 purchased one of the shops, again with a loan from ICOF, this time in conjunction with the Department of Trade and Industry. At the end of 1981 it was decided to close the repair shop, because its operation was very marginal.

Surprisingly, as the business gained strength labour turnover was quite high. Having reached a peak of seven permanent staff in 1980–1 the co-operative came down to five members, a reduction viewed with some relief by their accountant. From 1982 the business consolidated on one site and changed in orientation. Previously new members had been selected largely because of their sympathy towards co-operatives, but they now sought to stem the high labour turnover by employing people specifically interested in working with bicycles.

By 1983 wages had increased to £70 for a four-day week. Since then the co-operative has stayed on a sound commercial footing. Recycles is now Edinburgh's second bike shop and the leading supplier of specialist bicycle parts.

Suma Wholefoods
Suma Wholefoods (see Macfarlane, 1987a) was converted into a co-operative in 1976 using ICOM model rules. Its founder had been working in a wholefood shop that was a member of the informal Federation of Northern Wholefood Collectives (FNWC). He bought a van and started a delivery service to FNWC members, collecting orders, obtaining the goods from wholesalers and then delivering them to the various shops. As the business grew he took on workers, and started to keep stocks. However, he apparently began to feel it was becoming too much like a capitalist business and wanted to leave. It was decided that the workforce should buy the business and establish

it formally as a co-operative. The co-operative's initial capital took the form of a loan from the founder, which was repaid in two years.

Suma's turnover has grown rapidly, from £625,000 in 1977–78 to just under £4 million in 1984–85. Adjusting for inflation, the average increase in sales volume has been approximately 22 per cent per annum. The co-operative's membership increased from 10 in 1980 to 35 in 1985.

Wages levels at Suma before 1980 were quite low. This corresponds with a period when the proportion of internal funding of the business grew rapidly from 17 per cent to 40 per cent, as retained surplus was used to capitalise the business. After 1980 it was decided to increase wage levels, and they rose rapidly, almost doubling by 1982 to a flat £100 per week after deductions. Unfortunately this also coincided with a decision to decrease gross profit levels, because Suma's products were felt to be becoming too expensive. The result of these two decisions, despite improved efficiency in stock turnover, was a rapid decline in net surplus between 1980 and 1983.

If these trends had continued it would have spelt serious trouble for the business. However, there has been a conscious effort since 1982 to increase gross profit levels and to hold down wages. The need for more financial management and internal co-ordination has been recognised, and a marketing section was formed. The increase in mark-up on products has not led to a decline in demand. The business has continued to expand, leading in 1986 to the difficult decision to move from central Leeds to a better warehouse in Halifax.

One important explanation of Suma's growth given by members is that 'we were in the right place at the right time'. This view highlights the importance of the growing wholefood market, and the way that Suma's early growth was a reaction to demand rather than a planned effort. However, Suma, at least initially, shared ideological links with its market. Customer relations were based on trust and mutual support. Also, their drivers were knowledgeable about the wholefood business, so that Suma was able to provide a good-quality and responsive service.

Paradoxically the physical limitations of the warehouse appear to have contributed to Suma's success. The pressure on space, as demand increased, led to an increase in stock turnover rate from 6.3 to 8.5 times per annum, but handling this quantity of heavy goods in a three-storey building was inefficient. At peak times workers have had to work long hours under increased stress for what in real terms were decreasing wages. Members' needs for more money, better working conditions and less stress underlie the move to new premises. However, the move will increase operating costs, and so the co-operative is going to have to achieve greater labour efficiency, which should be possible in the new building and with more mechanisation. For the first time Suma has to grow to survive.

Finally, it should be noted that there has also been an element of good fortune in Suma's success. Suma has for much of its life operated with inadequate financial information, co-ordination and planning. This has led to periodic cash-flow crises. Suma has learnt from these problems and now takes financial management, co-ordination and planning more seriously.

Other 'self-developing' co-operatives
Wholegrain Foods (see Woolham, 1987) started as a partnership of three people running a restaurant in the early 1970s. In 1973 it became a shop selling wholefoods. Later expansion included setting up a bakery and a wholefood wholesaling operation. In 1978 the partnership was converted into a co-operative, which has continued to grow rapidly so that for the year 1984–5 it had a turnover of approximately £1.2 million, and employed over twenty people.

Although Wholegrain experienced some problems in raising external finance for expansion in the early days, and then again later when the bank wanted to take out a debenture against the loan, its main problems have been concerned with planning and managing this expansion. Much of the entrepreneurial work has been the responsibility of 'Simon', one of the original partners. This led to a serious competence gap between him and the other members. In addition, procedures for stock control and financial management have been poor. In two consecutive years the shop and then the warehouse made losses. However, the poor quality of information kept made it impossible to diagnose the problem adequately. In 1986 Simon and another experienced member decided to leave the co-operative: Simon to set up on his own. This has left the co-operative short of skills and experience, so the next couple of years are likely to be crucial to its development.

Lake School of English (see Cornforth, 1988a) is a phoenix co-operative teaching English as a foreign language (EFL) and based in Oxford. It was formed by some of the staff from a tutorial college whose EFL department was threatened with closure. The co-operative started with £200 in capital raised by a sponsored swim. It held its first courses in summer 1978 in hired premises in the town's suburbs. During the early years it was very much a hand-to-mouth existence with members taking very low wages. However, the co-operative has managed to increase its turnover each year, from about £15,000 in 1978–9 to over £70,000 in 1983–4. Today they operate from smart new premises in the centre of town, and pay wages at about the market rate.

A number of factors have been crucial to the successful development of Lake. First, the members had time to plan the new venture while in their old job, using contacts and knowledge of procedures and markets. Secondly, the commitment of the members was vital, particularly during the early years when wages and working conditions were poor. Thirdly, shortage of suitable, reasonably priced premises was a problem eventually overcome when they took out a short-term lease on premises owned by the council that were due for redevelopment. Fourthly, perhaps the major problem facing the co-operative was establishing their market, particularly during the winter. They succeeded by getting the British Council to use their school. Fifthly, members of Lake have good contacts, which has helped establish their credibility. Sixthly, members of the co-operative place a great emphasis on providing a good-quality, friendly service to their students, many of whom come because of personal recommendation. Finally, their decision to employ a full-time professional administrator has improved efficiency.

The Print Co-op (TPC) was started in 1979 by a small group who were concerned to provide more access to the print media for left-wing, community and women's groups who had limited funding. The start-up capital was a combination of money put in by the founders and an informal loan of £1,500. The co-operative survived due to the sacrifice of its members, who worked part-time for subsistence wages or sometimes nothing at all. They produced badges, leaflets and stickers, with an annual turnover of approximately £14,000.

In 1982 two of the founders left, and this marked the beginning of a shift in orientation. The co-operative began to debate the idea of providing training in print skills to groups such as women and ethnic minorities, who often find it difficult to gain access to the printing trade. This included upgrading the skills of existing members in a more equitable way. By the next year, it became clear that some members favoured expanding the business and improving capital investment, partly in order to pay better wages, whilst others, especially one founder, preferred to continue as they were. Eventually, after a turnover in membership, a policy of paying union rates was adopted in January 1984. By December that year a substantial loan from the London Co-operative Enterprise Board (LCEB) had been obtained to modernise their equipment and premises. The co-operative also expanded its market to include established organisations on the left such as trade unions, which were able to pay better rates for their work. The complexity of the new machinery, and the need to develop more competence in areas such as marketing, has led to a decline of job rotation and increasing specialisation. The co-operative's business has increased, and they are now able to pay wages at union rates, although this is still less than the market rate. Throughout these changes TPC's objectives have remained more or less the same; however, their mode of operation has changed dramatically.

Discussion
Why do some 'shoestring' co-operatives develop into commercially successful businesses, while others, as we have seen, remain commercially marginal?

One important factor seems to be market sector. All the self-developers we know of are in areas where small firms are able to enjoy at least a limited degree of independence. Some are in fairly open, competitive markets, like TPC, Lake and Recycles, within which these particular co-operatives have made conscious decisions to move from a less profitable to a more profitable part of the market. Others developed their own niches in relatively buoyant and expanding markets such as wholefoods.

To varying degrees all the self-developers have come to appreciate the importance of business skills such as financial management, marketing and stock control. Quite often this has been precipitated by some sort of crisis – for example, at Recycles the cash-flow crisis, and the decline in net surplus at Suma. There remains a question mark whether these management functions are sufficiently well developed at Wholegrain.

The recognition of the importance of skills has led to increasing specialisation. In some co-operatives, such as TPC, the technology required has meant job rotation has largely been abandoned. At other co-operatives, such as Suma, job rotation is still regarded as very important, giving people a broad insight into how the business runs, and increasing the co-operative's flexibility. In contrast, Wholegrain has perhaps become too dependent on key individuals and is therefore vulnerable if they leave the co-operative.

Outside support was crucial in several cases. SCDC and ICOF were important in financing Recycles and developing their financial and stock control systems. A co-operative consultant's report helped TPC to obtain their LCEB loan. Suma have made extensive use of their accountant, who helped to train one of the members to undertake the management accountancy role in the co-operative.

By definition all co-operatives of this type started under-capitalised. The willingness of members to take low wages in order to build up capital was important. Once established they did not appear to have too much trouble raising external loans, although members of Lake had to offer personal security for theirs. The ability to control wages and to alter the distribution of returns to members through both wages and bonuses does appear to give these co-operatives an advantage over conventional businesses in terms of greater flexibility. At Lake, for example, wages are kept deliberately lower than they might be until they can see how they are doing for the year. Payments are made up through a yearly bonus. At Suma the co-operative did not have a pay rise between 1982 and 1986 because of lower net surpluses.

However, although commitment, in this sense of willingness to put in 'sweat equity' and to reinvest in the business, has been crucial, another important factor in improving the business performance of these self-developers has been the desire for higher wages and better conditions, particularly when after a period of self-denial members may find themselves with heavier personal and family responsibilities. Finally, members are often well educated and able to learn and develop new management skills while trying to keep their original ideals alive.

'Capitalised' co-operatives

The final group of co-operatives includes those that began operating with higher levels of capitalisation and producing higher levels of value added per head than shoestring start-ups, although as we will discuss below they may still be relatively under-capitalised. All our examples are rescues or phoenixes. Typically they are in fairly capital-intensive sectors, though this is not always so.

However, we are aware that recently a number of new co-operatives are starting from scratch, much better capitalised, due to the availability of money from co-operative loan funds or through the use of other financial devices such as debentures (see Chapters 9 and 11). It is also worth noting that 'self-developing' co-operatives become better capitalised after a while, and perhaps after their start-up phase should be considered with these co-operatives.

The Engineering Co-op

The Engineering Co-op began trading in August 1983 as a phoenix arising from the failure of a small, jobbing engineering works supplying industrial customers. With extensive assistance from the local CDA, the owner and nine workers formed the co-operative and began trading within six weeks.

The members found it difficult to raise start-up capital, because potential backers were sceptical about co-operatives and unsure whether the co-operative would be able to do any better than the previous business. Fortunately the local CDA was able to draw on the contacts and experience of other well-established co-operatives in the area to arrange hire purchase to buy the equipment from the old firm. The rest of the capital came from ICOF, a bank overdraft and members' contributions of £1,000 each. The men feared the stigma of redundancy and wanted secure employment. To them this was a way of 'buying' their jobs.

After the co-operative's rapid start-up, two years of apparent growth were followed by a serious cash-flow crisis and consequent reorganisation. During the first two years productivity improved and orders increased, so the members thought they were doing well, although they were working a lot of unpaid overtime. However, they were not being given full financial information by one of the two managers, who thought they would not understand it and that he was doing his best for them. Unfortunately his strategy for overcoming short term cash-flow problems involved paying suppliers for raw materials to continue production, rather than paying VAT and PAYE, so that enormous debts to these most implacable of creditors developed. When the books went to be audited the crisis was discovered. Assisted by the local CDA and ICOF the co-operative reorganised and managed to reschedule its loan repayments. This and many hours of unpaid overtime saved the co-operative from liquidation, and by early 1986 they had gone into surplus and grown to employ sixteen workers. Price increases and more rigorous office procedures, especially credit control, have improved the financial position and even allowed a pay rise.

Being a co-operative handicapped the business originally in their search for start-up capital, but it came to their rescue in the form of increased commitment shown by members working long hours and making difficult decisions during the reorganisation. Their weaknesses were in financial management where they could only have been helped by the outside advisers if they had been kept informed. The co-operative has succeeded by its own criterion of keeping its members in continuous employment for three years on a living wage, with more jobs created. They had no wider social objectives, and are proud of their achievements as 'worker capitalists'.

Union Phoenix

Union Phoenix (see Thomas, 1988a) has its origins in a company rationalisation plan. Due to falling demand the parent company decided to close its plant and concentrate production elsewhere, making eighty-four workers redundant. The initiative to save the plant and form a co-operative came from one of their unions, the AUEW. Forty workers paid into a contingency fund while the project was negotiated between the union, the Wales Co-operative Centre, the Welsh Development Agency (WDA) and the parent company.

The co-operative has fifteen worker-members and is an AUEW closed shop. The sales manager (ex-convenor) has a strong leadership role. Consultants suggested that five production workers would be sufficient, but the men preferred more people to work for lower wages. All are single or with working wives; those with dependants were not chosen, because they would get more income from benefits. For the first year, the co-operative received the Enterprise Allowance for ten of the workers (the maximum allowed), and a European Social Fund small firms subsidy for most of the others. The capital to start trading came from the contingency fund as loans, plus a bank overdraft facility of £20,000 which was not called upon during the first two years. Loans from the WDA and Welsh Office were being negotiated but required the co-operative to formalise its proposed legal structure.

The workers are all skilled or semi-skilled, but they were willing to take on any work, even grass cutting or cleaning, to keep going while they attracted more engineering orders. Most have never worked anywhere else, and local unemployment is high. They expect that once the financial position has improved they will be compensated for the low wages with union rates and differentials being restored. The co-operative made a profit of £24,600 after tax on a turnover of £103,500 in its first year. However, wages were heavily subsidised during this period and were still below the union rates. Outside the period of these subsidies, the co-operative needs a turnover of over £200,000 to break even. It is not clear whether it can consistently attract this level of work in the future.

Other 'capitalised' co-operatives
Red Dragon Stores (Thomas, 1988b; see also Birchall, 1987; McMonnies, 1985c) had its origins in the closure of a small Fine Fare supermarket in north-east Wales in line with general trends in the retail and distribution trades towards larger supermarkets. Fine Fare were closing a regional distribution centre and several small stores, and suggested to USDAW, the workers' union, that they would be happy to assist management buy-outs for the seven stores that were still profitable. The area organizer for USDAW requested that Fine Fare should also consider the possibility of worker co-operatives. This was negotiated into the redundancy agreement along with a package of assistance for establishing the co-operatives.

The organizer presented this deal to the various shops. Three, including Red Dragon, decided to take over the businesses as co-operatives. The deal ensured the co-operative was well capitalized. The lease on the shop plus fixtures and fittings, valued together at approximately £20,000, were assigned free to the co-operative. Fine Fare paid for repairs, gave an interest-free loan for insurance and in effect another interest-free loan by giving the shop six to nine months to pay for the stock they took over. In addition, they delayed the closure date for a couple of months and made arrangements for VG to supply the store so that there was continuity at the change-over, in mid-1984.

The co-operative traded quite successfully for a couple of years. They paid off the stock before the six months and gave themselves a wage rise. However, they were always vulnerable as a small independent business in competition with large retailers with vertically integrated supply and distribution functions. In 1986 they changed from VG to another supplier, and when the latter ran into difficulties the co-operative had no way to protect its position, given its lack of assets (other than stock) on paper, and was forced to close.

The Clothing Co-op was a business that grew from the union-organised occupation of a sewing factory in a development area. The co-operative had a start-up grant and small member loans, plus some equipment from the old factory. They were lent some machines by customers at first (not unusual for CMT). The co-operative started with one customer, and were soon working regularly for three. Barely eighteen months later their business was profitable, wages were above the basic union rate, and they had doubled both the size of their workspace and the number of workers employed.

Then came the crisis. Everyone had been so busy working that regular meetings of the co-operative had ceased and the manager had been allowed to take more and more power. He suddenly announced that he and several of the workers, including two founder members, were leaving to form a rival non-co-operative business in the same town. Their very substantial Christmas bonuses went towards the financing of this new venture. The five remaining founders, bitter at this betrayal, struggled on to rebuild the co-operative around a more democratic foundation. They had to take on workers quickly to keep their orders fulfilled. In six months they had grown again to twenty-six workers, with four regular customers, but less than a year later they went into liquidation.

The co-operative's initial success was due to regular contracts obtained from local customers at the top end of the market, but they were not able to survive long when these were lost to rivals. The pressures in the cut-throat CMT business reduced them to a marginal position from which they could not recover.

Discussion
'Capitalised' co-operatives by definition need larger sums of capital from the beginning than the shoestring start-ups. They are often in more capital-intensive sectors. Many are rescues, and start larger in order to save as many jobs as possible. In fact, it is arguably a danger from a commercial point of view that pressure for jobs

can lead such co-operatives to start with too large a workforce. They are also taking over existing assets or trying to continue as a going concern, so have no cheap option. Also, rescue or not, the motivation is usually to create a commercial operation that will sustain proper jobs, so machinery and equipment are needed straight away to enable good productivity and quality.

Finance usually comes partly from the workers themselves, who may put in redundancy pay and also work for little or no wages for a while. Outside assistance from a union, a local CDA or both was vital in all the cases we studied, particularly in helping negotiate further finance for a rescue. This meant both getting a good deal from the old company or the liquidator and arranging external loans. Usually finance from all these sources together was still not enough. Both the engineering co-operatives had to start relatively under-capitalized, and Red Dragon Stores, though it acquired some assets free, found they were quite intangible and had no way of raising further capital when a crisis arose.

Rescues are usually in declining sectors like engineering or clothing, where firms are in a highly competitive or dependent market position. One might expect them to be highly constrained unless they diversify or move to another related sub-sector. However, although The Clothing Co-op did not reach a stable trading situation, there are other examples, like Wilshaw Rainwear, where, from a commercial point of view at least, a capitalised rescue of a dependent small clothing firm has been a success. So far there are fewer examples of rescues or capitalised new-start co-operatives in less dependent market positions.

As with any small business the quality of management is also vital to the successful development of a capitalised co-operative. In some rescue co-operatives management is distrusted because of its failure to safeguard jobs. Nevertheless, some managers may be willing to stay on. This is an asset only if they do not perpetuate the weaknesses which led to the closure of the original firm. Other rescue co-operatives have to develop or acquire management skills. At Union Phoenix these have come from a number of sources: the trade union convenor, the co-operative development worker and a new estimator. At The Clothing Co-op a general manager was hired from outside. He did not have the same commitment as the founder members to the co-operative, and used his time to gain the experience and contacts to launch his own business. The case highlights the risk in this strategy.

The creation of rescue co-operatives to save jobs can lead to increased worker commitment, which is often vital to their subsequent success. At both engineering co-operatives, for example, the workers' willingness to work unpaid overtime and long hours has seen them through the difficult start-up phases. However, unlike in new starts the workers may feel the decision to form a co-operative is forced on them as they would otherwise have lost their jobs. Probably they will expect reasonable wages and conditions after a relatively short time. It will be difficult to maintain commitment otherwise. However, the possibility is there for capitalised rescues to become stable businesses, or become 'capitalised developers'.

Factors affecting co-operatives' business development

As we have gone through this chapter outlining the various case-study co-operatives and their different patterns of performance, a number of factors have been suggested that might help to explain the differences. These factors can be grouped into five areas: how a co-operative is financed; in which sector it is trading and how it is related to the market; the skills and commitment of the workers; the management and organisation of the co-operative; and the availability and appropriateness of outside support and assistance. In each area, we can look for reasons for the success or failure of small businesses in general, and apply these to particular co-operatives. We ask also whether co-operatives are likely to be affected differently from other businesses and whether there are any special lessons for how to achieve business success as a co-operative.

Finance
In Chapter 3 we found little evidence for Vanek's suggestion that co-operatives tend to under-perform because of being financed from members' contributions and retained surpluses, though if they do become well capitalised co-operatives might be liable to this tendency. In fact, co-operatives, particularly in their early years, are financed largely by external loans, and it is the lack of finance rather than what type of finance that handicaps co-operatives. At its most basic, co-operatives are under-capitalised because their members typically have little money and lack assets to use as security for loans. This restricts them to the least capital-intensive sub-sectors. There is no evidence that the problems are worse than for similarly poorly endowed individuals trying to set up conventional businesses in those sub-sectors (though it could be that feeling a need to remain equal prevents individual members with private assets from using them for security for loans for the co-operative). In both cases under-capitalisation tends to exacerbate other problems, most notably that of obtaining suitable premises, and makes the business highly vulnerable to cash-flow problems during the early years. Dependence on loans that have to be repaid does bring with it the burdens of high gearing.

PA Management Consultants (1985) point to three areas where the co-operative form creates special business problems for itself, one of which is the restricted financial base, and suggest that co-operative structures be amended so that they can offer equity participation both to members and to outsiders. However, we argued in Chapter 3 that those co-operatives that develop and grow do so on retained surpluses and external loans, with the latter forming a reducing proportion of their capital base. The self-developers described here have succeeded in financing their growth in this way, as indeed do most growing small businesses. However, this leaves open whether other co-operatives might have come forward to join these commercially successful examples, had the possibility of equity participation been available. In particular, rescues and capitalised new starts are both more likely to be achieved if the financial package can be extended to include as many elements as possible. It is also possible that, as with small businesses, the next stage of growth will prove difficult for co-operatives restricted to raising external capital from loans. We return to this point in Chapter 11.

Sector

In Chapter 3 we argued that industrial sector, and hence the way a co-operative is dependent on large firms and the market, constrains performance heavily. We can note in fact that the main start-up types and patterns, used to describe our case studies in this chapter, occur quite unevenly in different sectors (see Table 4.2).

Table 4.2 *Approximate incidence of different patterns of business development in different sectors*

	Clothing	Printing	Wholefoods	Engineering
Commercially marginal co-operatives	****	***	**	(?)
Self-developing co-operatives	(?)	***	***	(?)
Capitalised co-operatives	**	*	(?)	****

Key
****   A definite majority of co-operatives in this sector show this pattern
***   A considerable number of co-operatives show this combination of pattern and sector
**   A substantial minority of co-operatives in this sector have this pattern
*   A very few co-operatives in this sector show this pattern
(?)   Virtually no co-operatives in this sector have this combination

Given the degree of dependence discussed in Chapter 3, it is not surprising that there are virtually no self-developers in clothing. In printing there are examples of all the patterns, though few capitalised cases. Perhaps this reflects the fact that the printing industry is not in such rapid decline as to generate many rescues, while also requiring considerable capital to enter the market on a fully commercial basis. Engineering, by contrast, has fewer co-operatives, but they almost all have to be capitalised. As for wholefoods, both self-developers and marginals are well represented, but there would seem to be scope for capitalised start-ups here.

This is a factor which would seem to constrain co-operatives in the same way as other businesses. For example, the more marginal a business, the harder it finds it to adjust to changing markets, and this is equally true for co-operatives like Oakleaf or WICC. However, as discussed in Chapter 3, the various sectors do give different scope for job control, identification with the product and political or social motivation.

Workers' skills and commitment

In a sense, a worker co-operative is its workers. Our so-called shoestring start-ups depend heavily on their skills and commitment as their main assets. Capitalised co-operatives also generate commitment, though it may be short-lived unless material rewards are forthcoming. This increased commitment is readily agreed to be worker co-operatives' one big advantage over other firms, though some argue that it has drawbacks. For example, PA (1985: 147) conclude that co-operatives need help to 'exploit the benefits of co-operative involvement whilst avoiding the pitfalls of confused lines of authority'. Cable and Fitzroy (1980) argue that workers' greater interest in the success of the enterprise will increase commitment as well as reducing the need for direct supervision and hence overheads. In contrast, it has been argued that workers' control will lead to indiscipline, shirking and 'freeloading' (Alchian and Demsetz, 1972). However, almost all our case studies showed the advantages of a committed workforce without any of these drawbacks. One exception was The Clothing Co-op, where omitting to involve and gain commitment from new workers as the co-operative expanded was one factor that contributed to its failure.

Skill is a less uniformly positive aspect. In some shoestring start-ups, members may have to learn some of the basic skills of the job as they go along, whereas in rescues it is almost certain that these skills are there. However, there is no reason to suppose workers' co-operatives differ in the availability of skills from other businesses.

Chapter 5 looks at the relation of the individual worker to the co-operative in more detail.

Management and organisation
On the whole, writing on the 'administration' or management of worker co-operatives expects a negative outcome. (For a review of the main arguments see Fanning and McCarthy, 1986.) One of the Webbs' main points against worker co-operatives was that they were bound to suffer poor management as well as 'want of discipline' (see Chapters 1 and 6). Co-operatives are said to be unable to attract and retain good-quality professional managers. They are also said to lack entrepreneurial direction (O'Mahoney, 1979: 76) because entrepreneurship cannot easily be subjected to collective control. PA (1985) found management, along with finance and involvement, to be one of the three main areas of 'factors inhibiting the growth of worker co-operatives'. They suggested more training in management skills, the need to persuade co-operators to heed professional advice and the possibility of appointing professional managers from outside who need not be members of the co-operative.

This last finds little favour with co-operators (IPP, 1987), and the story of The Clothing Co-op illustrates its dangers. However, the previous point demonstrates, by the fact that it needs to be made, how co-operators are often antipathetic to the very idea of management. This finds different forms in different types of co-operative. Alternativists, for example, may equate management with the alienating lifestyle they wish to break away from; socialists may regard managers as 'agents of capital'; trade unionists and workers in rescue co-operatives may have a history of struggling against exploitative conditions imposed by management, besides having a poor opinion of this 'management' that clearly failed to safeguard their own jobs. This latter feeling may be shared by some of those starting up new co-operatives following redundancy, but the predominant difficulty in new shoestring co-operatives, as with other new small businesses, is simply lack of appreciation of what is involved in management.

Co-operators are not likely to have previous experience of managing small businesses. Once the importance of management is realised, a major problem facing all new co-operatives becomes acquiring business and management skills, particularly in areas of financial management, marketing, production and stock control. Our case-study co-operatives had a variety of problems in these areas, depending on the nature of the business. They highlight the importance of good advisory, development and training services for people forming co-operatives (see below and Chapter 9). One should not, however, conclude too easily that the difference between self-developers and commercially marginal co-operatives is that the latter failed to learn to manage. This may be so, but marginal co-operatives often have heavier constraints in other areas, and may be politically motivated to pursue a line that cannot be a commercial success.

On the other hand, the existence of several successful examples of 'self-developers' seems to show that the various pessimistic theorists are wrong. Of course, whether such co-operatives can continue successfully is not yet proven. Chapter 6 looks at whether co-operatives are bound to degenerate and Chapter 7 at co-operative management in a broader sense than just the commercial.

Outside support and assistance

Several of the shoestrings and capitalised rescues were able to draw on a lot of support from local CDAs and other agencies. Most of the self-developers we looked at began growing before the period when such support was available, though Recycles and TPC used co-operative loan funds.

As we see in Chapter 9, the network of support organisations has been very largely responsible for the growth of the new co-operative movement. Co-operatives starting up have one advantage over other businesses in that the support available is often very intensive. However, looking at the patterns of development of our case studies one might feel that more of this support could go to improving the management skills and access to finance of shoestring co-operatives, and helping more of them turn into self-developers.

Note

1. Happy Hands closed during 1987 as this book was going to press.

5

The Costs and Benefits of Co-operative Working

As we have seen in Chapters 2–4, co-operatives can succeed in business terms – at least to some extent. But can they effectively combine co-operative and social goals with their business goals? For the next four chapters, we consider the social performance of worker co-operatives.

Within this, we look first at the relationship between the individual worker and the co-operative, for three reasons. First, workers' satisfaction is in itself an aspect of the performance of a co-operative as of any organisation. Secondly, co-operatives as such *consist* of their workers, so to a great extent they exist to carry out what their workers want. The essence of co-operative principles is that labour hires capital. Thus, co-operators' main asset is themselves. The third reason is to see whether their human investment can get sufficient 'return' to maintain or even increase commitment and combat the tendencies to 'degeneration' discussed in Chapters 1 and 6.

What is it like from the perspective of the individual to work in a co-operative? How do people's views on co-operative working change as they gain experience in a co-operative which itself changes continually in response to social and economic pressures? Does it help to be a dedicated idealist from the beginning, or can co-operation become highly valued having originally been an incidental part of securing employment?

Focussing on the interactions between the organisation and the individual can make an important contribution to understanding the creation of successful co-operatives. The creation, maintenance and increase of workers' commitment will not be likely unless their work-related needs are fulfilled. Some consideration of these needs must be an essential part of any attempt to judge the social performance of co-operatives.

Job satisfaction, participation and commitment
Co-operatives are frequently promoted on the grounds that they can provide a better working environment and a more satisfying job than more conventional businesses. However, these claims are seldom based on detailed empirical studies. It is frequently assumed that working in a co-operative not only leads to more worker participation, but that this participation is desired, welcomed and appreciated by

workers, so that workers are more satisfied with their jobs. It is also argued that increased satisfaction will lead to greater commitment and hence to higher productivity, which will improve the economic performance of the co-operative. These popular assumptions are over-simple and may impede our efforts to understand how successful co-operatives work. We have already seen that co-operatives vary enormously. Their origins, the intentions of their founders, the product or service offered and the size and age of the co-operative can all affect its character as a workplace and who is likely to join it. Workers also differ enormously. They are female or male, young or old, with or without dependants and with or without qualifications and skills. Their cultural and class backgrounds differ, and their requirements from and expectations of employment are likely to differ accordingly. It is important then to examine how workers from a range of backgrounds experience working in different types of co-operative.

Before we can study how satisfied workers are with their jobs and the democratisation of their co-operatives, we need to consider the concepts involved more carefully. Job satisfaction is essentially a relative concept. Its estimation can provide only a snapshot of the situation at a particular time. Commitment, a broader concept taking more explicit account of an individual's past experience and future intentions, also fluctuates considerably with circumstances.

Lischeron and Wall (1977) analysed participation by dividing it into three possible levels: local, medium and distant. Local participation involved control over the immediate job content; medium participation concerned decisions usually taken by middle management, such as those affecting a department, new personnel, promotion, training, etc.; and distant participation referred to involvement in such areas as long-term planning and major capital expenditure. (This is a much narrower definition of control than we use when looking at co-operatives from the labour process perspective, which we do in Chapter 6. In particular, it ignores questions of how far control over an organisation's affairs is located outside the organisation altogether.)

Lischeron and Wall carried out action research which involved introducing more participation into various organisations and monitoring its effects over six months. They found that there was no simple link between participation and satisfaction. A majority of skilled and unskilled workers had a strong desire to influence local and medium-level decision-making, whereas only a substantial minority had a strong desire to influence distant-level decision-making. The greatest increase in participation was desired at medium level. (Local-level participation was already available to many workers.) Workers showed a desire for considerable if not complete autonomy in their jobs.

Curran and Stanworth (1986) reviewed research on job satisfaction and worker involvement in small firms whilst reporting the results of their own study. They concluded that, contrary to popular belief, small firms were not necessarily either sweatshops or ideal working environments. These firms provided employment for younger, less qualified workers. Industrial sector and the characteristics of the labour force, such as age, qualifications and marital status, were all much better predictors of workers' satisfaction than the size of the firm. Older, married workers were less likely to be satisfied than their younger unmarried counterparts, unless their firms could offer very favourable terms and conditions.

Oliver (1986), in a thorough review of research on job satisfaction and commitment in co-operatives, comments on the lack of conceptual clarity in this area and casts doubt on the findings that co-operators are more satisfied than other workers because they are in co-operatives. His study of commitment in a large endowed co-operative confirms the relevance of context, and highlights the importance of the psychological investment a person has made by staying some time in an organisation, which makes them reluctant to leave. Oliver also found his sample of co-operators valued control over their work very highly, although it appears that this refers mainly to the local level of control as defined by Lischeron and Wall (1977).

All these authors recommend essentially that researchers should stop asking whether participation causes an increase in job satisfaction, and start inquiring what people think about various specific forms of participation that they are currently experiencing, and how their views change over time.

This is exactly what our qualitative research described in this chapter set out to do. We needed an appropriate framework to discuss the expectations and requirements of individuals and their interactions with co-operative working experiences. We needed to synthesise individual perceptions, which are essentially unique in their detail to each person, into a coherent whole that can begin to provide explanations whilst still doing justice to the original rich data. We drew upon ideas from exchange theory to investigate people's experiences of co-operative working, and found the literature on orientations to work useful in analysing and interpreting these experiences.

An exchange theory framework
Previous research (e.g. Oliver, 1984, 1986; Tynan and Thomas, 1981) had suggested that exchange theory ideas could be used as a basis to study the experiences of workers in co-operatives, and this provided the framework for our analysis.

As succinctly described by Tynan and Thomas (1981: 7), exchange theory (Homans, 1950; Thibaut and Kelley, 1959) postulates that:

> Human action is based on self-interest, and calculated to maximise benefits or to satisfice at least cost ... People reward each other by their behaviour and expect rewards in return ... Social behaviour is then seen as a form of tenuous contract which is in a constant process of renegotiation. Behaviour incurs future obligations and performance may cease when expected rewards are no longer forthcoming.

Joining a co-operative, working in it and participating in running it are all social behaviours. It should be emphasised that, unlike behaviourist learning theories, exchange theory need not be interpreted as rigidly deterministic or mechanistic, since it allows people to re-evaluate cognitively what they consider as rewards, costs, outcomes and comparison levels. For example, they might decide after a couple of years that the sense of challenge and access to power achieved by chairing an important subcommittee in their co-operative no longer outweighs the time it takes from their life with their family. This idea of exchange was used to organise our findings about people's subjective experiences of work in the wider context of their lives as a whole, irrespective of whether the people themselves actually conceptualised the work relationship in exchange terms.

It may seem paradoxical to study co-operators via a theory about individual self-interest, but because people themselves are viewed as deciding what is rewarding for them and what is not, it follows that working towards social ownership can be perceived as extremely rewarding by some individuals, in the same way that others prefer high pay levels in exchange for their labour. Using the exchange idea as an analogy makes it not only possible but useful to regard a proponent of any reasonably coherent set of work values as exchanging effort in their co-operative for the chance to enact or fulfil such values.

We found that co-operatives could provide their members with a wide range of new benefits via the control and responsibility involved in running a business. However, members also experienced new costs from co-operative working, although these were usually outweighed by the benefits.

Orientations to work
To discover and interpret patterns in the data on people's satisfaction and dissatisfaction with co-operative working, we also used the sociological concept of orientation to work. A person's orientation to work represents a cluster of associated attitudes about work and its place in relation to the rest of a person's life. We inferred a person's orientation to work from their opinions about the costs and benefits of co-operative working. We developed four

categories of work orientation, namely: instrumental, social, moral and control-seeking (see Table 5.1). The first three of these correspond closely to previous theory (e.g. Clark and Wilson, 1961; Etzioni, 1961). Adding the fourth gives emphasis to the politics of organisational life. However, a person's orientation will often be a combination of more than one of these categories; for example, most co-operators were found to combine a social orientation with other orientations towards their work. Some combinations were more usual than others; for example, the combination of strong instrumental and moral orientations was not found.

Table 5.1   *Orientations to work*

Orientation	What is highly valued
Instrumental	High earnings – to attain material improvements in own and family's lifestyle. Job security. Status.
Social	Working with friends. Working with people who share your beliefs and values, people you can be yourself with, people who are supportive. Feelings of loyalty to fellow workers.
Moral	Purposive work, that gives a sense of satisfaction at achieving a goal larger than personal material advancement. The satisfaction can come from the process, e.g. collective working, or the product or service, e.g. wholefoods as a means of promoting a healthy and ecologically sound life-style.
Control	Power and influence over work, at three levels: task, departmental and organisational.

The benefits of co-operative working

As shown in Table 5.1, each of the four categories of orientation corresponds to certain benefits. A person valuing a particular benefit highly is categorised as having the corresponding type of orientation. In what follows we describe the benefits felt by our co-operators in more detail under the same four headings as the categories of orientation. The costs incurred are dealt with later.

However, before breaking things down in this way, we should note that, overall, co-operative working was intense and involving, whether for better or worse. People were never indifferent about it. They felt a heightened emotional involvement with their work. The worries when things were going badly could be severe. But it was noticeable that when co-operative working was going well it gave rise to feelings of great excitement and satisfaction, 'a high', 'a buzz', that was far more stimulating than conventional employment had ever been.

Instrumental benefits

The best known illustration of the desire for instrumental benefits from work (i.e. an instrumental orientation) is probably Goldthorpe et al.'s (1968) 'affluent worker', who did not look for any intrinsic satisfaction from a job, but wanted high earnings to attain improvements in lifestyle. Etzioni's (1961) calculative involvement with work is similar and has been used in several psychological studies, e.g. Oliver (1986). Clark and Wilson's (1961) typology of incentives that motivate people towards specific types of organisation uses the term 'material incentives', which spells out more precisely what the person requires for their lifestyle: money, wealth and prestige. Often these are desired for the sake of the family rather than for the individual alone.

People setting up job-creation or rescue co-operatives are likely first of all to be trying to achieve secure jobs with a living wage. They may not know a great deal about co-operation, but they want a chance to use their skills or to continue doing the work they know, and a co-operative is a way to do this. Having a job at all is thus the most basic instrumental benefit of being in a co-operative.

The exchange framework helps relate benefits to alternatives. For some of our co-operators, work alternatives were seen as limited or absent, which made them value their co-operative and formed the basis of their early commitment to making it work. For example, the women of The Clothing Co-op felt that moving to other employment would have exposed them to the danger of further redundancies. Several of the men of The Engineering Co-op feared that they would never be re-employed as they were over fifty and took tremendous pride in the fact that they had never been unemployed. They too felt they had nothing to lose. 'It was a bit like buying a job.'

Workers involved in founding rescue co-operatives often mentioned that they hoped to expand eventually and provide secure employment for more people. This was in fact the only type of social objective held in these two co-operatives. The wish to provide instrumental benefits for others shows a moral orientation and will be further considered later.

Finding a job was also quite a common reason for joining a co-operative. Workers did not always realise that a co-operative was a different species of employer. Several workers in wholefood shops who had never previously heard of co-operatives joined co-operatives because they were unemployed and needed work. Some co-operators mentioned flexible working hours as a benefit for them – these were usually women with children who were working part-time.

Several of the co-operators interviewed considered that they valued a living wage as an important objective of their co-operative, although many were prepared to work for nothing for long periods in anticipation of financial rewards to come if the business succeeded. In some co-operatives, a policy of little or no wage differentials meant that for particular jobs, e.g. wholefood warehouse packing or shopwork, people received quite good wages for their locality. The comparison is difficult, because co-operators almost always combine basic jobs with an element of responsibility, so that if such jobs existed outside a co-operative they might carry higher wages than the minimum. In addition, some workers were better qualified than the job demanded and could have earned higher wages elsewhere doing different work. Thus it was possible for one co-operative worker to quote wage levels as one of the benefits, while another, receiving the same money, would give them as a cost, because either they had been there longer, had more dependants to support, had a more responsible role or realised what they could expect from another employer.

People with dominantly instrumental orientations were found in most of the co-operatives studied, but they were scarcer in alternative co-operatives, particularly among founder members. Workers in job-creation and rescue co-operatives nearly always held instrumental orientations, since having a job at all was important to them. Instrumental benefits, especially job security, can be a powerful spur to founding or working in a co-operative, and their importance should not be underrated by those who prefer to stress the idealistic nature of co-operation. The recent expansion of the co-operative sector, since its earlier revival by idealists (see Chapter 1), owes much to those with dominantly instrumental motives or who have come to take on such motives.

Social benefits
Social benefits cover all the advantages of working amongst friends. Clark and Wilson (1961) call them solidarity incentives: those which arise from associating with people who share similar attitudes and values. Co-operative members who showed no interest in collective working as a political or moral statement (see next section), such as those from some of the rescue co-operatives, were equally likely to state that they wanted to go on working with their friends. It was common for everyone to speak highly of the friendly atmosphere of their co-operative: 'It is important to be with people you know' (The Clothing Co-op). 'A lot of support' (Lake). There were aspects of loyalty in this for some people: 'They gave me a chance' (The Engineering Co-op).

It was a welcome luxury to work with people who were congenial, both politically (if this was a concern) and personally. They were people with whom you could be yourself at work: 'You feel freer to admit mistakes and so you learn' (Lake). 'You can grow as a person' (Suma). 'Not having to have a work and a personal personae. I know people closely and they know my strengths and weaknesses' (Lake).

Working in a co-operative is thus a way in which a person's basic self-esteem and identity needs can be met within a work environment. To this extent, virtually all co-operative workers, no matter what type of co-operative they work in, hold a social orientation to their work, but it is rarely their overriding orientation or the source of their motivation for forming or joining a co-operative. However, the trust between co-operators that is built up through appreciation of the social benefits can be a powerful force in generating and maintaining individuals' commitment.

Moral benefits

The category of moral benefits is derived from Etzioni's (1961) ideas of moral involvement, typified by the way highly committed people related to their churches or political parties. A moral involvement denotes a positive identification with an organisation and its goals based on shared values. Clark and Wilson (1961) describe a similar category based on what they call purposive incentives, those which give individuals a sense of satisfaction at accomplishing a goal that is larger than their personal material advancement, typical of social movements. Thus moral benefits are an appropriate description of those sought by the founders of idealistic co-operatives that were intended to promote particular political or social goals. This category can be extended to cover the practising of craft or professional skills when not used entirely for material advancement.

The wholefood co-operatives were all founded with the moral objective of promoting more knowledge of wholefoods as well as their consumption. The Print Co-operative (TPC) had the objective of enabling various community and left-wing groups to gain access to cheap printing facilities, and the language school, Lake, wanted to teach their subject in a way that did not exploit students and staff. The founders of these co-operatives also believed that working together as equals was politically desirable. 'There must be many people who, like us, have been driven half insane by the dehumanising straitjacket of the orthodox working world and yearned to be part of something better, more fulfilling' (The Bean Shop). 'I hate capitalist business' (Lake). 'A true community shop – involving everybody who uses it ... important decisions could be arrived at by all those interested and involved' (Wholegrain).

Many of the members of these co-operatives had joined because they felt attracted to the radical products or services and egalitarian working practices. For example, several members of Suma reported that they would not have joined unless it was a co-operative which aimed to be non-hierarchical. One talked of 'a real desire to do something political', while another referred to 'a sense of being part of something that ought to be more widespread ... I have a passionate interest in the products that we sell'. The printers agreed in that they wanted work that was 'facilitating political ends'.

Strong moral orientations to work were found, as expected virtually by definition, in alternative co-operatives, particularly amongst founders, although they were not necessarily present in all members. They also proved important in opposing any degeneration of democracy (see Chapters 6–8).

Control: the benefits of power

The category of control-seeking is the most complex dimension of benefits, and the most important from the point of view of its potential for fulfilment via co-operatives. It is an adaptation of Tynan and Thomas' (1981) power as an incentive, the wish to gain status and influence.

Many people spoke of the benefits of control at task level in their co-operatives. They positively enjoyed using their skills. 'There's some scope for personal creativity' (TPC). 'You can work at your own pace within the economics of it' (TPC). 'Not having someone who does not know the job telling you what to do...' (Lake).

These comments were much more frequent in co-operatives that practised some degree of job rotation. Where jobs had remained narrow, as in manufacturing, their restrictions were more likely to appear as costs, e.g. the boredom of operating a sewing-machine flat out all day. For some people co-operative working had involved learning new skills, which had increased their confidence at work. They appreciated the chance the co-operative had given them to be trained and to cope with a challenging job. 'I've got much more confidence ... I used to be shy and depressed' [when unemployed]' (WICC). 'People accept that you probably can do the things you say you want to do' (Suma).

The people valuing such opportunities to increase their control over their work were usually women or working-class men, precisely the people who are likely to be disadvantaged in conventional organisations.

Most co-operatives were too small to be divided into different departments, but in the larger ones people valued being able to exert more control over how their 'department' operated and to choose which jobs to take on.

Control over the direction of the whole organisation was also valued, despite the extra work and worries involved. 'Having a say in what wage I'd like, and receiving it' was given as a benefit by several people from rescue co-operatives. Influence at this level was also valued because it gave some control over the surplus earned by the co-operative. For example, at Lake members enjoyed being able to spend more money on materials to be used in the teaching, and providing the occasional scholarship for students.

Learning how to take control and run the business gave people better insights: 'You feel as if you are a little bit in control of your destiny' (The Engineering Co-op). '...greater satisfaction from being able to form a clearer picture of the business as a whole, seeing behind the scenes, as it were' (The Clothing Co-op).

Those with previous management experience in conventional firms who had become co-operative managers (The Engineering Co-op, Red Dragon) said they valued the chance to share some of their pressures and responsibilities with the rest of the workers without interference from a higher level of management.

Different views of the benefits of co-operative ownership were found according to the type of co-operative involved. Typically people from job-creation or job-saving co-operatives saw the benefits of co-operative ownership in terms of working for themselves, pride of ownership and their right to share in profits: 'You get a different feeling, working for yourself'; 'The profits are split, not creamed off' (The Engineering Co-op). 'There's more incentive to work harder'; 'It's your own little firm' (The Clothing Co-op). 'You're working more hours but you get more enjoyment ... it's your own' (WICC).

People from the alternative co-operatives were much more likely to emphasise their appreciation of autonomy at task level than to talk of ownership and direction. They valued control at organisational level partly as a political means to obtain the moral benefits of providing products or services that were social goods and for proving that non-hierarchical work organisation could be successful. 'It's stimulating ... trying to make it work' (Suma).

Members in job-creation or job-saving co-operatives who valued the benefits of organisational control still saw this at least partially in terms of personal ownership of resources (the results of their labour) to keep as wages as well as to continue the business, while the alternativists were less interested in these instrumental aspects but wanted to control their own working days whilst achieving their moral purposes. Many were radically inclined and did not believe in the accumulation of personal wealth. Some admitted to disliking management responsibilities. In some cases power as such over the destiny of the organisation did not seem to appeal to them, whereas the rescue and job-creation co-operators, often more personally disadvantaged, appreciated its attractions.

This was also reflected at task and departmental level, when alternativists were more likely to practise job rotation, whilst the more instrumentally inclined often continued to pursue conventional types of fragmented work organisation, because they believed these to be more efficient and therefore more likely to produce more financial rewards.

Interrelationships of benefits
Sometimes people found it hard to break down their overall praise of co-operative working into separate distinct benefits, because the benefits were closely related. One rescue co-operator may consider ownership and control as ends in themselves, while another sees control more as a means to job security, and an idealistic co-operator values it as a means for obtaining political ends or moral benefits. Fulfilling social needs by working with friends is likewise an end for some people, while others find in it the means for personal growth and the achievement of a collective and supportive work environment. It was also noticeable that some people were so used to working collectively that they tended to answer questions in terms of 'we feel or do such-and-such ' and not as individuals. Certainly, the 'buzz' of a co-operative working really well defies analysis into categories.

The costs of co-operation

It should first of all be mentioned that many co-operators found it difficult to think of the things that they liked least about their work. Many said their co-operatives provided the best jobs they had ever had. Others took great pains to explain that the costs they described were more than balanced out by the benefits. However, the exchange framework should again alert us to look for points of reference and comparison levels. Some co-operators' comparison will be with previous jobs, and we should note that many had experienced jobs with relatively poor terms and conditions and/or few opportunities for control; others had been unemployed. Others' implicit comparison may be more with their ideals.

The costs we found did not group together as tidily as the benefits. Not all the costs mentioned by our co-operators represent the mirror images of the benefits. Sometimes things seem straightforward; for example, a person with a strongly instrumental orientation, expressed as valuing the benefits of good pay in their co-operatives, would almost certainly regard low pay as a cost. However, another person may not value high pay at all, but finds subsistence wages a cost, although industry minimum levels would be acceptable.

We have classified people's expressed costs according to how directly they are attributable to co-operative working as such. First, there are costs intrinsic to the tasks performed, which would occur equally in conventional firms, particularly where jobs have been systematically deskilled over the years. Secondly, there are the instrumental costs, where material rewards are low. Finally, we examine costs that are directly attributable to co-operative work organisation and the stresses of working closely with others. These are an inseparable mixture of the costs of control and the costs of having a social orientation, and some are particularly heavy for 'activists' who take on substantial responsibilities or management functions.

Costs intrinsic to the tasks performed

Despite the advangates of co-operative working, for example in terms of task control and social needs, many jobs still involved boredom, monotony, dirt or danger. Sewing, for example: 'It's not a bed of roses ... there's nothing that exciting about work, it's something you have to do ... it's hard work ... you have to concentrate, you can't just gossip away and it can be boring.' Printing facilitates politically desirable ends but it also involves 'toxic chemicals, noise, oil vapour, carcinogens'; shopwork, however noble the product, can be monotonous behind the till; while warehousing and driving can have their dangerous aspects.

Some of these costs result from a lack of any serious attempt to reorganise work, but skill sharing, job redesign and job rotation can ameliorate only a few disliked features. There will still be some parts everyone hates, which have to be shared out fairly. We felt that co-operators sometimes have their expectations about pleasanter, more satisfying jobs raised unfairly, given that most work, however organised, still has its intrinsic costs. In fact, people of all orientations from all types of co-operative were likely to report the intrinsic costs of some jobs.

Instrumental costs

These costs are often referred to as extrinsic to the actual job done, and they are in a way the mirror image of instrumental benefits.

Many co-operators said their main costs were low pay, especially at the start of the co-operative, and tiredness due to long hours. Some also regretted that their premises were far from ideal. They usually qualified these complaints by saying that they would not mind for themselves but that low wages and long hours affected the quality of their home lives. Those with dependants found it difficult to provide for them on wages that satisfied single people, while single people as much as those with partners regretted the damage inflicted on their social lives by long and sometimes unpredictable hours of work. 'The worst part's when it's three o'clock in the morning and you've still got hundreds of pieces of chicken to do ... you wonder why you do it' (WICC). 'No time for outside activities ... we have to work ourselves stupid sometimes' (Lake).

Many co-operatives have been able to improve wage levels. For example, at TPC there had been an evolution since the early days when members took subsistence wages to give their customers access to printing. Eventually they had decided to raise wages to union levels to avoid under-cutting other workers and exploiting themselves. At Suma members began to resent the wage levels after several years, when they had often acquired dependants and could also make comparisons with friends in other organisations. As the business became more successful they were able to increase wages substantially, although in recent years wages have again fallen behind. In the early years of most co-operatives, as with the owners of small businesses, people had been prepared to put up with high instrumental costs while building up their enterprises. Eventually, though, they became less satisfied if wages and conditions did not improve.

Social and control costs
This group of costs arose specifically from attempting to work co-operatively with other people. In a sense they were incurred as the opposing face of the social benefits, the costs of interacting closely when decisions have to be shared, and they arose whether or not the co-operative had designated some individuals as managers. 'It's small and incestuous ... very wearing ... we're living in each other's pockets.' They were also the costs of control, especially at enterprise level. Collective working and democratic decision-making are unfamiliar to most people and may require difficult decisions to be made, so that when management problems arose, shared responsibilities could lead to stress.

A commonly stated cost of co-operative working was the financial and business worries. The job was no longer nine to five. It caused sleepless nights. 'Too many figures going round in your head'; 'You don't leave worries to bosses.' These worries were often worst during the start-up period, but could recur when the co-operative was expanding rapidly, or was experiencing problems.

Another common source of tension concerned the performance of other people in the co-operative – for example, that they were not working hard enough, had the wrong attitudes to work or lacked commitment. People in rescue co-operatives who were used to hierarchical working where supervisors controlled discipline found it difficult to confront colleagues who were not 'pulling their weight'. They were more used to colluding with them to evade management controls, and yet wanted to point out when the co-operative's money was being wasted by inefficient or lazy work.

Some felt that lack of feedback could be a problem for anyone in a collectively run co-operative, because there was so much autonomy. 'Nobody said a thing if you took the initiative whether you did it well or badly.' The opposite view, that everyone would comment and make you confused, occurred in the same co-operative and in others. It was obvious that co-operators had to learn to take control and that this learning took a considerable time.

In the more idealistic co-operatives some people felt that their organisations weren't as successful as they ought to have been at being collective or at keeping up their ideals. These people had started with extremely high expectations, which were probably unrealistic. A few felt that they had compromised too much over the products they sold, or that they had not been as successful as they would have liked in achieving wider social and political goals, but most complaints were about how decisions were made. There was a tendency as co-operatives grew older for informal hierarchies to develop around long-serving members who had the most information and skill, plus the personal qualities to speak out at meetings. It was felt that some people were not sharing information so that they could retain power (see Chapters 6 and 7). Although many people were committed to collective working they still found that it had costs: meetings took up considerable time and were sometimes boring and repetitive; there were painful and disagreeable conflicts; preparation for meetings was poor, etc.

Some members of the larger, older co-operatives felt there was a general inertia and reluctance to change in their organisations. Other problems encountered were a tendency to avoid open conflict in meetings when negative feelings were prevalent. Individuals from most co-operatives had encountered this at some time, and believed it was important for such feelings to be confronted and discussed.

Problems of activists
Whether or not a co-operative officially differentiates management from other roles, some individuals are bound to take on more responsibilities than others. Such activists often felt that their work was undervalued, particularly those involved in taking on managerial or specialist functions in the larger co-operatives. They would have liked more interest and support from their fellow co-operators.

In the older established co-operatives, some people who had strong orientations towards control, often combined with moral orientations, reported going through phases of high followed by low commitment, as the benefits they received decreased in proportion to the increasing costs incurred. 'A period of high commitment, of really getting involved with it ... it takes over your life ... you burn yourself out after a while, no job should take that much out of you'.

> I've always had this image of ... this great monster that swallowed you up and then spat you out again after about three years ... I found it very hard to get satisfaction out of the job and work reasonable hours ... it was a sort of 'work ethic' that someone set up that you had to kill yourselves or else you weren't a dedicated worker ... crazy.

This led to feeling negative about the co-operative, opting out of meetings and considering or actually leaving the co-operative. Similarly, Tynan and Thomas (1981) found that activists, both specialists and those who participate prominently in meetings, could become disillusioned if their efforts were not rewarded by changes in their co-operative.

The costs of control found in our study suggest that co-operators, especially those who were unused to management responsibilities, were discovering 'executive stress' (e.g. Evans and Bartoleme, 1980). This could happen in any type of co-operative but is more likely when the majority of members lack managerial skills or do not wish to exercise them.

Activists may grow to resent those whom they see as avoiding responsibility, doing less than their fair share by only performing their basic tasks: 'Selection procedures have been wrong: people see being a co-op not as a place where they have to take on responsibility but as somewhere where they don't have to take responsibility.' They may also feel that newer members do not understand enough about the history and workings of the co-operative to make useful contributions to important decisions. 'Old heads, new ideas, new heads, old ideas,' said a long-serving member criticising meetings at a wholefood co-operative. This could weaken the co-operative as a whole because responsibilities fell heavily on too few people. Founders of co-operatives had particular problems, and some of the founders we interviewed felt that co-operative entrepreneurs need more instrumental rewards than those who do the everyday work. Otherwise, for them the benefits of control will eventually be outweighed by its costs.

Balancing costs and benefits

Much can be done to reduce the costs of co-operative working, as will be discussed in Chapters 7 and 8. New methods of work organisation, better capitalisation and the rethinking of decision-making mechanisms can also increase the benefits. The main point to make here is that most co-operators accepted the costs because on balance they believed they were outweighed by the benefits discussed earlier. Just as a co-operative must balance its social and financial objectives, its workers balance their most valued benefits against any costs they incur through co-operative working. Several discussed this in terms of an exchange:

> Like all democratic processes it needs people to pull their weight, some people do more than others ... [but] I wouldn't want to work in any other way ... it's less frustrating and alienating.

> Everlasting meetings ... [but] I never liked hierarchy ... you're allowed to think, throw around ideas, you can grow as a person.

> I would not work for such low wages had it not been a co-op. The job retains interest, it is continually evolving.

Because human beings reflect on and interact with their experiences, people could and did change their orientations to work as their expectations were confronted by reality. Most of the co-operatives we studied had been established long enough for us to consider how people's original expectations and needs had been transformed by their actual experiences of co-operative working. It was noticeable that many who began sceptical came to value co-operative working after a time.

It will be remembered that many co-operators, even those who were founder members, knew very little about co-operative working when they started. Some co-operatives had no wider social objectives at all, yet nearly all their workers still felt a high sense of commitment. There were costs, but they found that benefits like a sense of success through achievement and ownership outweighed them. Learning to take control of their work and their businesses was stressful but rewarding, and most did not want to return to conventional employment. An interesting question for the co-operative movement in the future is whether such pragmatic co-operators will begin to pursue wider social objectives. The most likely social objective, already valued by some, would be to reduce local unemployment, and most individuals favoured creating more jobs in their co-operative, provided it did not have to grow too big and therefore become impersonal. They feared losing the social benefits of co-operation and at the same time increasing difficulties over democratic decision-making. They did not believe that co-operative decision-making could work in a larger co-operative because they were not aware of any examples.

The more idealistic co-operators had started with much higher expectations and often strived for a greater range of benefits. The moral benefits were the hardest to achieve. People tended to feel loyalty and commitment, but felt too that they could still have done better, that they weren't really achieving co-operative working at its best.

It was obvious that substantial personal (as well as organisational) learning had taken place as the co-operatives grew older. The general feeling overall was that the difficulties and costs of creating a new form of work were worthwhile and that they would persevere. Most people still believed in co-operative ideals, and those who had joined simply to get jobs were amongst the most enthusiastic:

> At first I resented the late hours and feeling tired … I didn't feel the same responsibility as the others… now my attitudes have changed … it is an enormous commitment … but you want to do it, there are tremendous rewards … much greater satisfaction in working in a co-op. (Lake)

> I started to take up the boredom [of being unemployed], I was unsure of it, now I have the same enthusiasm built on more solid foundations, I know where I stand. (WICC)

It seemed that the extra responsibilities taken on as a member of a co-operative were usually very rewarding; only if the associated costs in terms of personal stress and overwork or the erosion of home life became too severe would a person show signs of becoming disillusioned. Interpersonal conflicts at work where an individual felt continually pressurised, or alternatively ignored and unsupported by the other members, could also reduce commitment. Here a belief in co-operation as an ideology could help lessen the stress. Contact with other co-operatives which have faced similar problems could give people the sense that they are not alone but part of a wider movement, as well as providing a forum for the exchange of organisational skills. It could also reinforce the lesson that co-operation is difficult and won't necessarily work instantly. Trust has to be developed slowly within the group.

We believe there is a further problem. It has already been pointed out in Chapter 1 that people with entrepreneurial tendencies are not easily attracted to co-operatives. They are also difficult to retain, partly because of the lack of any career structure for those wishing to use leadership and management skills. In a conventional business, many employees will have expectations of promotion. There may be predictable career paths for the advancement of those who fulfil the organisation's criteria. Promotion means more money and more status, as well as (usually) more responsibility. Even in an organisation where time served is the main factor in obtaining promotion, the person promoted is likely to feel rewarded. There is no obvious equivalent of this for co-operators.

Transience has always been a feature of the US alternative collectivist movement (Rothschild-Whitt, 1976), but only a minority of UK co-operators are alternativists. The majority require secure jobs to maintain themselves and their dependants. However, if co-operative working is successful in developing skills and confidence, more people will feel the need to seek further challenges. If the sector is not large enough to provide these, valuable skills may be lost. Some people with notable leadership skills leave to help found new co-operatives or become advisers. Both of these options are good ways of sharing valuable skills more widely, but carry the danger that those skills will be diluted, leaving the co-operative unable to manage itself. More worryingly some able people have left the co-operative sector to found their own businesses or pursue their careers in the public or private sector. In future, as more co-operatives grow, there could be an expansion of opportunity for workers to move from one to another, allowing them to broaden their experience without having to move out of the sector.

The experience of the individual: further implications
Our findings agree with the literature cited earlier in the chapter, in that co-operators did show high levels of commitment, but that this could be partially explained in terms of their ages, family structures and lack of employment alternatives. As Lischeron and Wall had found, people did not always originally want the responsibilities of control at the distant (enterprise) level. The qualitative nature of our research also enabled us to examine the ways in which commitment increased as moral orientations began to be felt as well as instrumental and social ones. People became more and more identified psychologically with their co-operatives, into which they had put great efforts, but in return received considerable benefits, especially if they had learned to exercise control over work.

We have also seen that although individuals' orientations do not map exactly into our typology of co-operatives, we can point to some common patterns. Typically, alternativist co-operators start their co-operative careers with dominantly moral orientations. In the majority of rescues, phoenixes and job-creation co-operatives, people's orientations are a mixture of instrumental (especially wanting job security) and social. There is not necessarily any moral orientation towards working in a co-operative. All the types of co-operative can attract new members on the basis of providing employment, or providing work in a particular sector. Idealistic co-operatives also attract people because they believe in the product or service the co-operative is offering and/or in co-operative principles. In any co-operative some members will have or acquire control orientations, or their organisations will not get managed. If the responsibilities of control are shared whilst avoiding overload on any one individual, its benefits are more likely to be appreciated and therefore not easily relinquished. People who appreciate the benefits of control become more likely to acquire moral orientations towards co-operation. However, as co-operators grow older and typically acquire dependants, their instrumental needs are also likely to become more important, irrespective of whether they have ever been so before.

The exchange framework was useful to illustrate how co-operatives can serve individuals with widely differing needs. If people's original needs and expectations are fulfilled sufficiently by co-operative working, further unanticipated benefits may be discovered, such as those of control at organisational level, and these will then be desired from future work experiences. We found that people did not want to give back control over their working lives once they had experienced it.

Positive experiences of control can evolve into a moral orientation to co-operative working. This evolution is vitally important for co-operatives. As long as the external constraints remain so strong, it is unlikely that a purely instrumental orientation will be sufficient to maintain commitment. The development of a firm moral involvement, in Etzioni's terms, will be necessary to keep commitment levels high.

6
Democratic Control or Degeneration?

In this chapter and the next two, we move on to examine the social performance of co-operatives at the organisational level. To some extent, each co-operative has its own social goals, and so an examination of social performance must look at what members want for themselves and for their co-operative. We saw in the last chapter the great range of orientations to work found in co-operatives and the variety of ways that different co-operatives meet – or fail to meet – their members' various aspirations. Nevertheless, there are some generalised ways in which we can try to measure success in co-operative terms. The most basic questions perhaps concern whether it is possible to maintain co-operative principles such as open membership, equal democratic control, limited return to capital and the maintenance of social and educational aims. To put it in terms of control, we need to ask the following: Can workers in co-operatives gain control over their jobs? Can workplace relations be constructed and maintained on a 'democratic' basis? Can worker co-operatives pursue goals and priorities that go beyond profit-seeking? Can the slogan 'Labour hires Capital' be made meaningful?

As we discussed in Chapter 1, we reject the rather dogmatic and contradictory answers that these questions frequently attract. Co-operatives are not *bound* to 'degenerate', i.e. to fail in the long run as democratic businesses. Neither is the fact of setting up a 'co-operative' *bound* to succeed in terms of organisational democracy and worker control in the workplace. Instead, the answers to the above questions will depend on the particular constraints and pressures a co-operative faces, and the choices that its members make. In this chapter we examine some of the choices that co-operatives have been able to make over areas such as resource allocation, product choice, production technology, conditions of work and work organisation, and show how the nature and degree of constraint vary between these areas and between co-operatives in different positions in the market. However, we must first describe in more detail our own theoretical perspective. This is best explained through a critique of contrasting theories of 'degeneration'.

The degeneration thesis

The degeneration thesis, as it has become known, has a long history. It has its origins in socialist and Marxist critiques of worker co-operatives (or 'associations of producers' as they were known) as a means for transforming capitalist relations of production. Marx saw co-operatives as demonstrating the possibility of new modes of production, but believed that they must inevitably come to reflect the capitalist system in which they operated. 'The co-operative factories of labourers themselves represent within the old form the first sprouts of the new, although they naturally reproduce everywhere in their actual organisation all the shortcomings of the prevailing system' (Marx, 1966: 440). The most sustained critique of worker co-operatives came from the Fabian socialists Sydney and Beatrice Webb (1914, 1921). They did not believe worker co-operatives to be a viable form of enterprise. Based on their observations of associations of producers in Britain, they concluded:

> The most enthusiastic believer in this form of democracy would be hard put to it to find, in all the range of industry and commerce, a single lasting success. In the relatively few cases in which such enterprises have not eventually succumbed as business concerns they have ceased to be democracies of producers themselves managing their own work; and have become, in effect, associations of capitalists on a small scale.... (1921: 463–4)

More recently, Meister (1974, 1984) has presented a more detailed description of the process of degeneration, based on his studies of various democratic associations. He suggests that democratic associations have a life-cycle of four distinct phases. The first phase is characterised by high idealism and commitment which enables the association to get off the ground. However, over time there are clashes 'between a direct democracy jealous of its prerogatives and an economic activity still badly established' (Meister, 1984: 143). The need for greater efficiency leads to the establishment of full-time administrators or co-ordinators who come to be seen as directors. The second phase is a period of transition in which, if the enterprise survives, further economic consolidation takes places and conventional principles of organisation are increasingly adopted. These changes are not always accepted peacefully, and conflicts continue between idealists and managers. In the third phase co-operatives lose their radical ideals, and market values are accepted. Democracy becomes restricted to a representative board, and the gap between managers and workers increases as the business develops and production is rationalised. During the fourth phase members and their representatives lose all effective power as control is assumed by managers because of their superior expertise and ability to control information.

In these and other studies it is possible to distinguish three different forms of 'degeneration'. First, co-operatives may revert to a capitalist form where some or all of the workforce become excluded from ownership and the associated rights of control that go with it (Holyoake, 1906; Jones, B., 1894; Russell, 1985; Webb and Webb, 1914). We call this 'formal' or 'constitutional' degeneration. Secondly, what we term 'goal' degeneration may occur when the priorities co-operatives pursue become dominated by the assumed goal of capitalist companies – profit-seeking (Mandel, 1975; Webb and Webb, 1914). Thirdly, whether or not workers are formally excluded from ownership, control may become concentrated in the hands of a few and the form of organization become similar to that adopted by capitalist companies, with the same managerial hierarchy and division of labour (Kirkham, 1973; Meister, 1984; Shirom, 1972; Webb and Webb, 1914, 1921). We call this 'organizational' degeneration.

What different writers mean by degeneration can include any or all of the above. Their explanations of why degeneration occurs can also be divided broadly into three, though it is a slightly different division. First, some writers limit themselves to 'constitutional' degeneration, and offer an explanation of the tendency of worker co-operatives to revert to capitalist forms of ownership. The second and third group of theorists address themselves to degeneration as a whole process that can be manifested in any or all of the three forms outlined. One draws on Marxist theory of the labour process and argues that capitalist relations of production will force co-operatives to adopt the same priorities and organisational form as capitalist businesses. In contrast, the final group, drawing on theorists like Michels (1949), stresses internal organizational pressures that mean genuine democratic control is not possible in any social system, whether capitalist or not.

We thus have three types of theory of degeneration, which we now look at in turn in more detail.

Theory of constitutional degeneration

As we discussed in Chapter 1, various observers of worker co-operatives during the last century noticed the tendency in successful co-operatives for ownership either to be taken over by external shareholders or to become concentrated in the hands of a few workers. During much of this time there was no clearly articulated model of worker co-operation. Owen's original conception was that productive assets should belong to the community. As a result in early co-operative societies membership was open to all members of the community. The early producer societies had both external and worker shareholders and the law under which these co-operatives operated until 1852 allowed these shares to be traded. Although the Industrial and Provident Societies Act put limits on trading in and the returns on shares in co-operatives, an association of producers was not (and is not) obliged to register under this Act, and in any case it made no special provisions for producer or worker co-operatives in terms of safeguarding workers' rights of control.

Open membership and the lack of restrictions on share trading are seen by various theorists as the source of constitutional degeneration (Fanning and McCarthy, 1986; Holyoake, 1906: 283; Vanek 1970). The driving force behind this form of degeneration is economic self-interest. If membership is open to outsiders and the co-operative is successful, then external shareholders will be attracted to buy more shares and eventually take over the co-operative. If shareholding is limited to workers, but new workers are not guaranteed membership, then it is argued that existing members will not allow new workers into membership so that they can keep a greater proportion of the profits for themselves.

Although the debate on the most appropriate form of legal structure for worker co-operatives continues today (Ellerman, 1984), it is widely acknowledged that workers' rights to membership, and hence democratic control of the co-operative, should be based on their working in the co-operative and not on share ownership; that membership rights should not be tradeable and that any control exercised by external shareholders must be strictly limited. However, as we will discuss in Chapter 11, this still leaves a good deal of variety in terms of the ownership structure of co-operatives.

In Britain the lack of special provisions for worker co-operatives in the law means that it is the constitution a co-operative adopts that defines it as a worker co-operative, and is the main safeguard against formal degeneration. Most co-operatives register using ICOM model rules, which achieve this end by restricting membership and shareholding to workers who each own a £1 nominal share which cannot be traded.

While the theory discussed above presents a powerful explanation of constitutional degeneration it is limited in two important respects. First, while formal legal structures obviously have an important influence on behaviour they do not determine it. There have been examples of worker co-operatives where, despite legal safeguards, membership rights have effectively been restricted. Secondly, the fact that workers have formal rights of control does not necessarily mean that they can effectively exercise this control in practice, and so processes of 'goal' or 'organisational' degeneration may still occur. Either the enterprise may be so constrained by external circumstances that little opportunity for control exists, or control may become concentrated in the hands of a few members. These in essence are the explanations given for degeneration in the other two theoretical approaches examined below.

Marxist theories of degeneration: external forces under capitalism
Writers in the Marxist tradition identify the cause of degeneration in worker co-operatives with external forces which have their origins in capitalist relations of production. Marx himself had mixed views on co-operatives. Whilst he acknowledged that co-operatives demonstrated the feasibility of certain aspects of a socialist mode of production, he also felt that while they operated in a capitalist system they were doomed to

reflect that system. This has been a recurring theme in subsequent Marxist analysis of worker co-operatives. For example, Mandel (1975) argues:

> Not only is self-management limited to the level of the factory, workshop or assembly line, an illusion from an economic point of view, in that the workers cannot implement decisions against the operations of market laws, but, worse still, the decisions taken by the workers became more and more restricted to decisions about profits ... the fundamental principle underlying self-management, which is the liberation of labour, whereby workers dominate the process of production ... is unrealisable in an economy which allows the survival of competition.

The main thrust of this Marxist analysis is that isolated worker co-operatives cannot change the wider forces and relations of production that have developed under capitalism, but will be subject to these forces. In particular the need to survive in a competitive market will force them to seek to maximise profit in the same way as other capitalist businesses.

However, the analysis goes beyond this to argue that co-operatives will have to adopt the same forms of organisation as capitalist enterprises. For example, Mandel (1975) states: 'There have been many examples of workers' co-operatives that went wrong; there have been some that 'succeeded' – in capitalist terms that is! All they have succeeded in, however, has been to transform themselves into profitable capitalist enterprises, operating in the same way as other capitalist firms.' Nichols (1980: 25) makes a similar point:

> Second, about capitalist relations of production. The point about these is that they consist not only of intra-enterprise relations (capitalist/manager: worker) but also of inter-enterprise relations (that is, relations between private capitals, which are market mediated and unplanned...). Because of this it is difficult, for example, for worker co-operatives to break away from capitalist principles of organization (hierarchy, wage differentials, minimisation of wage costs, etc.).

As Tomlinson (1981) has noted, this analysis is based on the assumption that there is essentially one form of capitalist organisation and management that has to be adopted if the enterprise is to survive, and consequently co-operatives will have to adopt it. This assumption has been supported by a strand of the recent debates on the labour process, which following Braverman (1974) argues that under capitalism firms inevitably seek and impose Tayloristic forms of technology and work organisation that seek to reduce workers' skills and their control over the work that they do.

However, Braverman's views of the labour process have been the subject of much criticism and debate. In particular it has been argued that he neglected the ability of workers to resist managerial strategies of control and the implementation of new technologies, and that managers may pursue other strategies than direct control to obtain the compliance of workers (Friedman, 1977). In a similar vein Tomlinson (1981) has argued that management in co-operatives will not be entirely determined by external economic forces. Instead he argues that these external factors are better regarded as important constraints:

> Whilst I have argued that different organisational forms of enterprise are possible under capitalism, this is not of course to argue that such enterprises do not face constraints – but that these constraints are not the effect of 'capitalism' or 'the market' in general, but particular constraints of operating within particular markets (labour and product) with particular means of production and within particular national economies. (1981: 63)

This last point of Tomlinson's is particularly important in understanding the position of co-operatives. Many co-operatives are composed of 'peripheral' workers (Friedman, 1977) and set up in areas of the economy where they are likely to have very dependent positions as small firms (Chapter 3). This means that they are often highly constrained in the types of product they produce, or the price they can command for these products. In contrast, some co-operatives are more independent, established in new and growing markets or special niches where conditions are very different.

A specific feature of the Marxist explanations of degeneration is that the pressures towards degeneration stem entirely from wider capitalist relations of production. However, as Commisso (1979) has suggested in her study of self-management in Yugoslavia, the idea of wider forces constraining workers' control at the level of the firm could be applied not just to market constraints but also to constraints imposed by state planning.

Internal pressures towards degeneration

In contrast to Marxist explanations, various theorists have argued that the source of degeneration is the internal characteristics of worker co-operatives.

While the Webbs realised the marginal position that many associations of producers occupied in the economy, they believed that this was not the main source of their failure as businesses or co-operatives, because they argued that in similar circumstances consumer co-operatives had been able to grow and prosper:

> We cannot ascribe the failure of the Associations of Producers to the fact that they have to depend on voluntary recruiting or that they were exposed to capitalist competition, or that they were made up of manual workers and were entirely dependent for ability on what the manual workers could supply. For all these considerations apply, as we shall see, to the great and growing Co-operative Movement of Associations of Consumers. (1914: 20)

Instead they argued that associations of producers suffered from three inherent internal problems : indiscipline, stemming from their

democratic structure; lack of knowledge of the market; and unwillingness to adopt technical change. The more nearly these associations of
producers were democratically controlled by workers the worse these
problems became. The Webbs believed that as a result such associations
would either fail or be forced to adopt more conventional forms of
management and ownership structure, and hence degenerate.

Jones (1975) has suggested that the Webbs misinterpreted their findings on British associations of producers and were too pessimistic about
them. He concluded, on the basis of his research, that their survival
rate was very good, and that worker participation in many increased
over time rather than decreased. However, Jones' reliance on a few
formal measures of participation and the basis for his comparisons with
the work of the Webbs has been seriously criticised (e.g. Fairclough,
1986), which throws some doubt on his rebuttal of the Webbs.

There are perhaps more important weaknesses in the Webbs' case.
Their analysis of the failure of associations of producers was never
set against comparable failure rates of conventional small businesses
– which must have been high given the frequent economic cycles of
'boom and bust'. A comparison with consumer co-operatives is not
that meaningful given the different sectors they operated in and their
different structures. Their dismissal of external factors in explaining
the problems of producer co-operatives contradicts much of their own
analysis. Finally, even if the Webbs' conclusions were true at the time
it is not inevitable that they hold true today. As we have seen, constitutional safeguards make 'formal' degeneration more difficult. The
education and experience of workers have changed. The establishment
of support structures to assist co-operatives may help overcome internal
problems. This is not to say that co-operatives never experience the
problems identified by the Webbs, but to challenge the view that they
inevitably lead to failure or degeneration.

Other writers have suggested what are perhaps more important
internal pressures towards degeneration. Both Kirkham (1973), in
her detailed study of three producer cooperatives, and Meister (1974,
1984), in various studies of small democratic associations including
producer co-operatives, suggest that co-operatives are subject to
Michels' (1949) 'iron law of oligarchy'.

Michels studied political organizations but he believed that his
findings had general relevance. He argued that all democratic associations would eventually become dominated by ruling élites because
of a combination of factors. At a psychological level he suggested that
members of an organization experience a need for a leader, but once
in post, elected leaders tend to see the post as their own, and the skills
they possess become a powerful centralising force. The formation of
élites is also necessitated by various organisational factors which make

direct democracy inefficient: large *size* which makes meetings and other forms of communication difficult; the difficulty of resolving disputes in collectives; the degree of technical specialisation which requires *experts* who because of their expertise acquire greater power; the difficulty of large collectives in making quick *decisions*; and the need for a stable leader in order to preserve *continuity* of direction.

Michels' coherent and powerful thesis has become accepted wisdom. However, there are three important criticisms that can be levelled at it (Abrahamsson, 1977: 78–9). First, Michels' analysis assumes that direct democracy is the standard against which other forms of organisation are judged. As a result any form of representative democracy or delegation is regarded as a sign of oligarchy. Given that beyond a certain size every organisation will need, for reasons of efficiency, some form of delegation, then all large organisations must be oligarchic. Second, he argues that leaders by virtue of their position will move in a different 'social world' to those they lead. As they become socialised in this new world they lose touch with the ordinary membership, and their interests diverge from those of the members that elected them. It is possible that leaders in organisations can maintain good contact with the wider membership and try to act in their interests, particularly in organisations such as co-operatives which are much smaller than the trade unions and political parties studied by Michels. In addition, Michels' argument takes little account of the influence that 'public opinion' and the 'ballot box' can have on leaders. Finally, Michels' work largely ignores the historical processes that gave rise to the organisations he is studying. As a consequence he does not question the extent to which the processes that he observes might be influenced by wider economic, technological, social or political factors.

A combined perspective on degeneration: an empirical question

Our own theoretical position draws on these contrasting theoretical traditions, but accepts none in its entirety. First, we recognise that maintaining a formally democratic structure within a co-operative is not sufficient by itself to guard against 'organisational' or 'goal' degeneration. Secondly, we recognise that both external and internal forces will constrain, but not determine, the degree to which democratic control and alternative priorities can be maintained in co-operatives. The precise nature of these constraints will vary according to such factors as the co-operative's size, technology and its particular market position.

Thus co-operators are able to exercise at least some limited choice over both the organisational form and the priorities of their co-operative. However, this does not mean that they will inevitably pursue radical initiatives. How they exercise their freedom of choice will be influenced by their different orientations, knowledge and experience. As we saw in Chapter 5, co-operators differ quite widely in what they want from their co-operatives. In addition, there is no well-established, unifying body of knowledge about how co-operatives should be organised and run.

On this basis, the extent to which workers do actually achieve control over the process of work in co-operatives, and the way in which external and internal factors limit this control, become important empirical questions, which we will examine in the remainder of this chapter and the next. We look in turn at the three forms of degeneration, and see how far empirical evidence suggests that co-operatives in the new wave have been subject to degenerative forces and whether or not they have been able to resist them.

Avoiding constitutional degeneration: the open membership principle

The degeneration of a worker co-operative occurs most clearly when it departs from co-operative principles and thus ceases to be truly a co-operative. The most basic principles are perhaps those of open membership and democratic control by members on an equal basis. (Open membership in a worker co-operative means no discrimination between those employed, who should be equally entitled to be members.)

The potential for workers to control the process of work within co-operatives stems from the way co-operatives' formal legal structures embody these principles. As discussed earlier, the incorporation of constitutional safeguards into the rules of worker co-operatives has, so far at least, helped to prevent formal take-over either by external shareholders or by a minority of workers.

This is not to say that formal degeneration cannot occur, but it appears to be rare in Britain today. However, the common ownership constitution of many co-operatives can make raising external finance difficult because they cannot issue external shares. We know of at least one business that gave up its common ownership constitution in order to raise external finance (ICOM Training, 1987).

Although the vast majority of co-operatives retain their co-operative constitutions, this does not mean that membership rights are automatically extended to every worker, and membership can still be an important and sometimes contentious issue. There are both external and internal pressures which may lead to certain limits being put on the rights to membership.

Most co-operators regard membership as conferring certain responsibilities as well as rights. Before admitting new workers to membership they want to make sure that they will act responsibly within the co-operative. As a result the majority of co-operatives have a probationary period before new workers can become members. Usually this is for a formally agreed length of time, for example one year.

It was very unusual, in the co-operatives we studied, for workers who had served their probationary period to be refused membership. However, there was some evidence that admission to membership was by no means automatic in all co-operatives. In one case workers approaching what amounted to a personal review by existing members spoke of increased criticism aimed at them. They worried that existing members might not wish to see their profit share diluted, even though no probationer had ever been refused membership in this co-operative. In other cases the period of probation is not formalised. For example, at Happy Hands new workers are employed on a casual basis until after a period of months or years they are invited to be members. At one time, following a big expansion, the non-members outnumbered the members, and there may have been a possibility of existing members excluding newcomers, but in the event there was a general rethink and affirmation of the open membership principle.

It was also very unusual for membership rights to be withdrawn from a worker. We observed this in only one case. The grounds for withdrawing membership were that the member was not fulfilling his responsibilities. He seldom turned up to meetings, and it was felt that he did not have the right attitude or commitment to the co-operative. For example, it was said that he did not look for other work when his job was finished.

The nature of a co-operative's market can also place limits on membership. For example, Lake School of English does a high proportion of business during the summer months. This entails taking on casual staff for the summer period. Because these workers will be with the co-operative for only a short time they are not admitted into membership. However, the casual workers are paid somewhat more per hour than members because of the lack of holiday and other benefits in a short-term job. Casual workers are also employed for less regular periods at many co-operatives, Suma and Wholegrain being two examples.

The most obvious limitation on open membership is of course the fact that a co-operative's level of business can sustain only a certain number of employees and hence members. Quite often, as with both Recycles and The Bean Shop, friends and others may assist with work on a voluntary basis and then wish to become paid members. Whether this is possible becomes a business judgement.

In summary, then, the legal constitutions of co-operatives, notably the common ownership model promoted by ICOM and most local CDAs, have, so far at least, helped to prevent the common pattern of degeneration into capitalist forms of ownership observed during the last century. In all the co-operatives that we studied, membership rights were held by a majority of workers. However, our case studies do reveal that a blanket provision that all workers should be entitled to membership is too sweeping. There can be reasonable criteria for refusing to admit a person into membership, for example the need for responsible behaviour, and the seasonal nature of some businesses needs to be taken into account. In the long run the co-operative movement may need to consider developing institutionalised means for dealing with such questions, perhaps promoting a regulatory role for existing bodies such as ICOM or local CDAs.

The priorities of worker co-operatives: resisting goal degeneration

On the left an important critique of worker co-operatives has been that the priorities they pursue will have to reflect those of the capitalist system for them to survive. This critique maintains that workers' control over decision-making will be illusory, since their decisions will be dominated by the needs of the market and the necessity of making a profit. We have called this 'goal' degeneration. As we have argued, any economic system, be it governed by plan or market, will impose constraints on the control at the level of the firm. The question becomes one of whether members of co-operatives can exercise any meaningful control at this level. We examine this question by looking at the choices co-operatives have been able to make in four key areas of decision-making: investment and resource allocation; wages; choice of product or service; and choice of technology.

Control over investment and resource allocation
Decisions concerning the main flows of finance capital within the economy stand outside and above all but large corporations, the financial institutions and government. Generally speaking co-operatives, like small businesses, have access to only relatively small sums of capital for investment. They may build up reserves out of profits, or raise loans to make small purchases, but that is all. However, the capacity to do this often varies between businesses, depending crucially on which sector they are in.

As we have seen in Chapters 3 and 4, many co-operatives, particularly those that start from scratch, are severely under-capitalised. However, if co-operatives do start generating a surplus, then the workforce can exercise some control over how it is used. Often a high proportion needs to be reinvested in the business to maintain competitiveness, but there is some discretion as to how this is spent. For example, at Lake School of English the staff have invested heavily in books, teaching materials and aids. As a result the teachers felt that their school was better equipped than other places where they had worked and their job was made easier. They could also exercise more choice over the materials bought for their classes. At Suma the whole staff were involved in the decision to move to a new warehouse. Some move was necessary, due to increasing demand and the restriction on space in their existing warehouse, but all staff had the opportunity to influence the choice of new warehouse and its location. This was made after extensive discussions and a survey of all members to examine the impact of the move on individuals.

Not all decisions are governed by commercial considerations. Suma has also used some of its surplus in the past to help the establishment of other new co-operatives, and to assist existing co-operatives when faced with cash-flow problems. Clearly neither of these decisions was dictated by the market or a concern for their own profitability. At Wholegrain the members have used some of their surplus to make a major financial contribution to the establishment of a natural health centre next to their shop. The centre is a registered charity which organises regular classes, talks and demonstrations relating to natural health care. The decision to fund the centre is in line with the co-operative's objective of promoting natural foods and methods of health care, and has little to do with the dictates of the market.

Wages and wage differentials
Workers in co-operatives can also exert some control over the use of value added for wages. In Chapter 3 we showed how the proportion of value added used for wages tends to be higher than in conventional firms, though the total available is heavily constrained by market considerations, with considerable variations in wage levels between industrial sectors. In the early days of a co-operative the lack of external capital also often means that wage levels have to be kept low in order to capitalise the business.

Although the amount of money available for wages will be highly constrained, members of co-operatives are able to exercise considerable choice over how this money is allocated. The wage structure of the co-operatives we studied reflected the egalitarian ideals of co-operation.

Among rescue co-operatives that had retained specialist or managerial positions it was usual to keep some sort of pay differentials, although fewer in number and usually reduced in size. For example, Red Dragon Stores had replaced their previous employer's complex pay structure with a simpler system with reduced differentials. At

Union Phoenix it was agreed that all members should get the same wage whilst they were all having to take low wages in order to capitalise the business. It was expected that differentials would be reintroduced when the business could afford it. The only exception was the wages of the estimator, where in order to recruit a skilled person they had had to offer a higher wage than the others received.

The small job-creation co-operatives paid equal wages, where they were able to pay any wages at all.

All the alternative co-operatives had no or very low wage differentials, although The Bean Shop had introduced a long-service allowance. Suma and Wholegrain had more complex, but still very flat, payment structures. The highest differentials were at Wholegrain, although the maximum this had ever reached between members was 1.7 to 1. The few casual workers were, however, paid less than members.

Control over product choice

Decisions about the choice of product or service that an enterprise will provide are largely constrained by such factors as what the market will bear, available investment and the skills of the workforce. However, within these constraints there is still usually some degree of choice, and the issues surrounding this question vary between different types of co-operative. We distinguished in Chapter 3 between co-operatives dependent on one or two large firms as suppliers or subcontractors; co-operatives in a more independent position in a highly competitive, possibly declining market; and co-operatives in an independent position in a market niche usually based on innovation of some kind. These different relations with different markets are all constantly changing, throwing up new opportunities and threats, and in addition to the way markets themselves are expanding or declining, some co-operatives, particularly the last type, may be able to influence their markets in limited ways.

In co-operatives that are established primarily to create or save jobs the decisions about products are largely governed by considerations of the skills of the workforce and commercial viability. The founders of Happy Hands, for example, met on a training course. They decided to set up in the sewing industry because this was the area in which they were trained. Happy Hands would like to break out of the CMT business to design and manufacture their own range of clothes. However, they are in the dependent category, so that without a big leap in terms of additional marketing and design skills, organisation and additional capital, this development has been impractical so far.

In a similar way the product choices of rescue co-operatives have been dominated by the need to make these enterprises commercially viable in declining markets. The change from being a branch of a large company to a small co-operative can lead to better responsiveness to local demands. Union Phoenix was able to respond flexibly to different kinds of work, and Red Dragon Stores reported a 20 per cent increase in lines stocked, giving customers a better choice. These co-operatives had some independence, but within very competitive markets.

In contrast, some alternative co-operatives have helped to pioneer new markets in areas such as wholefoods and radical books. However, as the Oakleaf example showed, the move into the radical book market by large retailers and the decline of public sector spending on books has subsequently limited opportunities and squeezed a number of radical booksellers out of the market. There are also some warning signs that as the large and powerful private retailers move into selling wholefoods some co-operatives may again be squeezed out, as the market becomes less differentiated and more competitive.

Our case studies also show that alternative co-operatives' product choice and their relationship with the market have been influenced by their social goals, and that they have made achievements in pursuing these ends.

Two of the main objectives behind the founding of Wholegrain were to spread what the founders saw as a healthier way of eating and living, and to provide wholefoods at a reasonable price. They objected to what they saw as the excess mark-up of many health-food stores. Wholegrain has had considerable success in pursuing both these objectives, the first by its part in establishing the natural health centre noted above, and the second through establishing a wholefood supermarket.

At Suma the choice of product is governed by social and political as well as commercial criteria. They refuse to sell goods from South Africa and Israel. They have also been keen to support poor producers in the Third World and elsewhere. However, the nature of the commodity market and commercial considerations have made this difficult. They are often unable to get foods from specific sources. In addition, commodity prices can vary suddenly and sharply, so that buying involves considerable financial risks. This makes it very difficult for the co-operative to enter into a long-term trading relationship with particular producers.

The interplay between social objectives and market forces is also illustrated at Recycles. It is staffed largely by biking enthusiasts who pride themselves on the quality of the service that they provide. As a result members of the co-operative were reluctant to let any new bike leave the shop until it was properly set up. Because of the extra labour this involved their prices were slightly higher than some of the other large cycle retailers. Eventually the co-operative's own market research led them to realise that this policy was losing them sales, and reluctantly they reduced the amount of time spent on setting up bikes. Similarly Oakleaf was forced to stock a wider range of books than it would ideally have liked in order to increase turnover.

Control over the physical means of production, i.e. technology

The ability of small and medium-sized enterprises to influence the development of the technology that they use is usually minimal. Their choices are limited to what is available within the market-place. Given that many co-operatives are in very dependent positions or in highly competitive sectors, are still struggling to become established and find it difficult to raise investment capital, then it is not surprising that many are forced to use the cheapest and most basic technology available. However, within these constraints there are often choices that can be made to improve the quality of working life.

In the clothing industry the relative simplicity and portability of the technology has meant that workers in clothing co-operatives can potentially break away from conventional production lines, which were designed as much for reasons of easy supervision as for efficiency. For example, they have the possibility of altering the layout of machines to facilitate group working, social contact and quality control by peers. However, the limits on the choice of technology and how it is organised and used do not just stem from economic constraints. Co-operators often bring with them into their co-operative the dominant rationalities of production organisation that they have experienced elsewhere, and may not realise that viable and appropriate alternatives exist (see, for example, Cornforth, 1981).

Among some of the alternative co-operatives, increasing women's access to technology and jobs that have traditionally been a male preserve is a priority. As we showed in Chapters 3 and 4, this has been a particularly important issue in printing co-operatives. At Suma they attempt to ensure that there are no barriers to women doing any of the jobs; for example, women can train to obtain an HGV licence to drive their large delivery truck on the same basis as men.

Goal degeneration is not inevitable

We have seen so far that the amount of control that can typically be exercised by members of co-operatives over investment, wage structure, product and technology is quite limited. However, it is enough to demonstrate that goal degeneration is not inevitable. The constraints imposed by working within capitalist relations of production are not absolute, but allow some freedom of action, particularly for less dependent co-operatives. This is true for conventional as well as co-operative businesses. It may be seen in the charitable donations and work that some companies undertake, or their various sponsorship and secondment schemes, although clearly there are often indirect commercial benefits from these activities. Within the 'space' or 'slack' allowed by the need to survive in the wider economic system, the priorities an enterprise pursues will depend on the orientation, knowledge and experience of those in power within the enterprise. For some co-operatives the priority is to create stable jobs with reasonable wages; for others it may be furthering broader social or political goals. It is also possible for co-operatives to adopt the purely materialist priorities of maximising income per worker, as in Vanek's model described in Chapter 3, or, in theory, to aim to maximise profit like the 'ideal' capitalist firm.

The ability of workers to influence the priorities of their co-operative will depend on their ability to maintain their influence over decision-making in the co-operative. This brings us to the third aspect of the degeneration thesis, that over time a co-operative will become dominated by a powerful élite, and the workers' ability to influence decision-making will decline.

Resisting organisational degeneration

We will examine the ability of workers to exercise control over the organisation and management of work at two levels: the enterprise as a whole and the shop-floor. The next chapter is directed to examining co-operative management at enterprise level. As part of this it considers how successful co-operatives have been so far in resisting pressures towards oligarchy, and considers the sort of structures and roles that will have to be developed if democratic control is to be maintained. In the remainder of this chapter we examine the shop-floor level, and consider to what extent workers have been able to exercise control over three aspects of their jobs: (a) conditions of employment; (b) supervision and discipline; and (c) work organisation and job content.

Conditions of employment

The freedom of co-operatives to offer workers improved conditions of employment is severely constrained by the need to survive. However, many co-operatives have still been able to make some gains for their members in this area.

Happy Hands is one of a number of co-operatives that have been set up with the aim of providing flexible employment for women with young children (for another example see Tynan, 1984). It has succeeded in this by providing part-time work of 25 hours a week with flexible working hours, and we noted in Chapter 4 how even at very low wage levels women could be materially better off working there. Perhaps most importantly it is a supportive and understanding working environment in which the women are able to treat each other's domestic concerns seriously and with sympathy.

At Red Dragon Stores the absence of central control from head office gave the workforce greater freedom in arranging time off and holidays than they enjoyed under their previous employer. At Recycles the workers have chosen to work a four-day week. Suma has introduced some flexibility in working time as long as the work gets done. This can be a cost as well as a benefit, because during peak times it can mean working overtime without pay. Suma's commercial success has also enabled it to introduce generous paternity as well as maternity allowances.

Supervision and discipline
All the co-operatives studied exhibited a reduction in vertical supervision compared to previous arrangements (in the case of rescue co-operatives) or similar firms that members had worked in. In the co-operatives with designated managers, these managers retained some of the responsibilities for supervision. It was usually up to the managers, in the first instance, to 'deal with' a member who was doing a job wrong or not pulling their weight. Persistent problems were then to be brought to a general meeting to be dealt with by all members. However, in all cases the need for managerial supervision was reduced, partly because workers themselves would complain if one of their colleagues was slacking, and partly because the co-operative structure encouraged greater commitment among the workforce. In some cases the idea of bringing a dispute to a general meeting had not been tested because no such problems had yet arisen. As the shop manager at Red Dragon Stores put it: 'Now we're all in it together; then I was working for the company and they were just working for themselves.'

In other co-operatives there were no formal supervisory relationships. If a person was not pulling their weight they would usually be talked to by other workers, or the issue would be brought up at a meeting of their work group or of the co-operative as a whole. At Suma a more elaborate procedure had developed because of the size of the organization. Suma set up a specialist personnel committee elected by all the members to which persistent problems would be referred. If the personnel committee could not resolve the issue, or an important decision had to be made, then the matter would pass to the general meeting. As a result decisions concerning hiring, firing and membership could be discussed by all members of the co-operative.

It was a common feeling that the increased autonomy and responsibility that came from reduced vertical supervision was an important benefit of co-operative working. This was perhaps particularly true for workers in sectors such as clothing who had experienced tight supervision in the past. As a worker in The Clothing Co-op put it: 'One of the main benefits is that there is no boss on your back.'

Work organisation and job content
In nearly all the co-operatives we studied, workers experienced some job enlargement and enrichment, with increased autonomy and responsibility in comparison to similar jobs elsewhere. In some co-operatives these changes were quite small, but in others they were much more significant, with, for example, new patterns of work organisation which allowed extensive job rotation. However, the need for continuity and specialist knowledge and the introduction of technology requiring specialist skills can constrain the amount of job rotation that is possible.

The division of labour and job content were perhaps least changed in the three larger rescue co-operatives. At the engineering co-operatives workers tend to do the same jobs as they had previously, but they have more autonomy and control in how the job is done because of the reduction in supervision. As one worker said: 'There is more freedom in how you do the job – you know the job's got to be done but you choose when and how.' However, it is also expected that members are more flexible and responsible in their work. As we have seen in Chapter 5, whether this is experienced as a cost or a benefit will largely depend on a member's orientation to work. At The Clothing Co-op production jobs were more or less standard for the clothing industry, although there was a little more mobility between the specialisms. Similarly, at Happy Hands, though it is not a rescue, production tasks remained fairly standard.

The autonomy of a small firm can offer workers broader, more varied jobs in comparison to working for a large company. This was particularly evident in the case of Red Dragon Stores. In this co-operative all the workers including the manager felt that their jobs were much less restricted than when they worked for a large chain. Shopwork is characterised by an increasingly strict division of labour, and increasing centralisation. At Red Dragon the tasks of ordering, pricing, dealing with suppliers and book-keeping were all done outside the branch before it became a co-operative. While it was most obviously the manager's job that was enhanced, the other workers all took part in these jobs, and any one of them could fill in for the manager if he was away.

It was among the alternative co-operatives that there was the most explicit commitment to job rotation and multi-skilling of workers, although this varied between co-operatives. These work practices stem from the belief in equality and direct democracy. They are attempts to share out work so that all members have to share the 'good' and the 'bad' jobs, and so that important skills and knowledge do not become concentrated in a few key workers who could then exercise undue influence over the democratic processes of the co-operative. However, the need for efficiency does place limitations on the extent of job rotation and multi-skilling of workers.

Suma has a strong commitment to job rotation which it has maintained even though it has grown and the business become much more complex. These developments have led to changes in the way job rotation takes place. When Suma was small, people would rotate jobs on a daily or weekly basis, and everyone could do all the jobs. This is no longer possible, and today work is roughly divided into two types: (a) routine work which requires little specialist knowledge or continuity, for example order-picking, driving, and some office work; and (b) 'specialist' work which requires specialist knowledge and/or continuity. A new recruit starts their career as a 'rota-floater' – this means they do several routine jobs on a weekly basis. A typical week's work would be two days marking up orders, one day in the warehouse and two days in the office. This gives the newcomer a broad experience, and enables them to work with a number of different people. Experienced workers are also expected to do spells as a rota-floater. After about six months the newcomer will begin to specialise, perhaps doing a regular two days in the office and three days order-picking.

The work that requires more continuity and specialist knowledge is handled differently. Jobs such as marketing, sales, warehouse co-ordination, transport co-ordination, buying, sales accounts and management accounts are done on a full-time basis, although some may be job-shared by two people. It is expected that these jobs will rotate over time; for example, people in sales accounts typically stay in the job for one to two years. Even in the most specialised jobs, such as buyer, where it can take eighteen months to learn all aspects of the job, an incumbent is expected to stay only a few years. These specialist posts are preferably filled from within the co-operative, and a new worker will be trained up by the old worker.

There were contrasting views on job rotation and multi-skilling. Many workers appreciated the opportunities for variety and to learn new skills that it afforded. A few workers who had developed specialist skills were concerned that these skills were not fully utilised when they went back to other work. It is possible that over time this could develop into a degenerative force but at present there is no sign of it.

Wholegrain Foods provides an interesting contrast with Suma. There was little job rotation between the main departments at

Wholegrain, and the implementation of collective decision-making and job rotation varied considerably between departments. This can partly be explained by reference to the goals of the founders of Wholegrain. Their main aim was to spread the 'wholefood revolution', and organising the business as a co-operative was seen to be compatible with this philosophy but not a central aim. As a result there has been no sustained attempt to develop a shared understanding of co-operative principles or organisation throughout the co-operative, or to train new members in these practices, and so each working area has tended to develop separately. The small bakery is run collectively by the workers, whereas the warehouse has developed around one older worker with a more instrumental orientation to work, and now has a more conventional hierarchical structure. These differences have been reinforced by the functional and geographical separation between departments.

All the small alternative co-operatives we studied had a strong commitment to job rotation from the start, but for reasons of continuity and efficiency have had to modify their practices.

At Lake School of English the job of director of studies is rotated among all teaching staff, and the allocation of work is decided collectively. As a result the variety, scope and autonomy of the teachers' jobs are considerably wider than they have experienced elsewhere. Originally the job of administrator was also rotated among the staff, on approximately a yearly basis. However, after a number of years they decided the system was leading to inefficiency. There were problems of continuity and a feeling that not all members possessed the skills to do the job properly. As a result they now employ a full-time professional administrator. However, the practice of job rotation has not been completely abandoned. Two teachers also work half-time on administration, on a rotating basis. This way all the teaching staff get some understanding of administrative work.

At TPC the move away from job rotation has been more marked. Originally all jobs were rotated, production and administrative jobs weekly. Over time members became dissatisfied with the low wages and they decided to invest in training and new technology. The new technology is much more sophisticated than the old, and they have had to introduce specialisation in order to use it efficiently. In addition, the administrative and marketing jobs are no longer rotated. Again more specialist knowledge has been gathered here by a worker attending outside training courses. The co-operative has introduced a key worker system where each worker specialises in one area but also learns another area of work so that they can double for another worker. However, there is some evidence to suggest a further move away from this system towards total specialisation.

The development of work organisation went through three stages at Oakleaf Books. Initially each person would simply take on work as it came. However, as the work became more complex and record-keeping systems were improved it was decided to share out work according to a system. The specialist tasks such as accounts were to be rotated annually. The irregular tasks, such as the newsletter, were discussed at meetings and undertaken by whoever had the time and inclination. Everyone did routine tasks, such as shopwork, which were allocated on a weekly rota.

In the early days the job rotation worked well, but there were some difficulties in incorporating new workers because it took them time to feel confident about taking major responsibilities, and pressure of work made it difficult to give enough time to training. The situation became worse when two founder members left and the co-operative's financial situation worsened. At this time the rotation of specialist jobs ceased, because there was less time for training and the precarious financial situation meant that they could not afford to make mistakes. However, other responsibilities and tasks were shared.

The record to date: limited gains

In this chapter we have examined various aspects of degeneration in co-operatives. Our empirical evidence suggests that so far co-operatives have by and large been able to resist pressures towards degeneration. Constitutional degeneration has generally been avoided by co-operatives adopting rules which place stricter limits on who may own shares, the rights connected with share ownership and the trading of shares, though there are still important arguments whether this restricts co-operatives too much financially. We have shown that the priorities a co-operative pursues are not totally dictated by wider economic factors, although these do place heavy constraints on what can be achieved. Sometimes commercial success has provided the resources to pursue broader social goals, in other cases the resources have come from sweat equity or subsidy. The priorities that co-operatives pursue will also depend on the goals and priorities of their members, and as we saw in Chapter 5 these vary quite widely. Some co-operatives are inspired by radical social and political ideals, while others are a more pragmatic response to unemployment, and their goals vary accordingly. Equally the ability of co-operators to put their goals into practice will be constrained by the limits of their own knowledge and experience. As we discuss in more detail in the next chapter, models of co-operative organisation and management are not well developed.

Finally, we have seen that workers in co-operatives have been able to secure more control over the organisation and management of work on the shop-floor than is usually the case, although again limits are imposed the need for efficiency, the nature of the technology and the workers' own orientation, knowledge and experience. Their achievements include less supervision, more flexible working arrangements, more variety of work, lower wage differentials and more direct control over how they carry out their jobs. However, over time the increasing complexity of some businesses and the accompanying pressures for specialisation and greater continuity have led to limits being placed on job rotation, and the introduction of greater, though still small, differentials.

Our analysis so far leaves two important and related questions unexamined: Can workers exercise democratic control at the enterprise level, as well as over jobs on the shop-floor? And can this democratic control be maintained and enhanced over time – or must co-operatives come to be dominated by a managerial élite? These questions are addressed in the next two chapters. Chapter 7 considers the development of management in co-operatives, and examines how successful co-operatives have been so far in developing participative and collective forms of management. Again we suggest that co-operatives have not succumbed to organisational degeneration at this level, although we do identify pressures that could lead to degeneration in the long term. To resist these pressures, there is a need not only for new managerial structures and roles, but also for practices and procedures which safeguard and promote members' interests independently of management. We examine some of these in Chapter 8.

7

Co-operative Management

As we pointed out in Chapter 1, worker co-operatives start up in a variety of very different circumstances, and their members have very different orientations. This means that several different patterns of management can evolve, and the problems that arise in trying to develop 'co-operative management' that is both democratic and efficient will be correspondingly diverse.

The first problem that many co-operatives face is establishing the legitimacy of management at all. For many alternativist co-operators, whose inspiration came from the radical political and social movements of the 1960s with their anti-authoritarian and anti-establishment philosophies, managers were agents of the rich and powerful in society, whose prime function was to control those below them. In rejecting this aspect of management many failed to see that other functions performed by managers such as planning, co-ordination, marketing and financial control were necessary to the survival of any organisation.

Redundant workers involved in new or rescue co-operatives may reject management for different reasons. They may blame the failure of their old business on bad management, or there may have been a history of poor industrial relations. In addition, hierarchy, the strict division of labour and poor management–worker communication often mean that workers have little understanding of the functions of management.

However, the problems go beyond just recognising the importance of management. Many members of co-operatives have little or no experience of working in other co-operatives or democratic forms of organisation. In addition, there is little in the way of theory on co-operative management that they can draw upon, apart from two rather simplistic models of limited utility.

The first of these is the 'collective' in which, in theory at least, the only legitimate authority is the collectivity as a whole. According to this model all important decisions are taken collectively, although the execution of these decisions may be delegated to specific individuals or groups. However, as Michels and others have pointed out, the increase in transaction costs as collectives grow makes this model really viable only in very small organisations.

The second model is based on the principles of representative democracy, and effectively substitutes workers for the shareholders in a conventional capitalist business. In this model workers elect the board of the co-operative who are responsible for policy and appointing senior management. A managerial hierarchy is in theory responsible for implementing the decisions of the board. We call these 'dual structure' co-operatives because they have two systems of control – a managerial system and a democratic system. In practice the weakness of this model is that managers, because of their expertise, access to information and ability to meet regularly, are also in the best position to formulate policy as well as to implement it. As a result there is a danger that they come to dominate the co-operative.

The degeneration thesis suggests that co-operatives will not be able to maintain democratic forms of management, becoming progressively more hierarchical and élitist. As we saw in the last chapter, Meister (1974, 1984) suggested that co-operatives will move from direct democracy and collective management to representative democracy and professional management, until eventually the co-operative is dominated by this managerial élite. The focus of this chapter is on whether co-operatives can develop and maintain democratic forms of management. The experience of various co-operatives is examined to see how they have attempted to cope with degenerative pressures, in particular how they attempt to reconcile the often conflicting pressures for democracy and efficiency. On the basis of this experience we argue that degeneration is not a continuous and irreversible process, and that co-operatives can become more democratic (i.e. regenerate) as well as degenerate. However, many of the co-operatives we examined are still very young, so we cannot say what the long-term tendencies will be, although Batstone's (1983) study of long established French co-operatives suggests that older co-operatives are also likely to experience periods of 'regeneration' as well as 'degeneration'.

Many new co-operatives start off with simple collective structures. The chapter examines the problems that these co-operatives face as they develop and grow. It considers the limitations of simple collective management, and the problem of 'structurelessness' that can occur if co-operatives stick too rigidly to collective ideals as they grow. It describes how some co-operatives have developed more complex structures to overcome these problems. In contrast to these collectives, the chapter also looks at co-operatives converted from existing businesses, which often start with established management structures more or less intact. Perhaps the most pertinent question to ask with regard to these co-operatives is not do they degenerate but can they be democratised. The chapter also deals with the implications of co-operative structures for the roles of leaders and managers.

However, before analysing the experience of management in co-operatives, we first introduce some concepts about management.

'Maintenance management' and 'management for change'
Even in the smallest co-operative there will be a wide range
of necessary management activities. Perhaps the most important
distinction to make is between those that keep the co-operative
functioning as it is ('maintenance management') and those aimed at
finding new directions for the co-operative or developing it in new
ways ('management for change'). (We are indebted to Jim Brown,
co-operative consultant, for the formulation of this distinction.)

'Maintenance management' includes what might be termed co-
ordination tasks such as organising production schedules or rotas and
keeping a check on budgets, as well as purchasing, pricing, debtor
control, selling, customer service, etc. There is a fuzzy dividing line
between management of this type and purely routine administration
such as book-keeping, maintaining personnel records and so on. These
'maintenance management' tasks can be conceived of as separate jobs
like productive jobs. Co-operatives that apply job rotation can fairly
easily include some of the administrative and co-ordination functions
on their rota. Equally, it is quite possible for a role of administrator or
co-ordinator to be given to one person, or for different maintenance
management tasks to be given to different people, without that role
being seen as carrying managerial authority, as we saw in Chapter 6,
at Lake School of English and Oakleaf Books.

The 'maintenance' of an organisation, particularly a co-operative,
also depends crucially on the maintenance of human relationships at
work. It is perhaps in the areas of supervision and personnel matters
that co-operators tend to shy away most strongly from conventional
ideas of 'management'. It is important here to distinguish between
management as a set of 'functions' and management as a set of
'positions'. Many co-operatives want to avoid creating individual
positions with supervisory authority, believing that this authority
must be exercised collectively in some way. We saw in Chapter
6 how most co-operatives succeed in operating with a reduction in
vertical supervision compared to other similar businesses. Although
high levels of commitment and good working relations can carry most
co-operatives through on a day-to-day basis, co-operatives still need to
ensure that the quality and effort of members' work are adequate.

Co-operatives often find it difficult to develop new ways of
dealing with these issues. One of the workers at Oakleaf Books
wrote:

> Because of our joint responsibility for the whole undertaking, I think we
> felt a justifiable interest in how well other people were working, but were
> loath to say anything if we felt something was wrong for fear of damaging
> important work relationships or seeming to act in an authoritarian manner.
> I felt we were extremely bad at dealing with these problems; they tended

to flare up in occasional arguments but were rarely discussed and dealt with. (Plumpton, 1988)

These issues of authority and discipline are more likely to be resolved fruitfully if it is recognised that the interests of workers may differ from those of the co-operative as a whole, and consequently there is a need to develop formal procedures for reviewing members' performance and for handling grievances and disciplinary matters. This is much easier to say than to do. In Chapter 8 we take further the discussion on conflict and differences of interests, and suggest ideas for coping with them.

'Management for change' is completely different. It involves decisions about growing in numbers, spending money on large items of new equipment, moving into new business areas and so on. It means being able to respond to changes in the business environment and being able to initiate change within the co-operative.

Quite often, the immediate concerns that 'maintenance management' copes with are so pressing that co-operators have difficulty finding time to think more strategically about change. This is a problem they share with many small businesses (Curran, 1986: 26–7). As a result it is common to relegate the activities required for change management to a very part-time basis. Some of the longer-standing members of collectives report spending a lot of time out of work hours worrying about strategic questions or even discussing ambitious ideas for change in the co-operative with friends, but not feeling that these issues are legitimate concerns for spending paid time when there are pressing production tasks. The danger here is that not only do these strategic issues not get the attention they require, but important discussions occur outside the co-operative's formal procedures, and decisions get taken by an informal élite.

The skills required for change management are more like those of an entrepreneur, and harder to pin down than the skills of 'maintenance management', which tends to need specific knowledge of a particular area. 'Management for change' calls for knowledge of changes in the business environment, the ability to discover new opportunities, creative thinking, general problem-solving skills, ability to analyse and organise information, making informed judgements based on incomplete evidence, and leadership qualities. Even with the provision of training courses, developing such skills can be difficult, and those members who do have some entrepreneurial flair can find it hard to use these management skills sensitively within a co-operative context.

'Change management' is not readily divided up into tasks, allocated or rotated. It is more likely to be effective if several people have inputs, some initiating ideas, some giving leadership, others gathering information and developing proposals. One way to achieve this is to set up an *ad hoc* project group or team to tackle specific issues. For example, at Suma a small team was established to examine the options open to them in their move to new premises. Different issues can be addressed by different project teams, which may help to avoid the concentration of power with one 'management' group. However, in a small co-operative it might only be possible to delegate looking at a possible change to an individual, and this might not sit well with the simple collective ideal.

Management in simple collectives and its limitations

The 'simple collective' may be regarded as an ideal type for certain small co-operatives. In such co-operatives the authority for making decisions is in principle the collective of all members. The only structure the organisation has is the meeting of all members. The norm is that important information about the business should be widely discussed and shared. Decisions will ideally be by consensus – if there are disagreements, they should be 'talked out'.

Specialist 'maintenance' functions such as doing the accounts, customer relations, purchasing, etc. may be rotated or may be delegated to individuals. However, the allocation of work and supervision are usually undertaken collectively.

This pattern of management occurs most commonly among the small alternative and job-creation co-operatives. Of the co-operatives we studied, Oakleaf Books was probably most consciously trying to follow this pattern as an ideal, though The Bean Shop, Recycles, Lake and several others started – and some continued – with this kind of model.

Almost all the examples that fit this model closely employed less than ten workers. The one exception was Happy Hands, which with over twenty workers maintained regular general meetings for major decisions, supplemented with easy informal passing of information and the allocation of various 'maintenance' tasks – doing the wages, answering the phone, organising outings – to individuals. This was possible because of the relatively simple and undifferentiated nature of its business.

As the importance of management functions is realised, co-operatives such as these often begin to move away from pure collective management towards increased specialisation. All the alternative co-operatives started with quite a strong commitment to job rotation including specialist 'maintenance management' tasks, but over time it was common for people to occupy specialist roles on a more permanent basis. Even at Oakleaf Books the financial control function stayed with one person for several years towards the end. There are both external and internal pressures that underlie this trend. First, as the business becomes more complex, the specialist knowledge required becomes greater and this takes longer to acquire. Secondly, co-operators may feel, after the first flush of enthusiasm for working in an anti-bureaucratic way, a need for greater continuity and specialisation in order to increase efficiency. Thirdly, financial pressures tend to reduce the time available for training and the willingness to take risks with inexperienced people.

As Michels suggests, these changes would appear to increase the potential for decision-making to become dominated by specialists, particularly since they frequently control the information needed for decision-making. However, a number of factors tend to counteract this happening. First, in some co-operatives specialist jobs are quite widely dispersed rather than concentrated among a few people. For example, at Recycles the administrative jobs were shared among six people. Secondly, in some of the co-operatives we studied, specialist knowledge was quite highly diffused already because of past job rotation, collective meetings and information sharing, or because a limited form of job rotation was still practised. Thirdly, members of co-operatives were often aware of the potential problem of domination by experts and took action to deal with it. For example, at Lake School of English the administrator was aware of the issue and saw her role as presenting the advantages or disadvantages of the various alternative courses of action, rather than presenting only the view that she favoured. These factors, coupled with the small size of these co-operatives and their open and informal style, ensured that most members felt that they were able to influence decisions and that their views would be taken seriously by other members of the co-operative.

In terms of both structure and role, the examples of Lake and Recycles stretch the notion of the simple collective, with decision-making by consensus among equals, as far as it will go, or further. Once management is taken seriously and the business reaches a certain complexity then even a co-operative with as few as six members begins to need some form of specialisation if it is to function efficiently.

It is instructive, however, to look at the kinds of problem that arise if the ideals of collectivism are held too strictly in a co-operative that develops and grows. This is not necessarily a well thought out, deliberate strategy; more likely it is simply a reluctance to adopt a formal structure.

'Structurelessness'

As pointed out above, the inspiration behind many of the new co-operatives formed in the 1970s was the alternative and counter-culture movements of the late 1960s and early 1970s. Essentially libertarian in orientation, these movements rejected formal bureaucratic structures, which they saw as representing and perpetuating existing inequalities of power. Instead they advocated small-scale organisation, direct democracy and the value of informal networks and groupings. Hierarchy, specialisation and the division of labour were rejected in favour of collective management, job rotation and skill sharing. These organisational characteristics are common in alternative co-operatives. While small they may function effectively, although as we have seen there is likely to be some increase in differentiation and specialisation, but as these co-operatives grow the costs of a purely collective structure increase.

As Michels observed, two major costs of direct democracy in organisations are the inability to make decisions quickly and the transaction costs associated with wide information dispersal. While Michels ignored the benefits that democracy can have in improving the quality of decisions and the ease of implementation, these problems remain and are clearly illustrated by examples from the experience of Recycles. The first type of cost occurred on more than one occasion when the membership was split evenly on a major issue. In one case inability to decide between two strong candidates for one permanent job led to 'two weeks of interminable meetings, most of them carbon copies of the first two', after which both people were taken on even though it had been thought the business could support only one extra member. Another time there were competing opinions on how to break into a new market sector, a decision requiring considerable capital investment and action by a certain deadline. Perhaps inevitably, given dispersed authority and differences in opinion, what occurred, by default, was the option of doing nothing. Transaction costs were apparent not just on particular occasions but constantly, not only in terms of the resources required to spread information and the time taken for meetings, but indirectly in the feelings expressed by members that they did not know all that was going on, but ought to.

The only way of decreasing transaction costs is to develop a structure in which not everyone is equally involved in all decisions. However, some alternative groups have been reluctant to introduce more structure because they feared that it would lead to inequality. What they failed to realise is that this process is likely to occur informally, and that informal élites may be more difficult to subject to democratic control than formal ones. Freeman (1972) was one of the first to challenge what she called 'the tyranny of structurelessness'. She argued that it was impossible to abolish structure. Power continued to be exercised in groups; the abolishment of a formal hierarchy usually meant that an informal hierarchy would emerge. As the power of informal élites is not explicitly recognised it is extremely difficult to place limits on their power or to hold them accountable.

Landry et al. (1985: 10) summarise the problem as follows:

> The problem is that informal élites are not accountable to anyone. Because power has no explicit basis there are no straightforward mechanisms for removing their influence. Unless you are part of the influential group it is hard to know who has real power in an organisation run by an informal élite: who you should lobby for what purpose; what are the criteria on which decisions are based; which of the organisation's goals should take priority.

At Recycles this problem has been minimised as founders have left rather than continue in a dominating position. In the words of one: 'I felt I'd been there for years and was taking up more space than other people ... you can crowd the new people out.'

However, Recycles has not grown beyond seven members. At Suma, both the increasing costs of collective decision-making and the emergence of an informal élite became apparent as the co-operative began to approach twenty members (Macfarlane, 1987a). Decision-making in the co-operative was by consensus. This meant that minorities could veto decisions. The increase in size led to a diversity of opinions which made reaching decisions more difficult. Some members felt that it was not even worth discussing some issues because they knew it would be impossible to reach a consensus. In addition, it was not possible for members to attend all meetings because some would always be out delivering goods. The co-operative was able to deal with these problems by introducing majority decision-making and the rule that decisions had to be ratified at a second meeting to give other members a chance to have their 'say' if they desired.

A more difficult issue was the feeling that the co-operative was being run by an informal élite. The dominant group consisted of long-serving (mainly male) members of the co-operative. Their dominance was built upon the expertise and knowledge that they had built up over time and their close association with each other. Clearly knowledge and expertise are likely to be an important power base in any organisation; however, this was exacerbated by the lack of structure and formal procedures in the co-operative. The co-operative lacked procedures to introduce new members effectively to its decision-making structures. There was a shortage of management information in the co-operative, and much of what was produced was held in people's heads rather than written down and circulated. As a result many members lacked the information necessary to make decisions. In addition, the informality of meetings meant that it was easier for those with greater knowledge or stronger personalities to dominate.

Similar problems occurred at Wholegrain. When the business was converted from the original partnership into a co-operative, the only decision-making body was the general meeting. However, 'Simon', one of the founders, recalls that an informal hierarchy had already developed:

> When it became a co-operative it had a management structure which was a sort of residue from the partnership days ... there was a control mechanism and there were definitely people in control of it, although it was very much open meetings ... it was effectively me and Thomas and Julia who ran the place ....

Complex collective structures

As it grows, the very democracy a collective is trying to preserve is in danger unless more complex structures are evolved. The formal structure of an organisation is an attempt to make explicit the main areas of responsibility in an organisation, who is responsible for those areas, what authority they have to make decisions and to direct the work of others and who they are accountable to. This is not to say that informal processes of power and influence will not still exist within the organisation. However, it does give an explicit 'frame of reference' for organising and judging people's actions. An organisation's formal structure can be thought of as a tool for trying to shape the processes of power and influence in the organisation.

Perhaps one of the reasons why a more complex structure is rejected in co-operatives is that it is commonly associated with the hierarchical structure found in many conventional organisations. However, there is a great deal of variation that is possible among structures. For example responsibilities can be given to subcommittees and groups rather than to individuals. Committees can be elected or appointed. Responsibilities can be spread widely or concentrated. Positions can be permanent or rotated. Limits can be placed on authority. These alternatives allow the possibility of democratic control at other levels within the organisation, and for many people to have access to positions of responsibility.

Suma has evolved a more complex structure to deal with problems caused by growth, mindful of the need to improve both democracy and efficiency. The first response to these problems was a proposal that a management committee should be established to create a decision-making group of a more manageable size than the general meeting. This proved a contentious issue, and the proposal was eventually rejected, since some feared it would formalise the power of the 'élite' of long-standing members and increase the barriers to involving new people. Instead it was decided to create two subcommittees of the general meeting, one to deal with finance and the other with personnel matters. The role of the subcommittees is to raise issues and prepare information for decision at the general meeting, and to carry out a number of executive functions delegated by the general meeting.

The composition and role of the subcommittees have evolved over time. In particular the composition of the finance committee has been changed to make it more representative of different functional interest groups within Suma. In addition, the co-operative has established the position of management accountant within the co-operative. Like other specialist posts this job is rotated after a few years. These developments have enabled the co-operative to undertake more detailed financial planning than was possible before.

There is a widespread feeling at Suma that the move to setting up subcommittees has improved democracy within the co-operative as well as improving efficiency. Although there are still inequalities in power, the committee structure and the rotation of jobs mean that power is much less concentrated than in most firms, or than it had been in Suma. However, some problems remain. Workers have a good deal of autonomy at Suma, and this has led to problems of co-ordination, which are beginning to be addressed by the setting up of inter-departmental meetings. In addition it is often difficult to discuss complex issues in the general meeting.

The Suma case study is particularly interesting from the point of view of 'organisational' degeneration. It shows that as the co-operative grew and the business required more specialist knowledge there was a tendency towards oligarchy. However, the membership were aware of this trend and have acted to deal with it. The development of other representative structures to supplement the general meeting has increased democratic accountability and control, rather than being another sign of oligarchy. 'Regeneration' as well as degeneration is possible, at least in the short term.

The structure of Wholegrain is more differentiated than Suma but it too has gone through phases of degeneration and regeneration, with different departments experiencing those processes in different ways. Its business is more diverse, and it operates from two geographically separate sites. It has five departments: the shop, office and bakery on one site and the warehouse and packing room on the other site. Originally the only decision-making body was the general meeting. As the co-operative grew all the main departments came to hold regular weekly or fortnightly meetings. The co-operative also elected a management committee with representatives from each department, which normally met fortnightly to deal with financial and other affairs that affected the co-operative as a whole. Finally, general meetings continued, usually once a month, to discuss, and vote upon, recommendations of the management committee. One of the founder members, 'Simon', had a special entrepreneurial role in charge of new business developments, and was formally accountable to the management committee.

Problems developing structures that reconcile democracy and efficiency have been apparent in both the shop and the warehouse, the largest departments of the co-operative. The management of the shop has gone through a number of phases. The shop meeting has formally remained the main decision-making body throughout. Initially there was a strong commitment to collective management and job rotation in the shop. Over time, partly due to high staff turnover and poor efficiency, one of the workers, 'Mandy', began to take more responsibility for the administrative functions concerning the shop. Eventually, Mandy asked that her role and responsibilities be formally recognised and that she become the shop manageress. This led to an important conflict in the co-operative. Some members felt that it was just recognition for the work she did, others felt that it would undermine the egalitarian nature of the co-operative. After she threatened to leave the co-operative, and it was discovered just how dependent the success of the shop was upon her, Mandy was made manageress. However, a subsequent manageress, 'Sarah', encouraged collective working in the shop through the delegation of managerial tasks and when she left the co-operative members of the shop decided to return to a more collective form of management. 'Clare' took over most of Sarah's administrative duties when Sarah left, but increasingly other members of the shop and bakery took responsibility for particular areas of office work. (Basic shopwork has always been rotated.) Clare commented on this change as follows:

> Since Sarah left, there's been talk of ... do we need someone with special skills. I changed my mind on this one ... if people were paid more (for having special skills) how would it be after a year? Would it block the chances of other workers to do more? Most are graduates and quite intelligent!

The warehouse was established later than the shop and grew around 'Ian', who, due to his length of service, age and detailed knowledge of the warehouse's business, assumed an informal managerial role as the numbers in the warehouse increased. Ian was less interested in collective working than many of the shop members and saw his role as increasing the efficiency of the business. Ian was largely responsible for recruitment to the warehouse, so it is perhaps not surprising that this view predominated there. This more instrumental attitude to work was probably partly due to the fact that Ian was older than many of the shopworkers and had a family, which meant that he had greater financial commitments than the others. Having said that, responsibilities for specialist activities such as book-keeping and vehicle maintenance were distributed among a number of members, and the warehouse still maintained regular meetings of all members.

The different cultures and structures that developed in the shop and the warehouse led to conflict. After a poor trading performance by the shop the warehouse accused them of inefficiency and poor management. The shop on the other hand thought that the warehouse was not run co-operatively.

Wholegrain also experienced problems over Simon's role. While it was commonly acknowledged that the success of the business owed much to his entrepreneurial ability, some members felt that he had taken over important areas of decision-making but was not really accountable for his actions. Over time a competence gap had developed between Simon and even the longest-serving member. In addition, Simon did not always succeed in communicating what he was doing, and many members found his attempts to explain the co-operative's finances above their heads.

What can be learnt from these experiences so far? Perhaps first and foremost collectives as they grow need regularly to review both their structure and procedures from the point of view of both efficiency and democracy. Perhaps one of the weaknesses of Wholegrain was that these issues always took second place to achieving the organisation's external goals of promoting healthy eating, etc. (Woolham, 1987).

As collectives grow then general meetings become unwieldy forums for decision-making. As we discuss in Chapter 8, much can be done to make these meetings more effective, for example through well-prepared documentation, the use of small discussion groups or the introduction of majority decision-making. However, inevitably some form of delegation of decision-making powers is required.

The best structure for a growing collective will depend on a range of factors including size and technology. A decentralised structure has the advantage of dispersing power and militates against the formation of a narrow élite, while bringing some decisions close to all members of the co-operative. However, decentralisation brings a need to develop clear procedures to ensure co-ordination, which may be overlooked. This became apparent as Suma grew. Equally there is a danger of different orientations developing which may lead to damaging conflict. It is important then that co-operatives that follow this strategy also devote effort to developing and maintaining a shared culture and understanding – through, for example, common recruitment and induction procedures, training and the periodic rotation of at least some staff between departments. It was partly through the absence of procedures like these that differences emerged at Wholegrain (Woolham, 1987).

It is important that opportunities for participation are developed at all organisational levels once different levels develop. For example, self-managed work groups or departmental meetings might be created. At higher levels representative groups might be elected to carry out or oversee important functions, as for example the personnel and finance committees at Suma.

Inevitably increased specialisation will lead to competence gaps between people. However, the co-operative should aim to increase and spread competences as widely as possible through procedures such as skill sharing, training and job rotation. Again the right balance must be struck between promoting democracy and efficiency. Too much job rotation can reduce competence, continuity and hence efficiency. However, dependence on a few experts, as well as being bad for democracy, can reduce a co-operative's flexibility, making it vulnerable if an expert is ill or leaves the business. At Wholegrain the business was seriously threatened when Simon and Ian decided to leave.

Leadership and initiative

The example of Simon at Wholegrain demonstrates the other side of the problem of trying to maintain pure collective management as an organisation develops and grows. Up to now in this chapter we have thought of management as a set of functions that could possibly be distributed consciously to different individuals or groups or kept as collective responsibilities. However, individuals themselves take on more or less in accordance with their own wishes. As we move from 'maintenance' to 'change' management, the functions required are less easily defined and parcelled out. Irrespective of what the group may wish to legislate, some individuals will be more active than others. Indeed, one of the positive features of co-operative working is the opportunity it affords to certain individuals to develop themselves and take on responsibilities where in another business they might stay in an inferior position in the hierarchy. This should be positive also for the co-operative, if it can harness the human resources in terms of leadership and initiative that are represented by its members' wishes to develop themselves as much as they can.

To understand the role of leadership in co-operatives it is necessary to understand a little more about the nature of leadership itself. Leadership is not some mysterious personal quality but is a set of skills (Brown and Hoskins, 1986) and the motivation and drive to use these skills to achieve desired ends. A leader needs the ability to perceive threats and opportunities, to conceive courses of action to deal with these threats and opportunities and finally to mobilise people and resources to pursue these actions. It is perhaps the ability to motivate and mobilise oneself and other people that really marks out what is involved in leadership from the other skills, which are essentially those of 'change management' described earlier. Ideally, in a co-operative, the changes initiated by leaders should be based on the informed consent of members. Simon's isolation from other members of Wholegrain, and the difficulties of communication, meant that consent to his proposals was not always fully informed.

In conventional businesses it is expected that managers should exercise a leadership role within the organisation. It is their job to ensure that changes are carried out. In a co-operative it is ultimately the responsibility of the membership as a whole to direct the enterprise. Leadership may not be seen as the responsibility of any specific group, which can mean that the need for leadership gets overlooked.

There may also be ideological barriers which question the legitimacy of leadership. Commonly leadership has individualistic, élitist and sexist connotations as a quality of great and powerful men. This often fits uncomfortably with the egalitarian philosophy of co-operation. As a result leadership like management has been regarded as taboo among more radical groups. If this results in a denial of the importance of leadership then co-operatives are likely to stagnate and die. Rather than questioning the legitimacy of leadership it is more appropriate for members of co-operatives to ask whether any suggested initiative will further their interests and objectives or not. In this way a leadership that is guided by and accountable to the members of the co-operative can be developed. The appropriate ideal for a co-operative is not that there should be no leaders, but that many people should have leadership skills and feel capable of using them.

The ideological barriers to leadership are more frequent in radical or idealistic co-operatives. However, once these barriers have been overcome many members within the co-operative may have the educational background and skills readily to assume leadership roles. The problem then may be a clash over different leadership styles, as we saw at Wholegrain. It is vital if major conflicts and splits are to be avoided that issues of leadership are discussed openly by members of the co-operative, rather than treated as taboo, and that a conscious effort is made to define what are acceptable forms of leadership. However, there will always be some differences in leadership styles, and it is important that co-operative members show a tolerance and an awareness of the strengths and weaknesses of different styles.

In some co-operatives leadership capabilities may be lacking or undeveloped. An important task for CSOs is to help workers to acquire the skills needed for leadership and the confidence to use them, and encourage people to take on responsibilities. Co-operatives themselves must also encourage the development of leadership skills on a day-to-day basis, through decentralising responsibilities, through training and perhaps most importantly through giving support and encouragement to people who exercise initiative.

Whilst we believe it is important for co-operators to remain constantly aware of the need for checks on leadership and management roles, we also see a problem for co-operatives in attracting and retaining people who already possess some leadership and management skills. As we saw in Chapter 5, members who take an active part in directing their co-operative enterprises can encounter high costs as well as the benefits of control. Being an activist and leader in a co-operative often means long hours and increased responsibilities with the associated problems of increased stress and occasionally 'burn-out', without the usual economic rewards. In addition, many activists feel that the membership do not appreciate their efforts, being quick to criticise when things go wrong but slow to praise or reward when things go well. As well as ensuring accountability, the other challenge for co-operatives is to develop a culture where good leadership and initiative are rewarded at least through recognition and support, if not financially.

Democratising established structures

Not all co-operatives start from scratch or with a strong commitment to collective working. Quite a different situation arises when management structures are already well established. This occurs most clearly in endowed or rescue co-operatives, but it is also possible for a philanthropic entrepreneur or CSO to start a 'top-down' co-operative (Oakeshott, 1978; Tynan, 1980a, 1980b) with the intention of moving from a strong leadership role for management to a more participative situation later.

These co-operatives are likely to adopt a 'dual structure' for several reasons. Perhaps most importantly they are used to having a management structure in the old firm, and it is often difficult to break existing patterns of social relationships. The workers' motivation for forming a co-operative may have little to do with a desire for collective management. In addition, the larger size of many endowed and rescue co-operatives makes some form of differentiated structure inevitable, and for many a managerial hierarchy is the most obvious solution to this problem.

Perhaps the most appropriate question with regard to these co-operatives is not so much 'Can democracy be maintained and degeneration avoided?' but 'Can a process be set in motion that will allow existing structures and procedures to be democratised, while maintaining efficiency?' Two of our case studies illustrate some of the problems that can occur.

The Clothing Co-op was established with the help of a development worker from a local CDA in a neighbouring town. The co-operative was short of a cutter and of management skills among the founding group. As a result they decided to appoint from outside a cutter who had a lot of experience in the trade to be their manager. During the early life of the co-operative general meetings were held fortnightly. The division of responsibilities between the general meeting and the manager was not formally specified, but evolved through custom and practice. There were disputes about how much autonomy the manager should have and exactly what sort of decisions should be brought to the meeting, but these gradually declined. The manager's main responsibilities were sales, recruitment and to oversee the admin- istration and financial affairs of the business. He had considerable autonomy to make decisions in these areas. If there was time he would consult with members of the co-operative, but if not he would take decisions and report back afterwards.

After the start-up phase the number of meetings declined until they were quite infrequent. The efforts of the development worker to keep in touch were also gently rebutted. The co-operative was progressing well commercially, and members saw no need to hold meetings, or take up the development worker's time. This situation continued until, out of the blue, the manager announced that he and one of the founder members of the co-operative were leaving to start their own business.

The case study suggests that, although founder members were able to help define managerial responsibilities and to influence key decisions in setting up the co-operative, they remained quite heavily dependent on the manager. Perhaps most importantly, though, they failed to establish a common understanding of co-operative principles and practices and a shared commitment to the co-operative. The decision to leave recruitment to the manager, the decline in meetings, and the lack of any procedures to introduce new members to the theory and practice of co-operation meant that new members were prepared to give their loyalty to the manager rather than to the co-operative. Ultimately when the manager decided to leave and take much of the business with him there was little the remaining members could do to prevent him.

The Engineering Co-op was also formed with the help of the local CDA. General meetings are held monthly. Anyone can put items on the agenda for the meeting. The meeting receives a financial report in the form of a monthly profit-and-loss statement from one of the managers, and usually statements about production from the other manager. Typically issues raised by workers concern production matters, discipline or membership. Apart from the general meeting the management structure has remained largely as in the old firm.

Unlike The Clothing Co-op, The Engineering Co-op, with the guidance and support of a development worker, has maintained regular meetings. These now appear to have become accepted and institutionalised. The meetings are open and frank, and criticisms are often voiced and discussed. However, workers like shareholders can have problems ensuring that the management they appoint are adequate. As we saw in Chapter 4, one manager, the former owner of the business, under pressure of cash-flow problems, did not pay VAT and PAYE and withheld this fact from other members and the co-operative's advisers.

Fortunately the co-operative was able to rescue the situation with assistance from the local CDA. A financial control committee was established with the managers and chairman of the co-operative as members, plus the development worker and an outside accountant in attendance. The ex-owner has decided to leave the co-operative and concentrate on other business commitments. The members of the co-operative were able to hold him accountable after the event, but their lack of expertise and the shortage of management information meant that the co-operative nearly failed.

These case studies highlight some of the key problems in democratising existing structures. How can democratic practices be sustained and institutionalised? How can responsibilities be divided between the democratic and managerial systems of control? How can members ensure that managers act in their interests and be held accountable for their actions? Clearly there are no easy answers to these problems, but these and other studies do suggest a number of useful lessons.

Some of the main barriers to democratisation may lie with the workers' and managers' own attitudes, knowledge and skills. Tynan and Thomas (1984) show how old orientations and attitudes to work can clash with those necessary to sustain co-operative working. Workers and managers may lack knowledge or understanding of how a co-operative can be organised and run. In addition, they are unlikely to have had experience of democratic decision-making or participative forms of management and so lack the skills and experience to operate effectively. As a result outside advice, assistance and training are likely to be necessary, at least during the early stages of democratisation. The continued assistance of the development worker was probably significant in the relatively successful development of The Engineering Co-op. The importance of outside assistance and training has been recognised in the study of a variety of conversion co-operatives (Clark and Guben, 1983; Lindenfeld, 1982).

Another important factor is that all members must have the opportunity to experience some form of democratic working, if they are to gain the skills and experience to participate effectively. Particularly in large co-operatives this will mean introducing forms of participation and democratic control at lower organisational levels as well as the general meeting. Bernstein (1976) suggests that there is a minimum threshold level of participation before a process of democratisation is likely to take off.

The development of 'dual structures' in co-operatives raises the problem of how responsibilities should be divided between the two systems of control (Cornforth and Thomas, 1980; Paton, 1978b). Many co-operatives try to operate a distinction between policy, which is decided democratically, and implementation, which is left to management. However, by itself such a distinction provides a poor guide to action. As Paton argues, policy may be interpreted either narrowly or broadly, and it is difficult to decide policy issues without understanding what other options might be available or what might be the problems of implementation. Perhaps a better solution is that questions of responsibilities and who should make what decision should be the subject of regular review and decided democratically. Important new issues should be brought to the attention of the co-operative's democratic bodies as soon as possible so that members have a chance to decide how the issue should be dealt with, and influence the formulation of policy.

An important source of organisational power is the ability to control the agenda for decision-making (Bachrach and Baratz, 1963; Lukes, 1974; Walsh, et al., 1981). It is important that workers as well as managers are able to define what they believe to be the issues facing their co-operative. However, agenda setting is often by default left as the responsibility of management. A better alternative is to give this responsibility to the chair or secretary of the co-operative, part of whose job should be to ensure that the democratic procedures of the co-operative are serviced and safeguarded.

Management information must be freely available and be as far as practicable presented in a form that is easy to understand. As we will discuss in more detail in the next section, an important aspect of a manager's new role is to ensure that the membership is well informed and understands the issues involved in important decisions.

No democratic structure by itself can guarantee that members are able to participate in and influence the management of their co-operative. Another important factor concerns how managers themselves behave. It is vitally important that those who manage are committed to working co-operatively, or as we saw at The Clothing Co-op they are likely to undermine the co-operative. However, commitment alone is not enough. Managers must also be prepared to develop new roles for themselves that are more compatible with co-operative principles.

New roles for managers

Certain individuals may be designated 'managers' in both complex collectives and conversions. If there is going to be greater equality than in conventional organisations between workers and those who carry out management functions, and if workers are going to have an effective say in decision-making, then new relationships between workers and managers have to be developed which will change the role of managers. Unfortunately there are no well-developed or widely accepted models of the manager's role in co-operatives.

One of the main problems is the 'competence gap' between those who manage and ordinary members. If this gap becomes too large the membership are likely to become over-dependent on managers. They will not understand management issues and not have the confidence and knowledge to take part effectively in decision-making. It must be managers' responsibility, at least in part, to ensure that this gap does not become too large. Consequently perhaps the most important aspect of managers' new role in co-operatives is that of educators. They need to present information and ideas in such a way as to increase the competence of all members and their ability to make decisions and to hold managers accountable for their actions.

The management accountant at Suma clearly saw his role in this way. Before his appointment most of the management accounts had been done externally, and awareness about these issues was quite low in the co-operative. He originally saw his role as presenting accounting information to the general meeting so that it could make decisions. However, he found that the information he presented was too complex and poorly understood. As a result he devoted a lot of effort to finding ways of simplifying the accounts and trying to communicate the main issues involved. Two years later he was able to say: 'Now people are speaking about it as if it is second nature.'

Another aspect of managers' power often stems from their job of formulating proposals for action (Lukes, 1974). Frequently, by the time proposals reach members for decision, many options may have been considered and rejected, perhaps leaving only one option for members to consider. In such cases members may not fully understand the reasoning behind the option they are being presented with, and may feel they have the choice of the option presented to them or no policy at all. It is important, then, that in major areas for change managers should involve members in the process of formulating proposals. Managers' task may then be more appropriately seen as examining the costs and benefits of competing options, which they present to the membership for decisions. This was the strategy that both the management accountant at Suma and the administrator at Lake tried to follow.

If both the above roles are to be carried out effectively then the membership must have access to management information in a form that can readily be understood. In most small co-operatives this can often be done through informal discussion and contacts. However, as co-operatives grow it is likely that more formal channels will have to be used. It is probably a mistake to leave this function just to meetings. The danger in this case is that the majority of the meeting is taken up with managers presenting information, often leaving little time for discussion or questioning. Briefing meetings or written reports before meetings are likely to be more effective. In larger co-operatives it may be necessary to develop 'worker information systems' (Robinson, 1988; Robinson and Paton, 1983) in the way large companies have developed management information systems.

If managers are going to be democratically accountable then they must be willing to accept direction and criticism from the members of the co-operative. This may be the most difficult aspect of managers' new role. All too often the reaction to criticism is to defend one's own position and to hide mistakes. This point really applies to all members of co-operatives and not just managers, and is perhaps an area where co-operatives could benefit from group training techniques. However, as we have already pointed out, managers and leaders are particularly exposed to criticism because of the position that they occupy.

It is perhaps also worth pointing out that if those with management responsibilities are going to adapt well to their new roles, members may need to change their own behaviour. Members need to encourage managers to provide information and to explain their actions in a way that can be understood. Managing can be a highly stressful job, particularly given the criticism and questioning that democracy can give rise to. It is important that members understand these difficulties and are willing to give support and encouragement as well as criticism. In reviewing managers' actions co-operators need to bear in mind the possible dangers of over-stressing the need for equality of influence. This point is discussed further in Chapter 8. Instead co-operators should be looking to whether management proposals serve their and the co-operative's interests.

Conclusions

In this chapter and the last we have seen that at least in the short term 'organisational' degeneration, like 'goal' degeneration and 'constitutional' degeneration, is not inevitable. Clearly simple collective management is viable only in small co-operatives. However, the transition to more complex structures does not have to mean the development of a conventional managerial hierarchy. It is possible to develop complex collective structures which combine features of representative and direct democracy and which both are efficient and allow a lot of scope for workers to influence the management of their organisation. We observed that processes of regeneration as well as degeneration can occur as collectives grow.

We have suggested that many co-operatives, particularly rescues and other conversions, do not start with a high and widespread commitment to democracy. As a result it is less appropriate to look at whether or not they degenerate but whether a process of democratisation can take place which gives meaning to the co-operative's formal rules. Our case studies showed that this is not easy. Problems can arise in institutionalising democratic procedures, in dividing responsibilities between managerial and democratic systems of control and over the role of managers. These co-operatives are likely to need outside support and assistance to deal successfully with such problems. However, as we observed in Chapter 5, members can develop a commitment to democracy, and as we saw above democratic procedures can become accepted and institutionalised. Again this shows that processes of democratisation, as well as degeneration, can occur.

This is not to say that there are not pressures towards degeneration, and we have identified some of them. Growth increases the transaction costs of collective decision-making. The need for efficiency frequently requires greater specialisation and continuity, reducing scope for job rotation and the sharing of management tasks. The co-operatives we studied are still relatively young and small, and may yet succumb to degenerative forces, although Batstone's (1983) study of French co-operatives suggests that co-operatives can experience processes of regeneration much later in their 'life-cycle'.

Another way of trying to prevent degeneration is to build into the co-operative various safeguards of members' interests independent of management. Ideally this should also include a more educational and philosophical strand, aiming to develop the 'democratic consciousness' which is so vital for keeping the co-operative spirit alive. These matters are the focus of the next chapter.

8

'For the Benefit of the Members'

In the constitution of most co-operatives the 'objects' clause states: '... to carry on for the benefit of the members the trade or business of ...'. In other words, the management of the enterprise has to be carried out in the interests of the members – in the case of a worker co-operative, in the interests of the workers.

In the last chapter we made a distinction between a *collective*, where authority lies with the members as a group of equals, all of whom may be involved in management, and a co-operative with a *dual structure*. In the latter, authority is divided in some way between the membership of the co-operative and those who are identified as managers of the co-operative.

However, even if, as in a small collective, all members are involved in management, this does not necessarily safeguard all their interests. There is always scope for basic differences over interpreting what is 'for the benefit of the members'. This is perhaps most easily seen in dual-structure co-operatives where managers could interpret members' interests differently from non-managers. Managers may tend to look first at building up a successful enterprise in business terms, and assume that members will automatically benefit from belonging to a successful enterprise. However, this could mean preferring to build up reserves or plough back surplus into new investment rather than to raise wages or pay a bonus; it could mean growth rather than consolidation; taking risks rather than securing existing jobs; or following the dictates of the market rather than supporting members' social goals for the co-operative.

The two main theoretical perspectives reviewed in Chapter 6 suggest that, for different reasons, managers' and members' interests are likely to diverge. In Marxist labour process theory managers are seen either simply as agents of capital or in a mediating role between the enterprise and the market environment. Either way, they are the ones who because of their position are most likely to see market constraints. They will be the ones explaining how the market gives no room for manoeuvre, and how this or that just has to be done to meet outside demands. Alternatively, in Michels' theory of oligarchy, managers are seen as acting in their own interests, both materially and politically, rather than in the interests of members. In addition,

Michels argues that those in powerful positions are more likely to act to consolidate power than to share it.

In practice 'managerial interpretations' of members' interests are often accepted as common sense. It is a dominant line of thought in our capitalist society that 'efficiency' in organisation or 'good management' is somehow an absolute ideal, derived from the world of business, but applicable in all organisations irrespective of the ownership or purpose of the enterprise. Indeed, the phrase 'for the benefit of the members' may be legally interpreted as implying the responsibility to try to maximise long-term profit to distribute to members for their material benefit, even if they were to vote for some other kind of 'benefit'. Hence, the idea that all the co-operative needs is 'good management', and that promoting the business interests of the enterprise will best serve the members' interests, may be an opinion honestly held by managers and readily accepted by members.

However, we argue that members' interests may differ from this managerial interpretation. 'Ownership' or 'common ownership' gives workers shared control over their *jobs* first and foremost; other benefits of ownership, such as the right to the residual surplus or control over disposal of the assets, are likely to be of secondary concern in practice. It follows that, in material terms at least, members' interests are primarily in conditions of employment, wages, quality of working life and so on, rather than in the success of the enterprise *per se*, although clearly the two are often related.

Different workers will have legitimate variations in their interests, too. We saw in Chapter 5 how co-operative working can bestow a variety of benefits: instrumental, social and moral benefits, as well as the benefits of a share in power and control. It is not purely a matter of personal choice. Different personal circumstances, skills and abilities will play a part in determining whether a particular member is more interested in high wages or in long-term job security, in skill sharing as a principle or in personal development.

Two further points need making here. First, members may have a collective interest, for example in maintaining an egalitarian pay structure or pursuing some external social or political goal. This may well differ from individual interests, particularly when, as so far in this chapter, the latter are expressed as objectively as possible. Secondly, there may be minority interests or sections of the workforce whose interests need safeguarding against the majority. To give some examples, the idea of equal opportunities as an important goal for co-operatives spans both of these points, whereas the promotion of healthy eating or of radical political views would involve only the first.

Promoting members' interests positively is therefore a different matter from trying to ensure the maximum involvement of members in management, whatever type of co-operative is involved. As we have argued above members may have a plurality of interests. As a result the first and most basic necessity is to recognise conflict as both legitimate and inevitable in a 'healthy' co-operative, and to develop ways of dealing with conflict constructively. This requires some understanding of the likely sources and dynamics of conflicts in co-operatives; we examine these issues in the next section. We then consider some practical suggestions for enabling co-operatives to deal with conflict more constructively and both to safeguard and to promote their members' interests.

In this chapter we focus on one interpretation of co-operative – a vehicle for promoting members' interests on an equal basis. At the end of the chapter we re-examine briefly the meaning of co-operation. We suggest that co-operative principles are open to different interpretations, and their implementation will be constrained by the need for efficiency. In fact, one important means of resisting degeneration is for co-operators to maintain a debate on co-operative principles and ideals and how they can best be put into practice. This debate is more likely to be sustained if a co-operative has links with an active co-operative movement.

Conflict in co-operatives

Co-operation is often taken to imply harmonious working rela-tionships. Indeed, one popular justification for co-operatives is that they are supposed to overcome the structural conflict of interests between workers and management (Oakeshott, 1978; Young and Rigge, 1983). However, as we have argued above, this conflict of interests persists, although the divisions between workers and managers may be reduced, and the potential for sectional interests to emerge remains in co-operatives as it does in other forms of organisation. In many ways the potential for conflict in democratic organisations such as co-operatives is higher than in conventional organisations because of the greater number and diversity of people involved in the decision-making process. Also, the fact that co-operatives are a relatively new and unusual form of organisation can lead to confusion, uncertainty and sometimes disagreements over the rights, roles and responsibilities of members. So it is perhaps not so surprising that in practice co-operatives are often characterised by a good deal of overt conflict. It is vitally important for co-operators to develop an understanding of the likely areas of conflict and their dynamics if this conflict is to be handled constructively.

Conflicts over objectives

The process of setting objectives in co-operatives differs from that in conventional businesses in two important respects. First, the objectives are not constrained by the expectations of a group of external shareholders. Secondly, the job of formulating objectives is not restricted to an élite group of owners or managers, but is open to all members of the co-operative. This additional freedom can mean that the co-operative framework opens up a Pandora's box of competing and conflicting objectives.

It is useful to distinguish between a co-operative's business objectives and its social objectives. The latter can usefully be further divided into internal objectives, concerning how the co-operative is run and organised for the benefit of its members, and those external objectives which concern how the co-operative intends to benefit the wider community. Conflicts frequently exist between these objectives.

A common conflict that emerges in alternative co-operatives is between the external and internal social objectives. At TPC, for example, the goal of providing a cheap printing service to political and community groups created tension with the goal of providing members and their dependants with a decent living. To some extent this dilemma was resolved by deciding to increase efficiency by investing in new technology, although prices also had to rise. The Bean Shop faced a similar dilemma, and again sought a way out through increasing efficiency.

Various co-operatives experienced conflicts between their social and business objectives. At Oakleaf Books their political goals dictated that they should stock only certain 'radical' books. Yet they knew that they could not sell enough of these books to make the business viable, and they had to compromise. At Recycles members were keen to provide a high-quality service to customers. However, they found that the higher prices they had to charge were beginning to threaten their business, and they had to reduce service and prices accordingly. At Suma the desire to help certain Third World producers had to be balanced against the commercial risks involved.

Some co-operatives have found it more difficult to reconcile conflicting objectives. At Wholegrain Foods the original objectives centred on external social goals: providing wholefoods at a reasonable price, opposing the over-commercialisation of health foods and running a community shop. The idea of co-operative working was seen as compatible with these goals but secondary. The co-operative expanded rapidly, and there was also quite a high turnover of staff. However, little attention was paid to explaining the co-operative's objectives to new workers or to developing any shared understanding of the meaning of working co-operatively. As a result different groups of workers tended to emphasise different objectives. Some of the older members gave most emphasis to the co-operative's external objectives; members in the shop gave more emphasis to working co-operatively; whereas the members in the warehouse emphasised business efficiency and improving their own wages. These differences have been reinforced by the decentralised selection procedures in the co-operative and the lack of job rotation. They have resulted in a feeling of lack of common purpose and a number of serious disputes (Woolham, 1987).

It is important that co-operatives are able to maintain a constructive debate over objectives. They need procedures to enable objectives to be made explicit, to examine the relationships between them and to review performance. Later in this chapter we suggest that a regular self-audit, which reviews both social and business goals, can help to meet this need. In addition, it can help to keep social objectives on the co-operative's agenda and resist goal degeneration.

'Personality clashes'

Another type of conflict in a co-operative may come into the open as a disagreement about a particular individual's competence or as a disciplinary complaint. Frequently these disputes are described as personality clashes, but we believe that this is usually not the whole story. Many of the co-operatives we studied had experienced some form of 'personality clash' during their existence, and sometimes these had been so serious that the individual(s) affected had left the co-operative. These were deep, long-standing differences rather than the minor brief flare-ups that occur when people work closely together.

For example, at The Clothing Co-op a founder member who had shown great enthusiasm for co-operatives left abruptly after several months of arguments. She was said to have been a disruptive influence, frequently accusing others of not working as hard as she did. Probably having lost her previous status as supervisor contributed to this. Eventually the other members demanded that she should reform or be voted out of the co-operative. She did not return, and so was dismissed. Her absence, accompanied as it was by bad feeling, was taken as evidence of a lack of commitment to the co-operative, although it was also felt she wanted too much influence over the business.

The conflict over whether 'Mandy' should become the shop manageress at Wholegrain, mentioned in Chapter 7, provides another example. The conflict arose when Mandy criticised the quality of work of another worker whom she informally regarded as her deputy in the shop. The conflict took on very strong personal dimensions where both workers felt that their personal integrity was challenged. Feelings ran so high that the 'deputy' felt he had to resign when Mandy was eventually made formally the manageress. Other workers tended to see the conflict as a personality clash, obscuring the fact that there was an underlying disagreement about how the shop should be managed.

It can often be more illuminating to regard a 'personality clash' as representing an underlying conflict of interests between an individual and the collective membership of the co-operative. Where the clash appears to be between two individuals, it can often be that one of them is asserting personal rights while the other is taking it on themselves to act for the co-operative as a whole. Without this attempt at a broader perspective, each 'awkward individual' represents simply a separate case with few wider implications for co-operative working. Whilst not ignoring temperamental incompatibilities completely, it is often better for co-operators not to think in terms of personality clashes, but to concentrate both on devising formal grievance, disciplinary and appeals procedures and on informal norms that reduce the chances of an individual becoming isolated as a deviant, whilst still safeguarding the co-operative's collective objectives.

Conflicting orientations to work
As these examples show, despite group pressures towards conformity, individuals do disagree within co-operatives. If they feel strongly enough, group pressure will not be enough to enforce compromise; indeed, group pressure is at its least effective when internalised (deeply valued) principles are at stake. Over time orientations to work may become deeply internalised, and as we saw in Chapter 5 members' orientations to work can vary widely so that they can be a source of tension and conflict within co-operatives.

We have already discussed how *interests* can differ according to factors such as age and experience, skills, family responsibilities and so on. These personal factors are in turn one source of differences in orientation to work. However, we also saw in Chapter 5 how individuals bring with them to a co-operative different experiences of previous working situations and different expectations of the promise of co-operative working. Many will have been socialised into an individualistic culture and will be used to hierarchical work situations. Few will give up established defensive and calculative orientations for long unless the rewards from the new way of working quickly become apparent. It is easy to see how conflicts can arise when some members have reverted to old, familiar orientations, to acting more in their own interests, whereas others see themselves as upholding the new co-operative ideal, perhaps over-zealously.

We found that, particularly in job-creation or rescue co-operatives, members were often quick to criticise others for not working hard enough, but disliked telling another person this face to face. Shop-floor workers were more used to occasional collusion with each other to fool the management about how hard they were working. They felt that it was the responsibility of management to discipline those who were not working hard enough. In one co-operative, as soon as this topic was discussed, it was obvious that there were underlying uncertainties over what sort of behaviour constituted commitment, and everyone held strong views on this. For some people working hard in normal hours was regarded as sufficient, provided that a worker was ready to help out others and look for work if there was a slack period in their usual tasks. For others, a committed co-operator was someone who must be willing to work plenty of overtime to boost productivity, even if this overtime was poorly paid or left in the bank as 'sweat equity'.

One worker was good at arguing from both sides: he would frequently join in the criticisms about people who were not present and how they did not contribute their fair share to the co-operative's takings, yet five minutes later he would be saying 'Why ever should they?' and sympathising with trainees who could see that the co-operative earned more money per hour out of their work than they were paid. This man, perhaps because he loved a good argument, was effectively articulating the dual roles that co-operators must play, as employers safeguarding their organisation, and as employees defending their rights as workers.

Conflicts arising from different orientations to work or different interpretations of the meaning of co-operation arise in other types of co-operative, as the conflicts at Wholegrain described earlier demonstrate. It was also suggested in one co-operative that conflicting orientations to work arose from gender differences. One woman observed: 'Men see their career in the co-op as progress from manual to the managerial functions. Women see it more as a cycle and are more prepared to move back to manual functions.' Conflicts over issues of gender and equal opportunities were of growing importance in many alternative co-operatives.

Conflicts involving deeply held principles are difficult to deal with, because people are unwilling to negotiate over matters of principle. A compromise solution is difficult or impossible to achieve, while a majority decision is unlikely to be acceptable to the minority who feel that their principles are being ignored. As a result conflict in co-operatives is more likely to remain constructive if members share common values and orientations to work. As we discuss later, one way of trying to achieve this is through careful selection, induction and training.

The dynamics of conflict

As we have seen, the potential for conflict remains in co-operatives and may even increase. At the same time, as Mansbridge (1980) has argued, conflict can be more difficult to handle in small democratic communities and groups like co-operatives than in bureaucratic organisations. There is a danger that destructive patterns will emerge.

Perhaps the most important problem to be aware of is that conflict can be extremely threatening in co-operatives. Relationships in co-operatives are often based on friendship and the ideal of community rather than just work roles. In this setting conflict might damage highly valued relationships. Additionally, the majority of decisions are made in open meetings, so any conflicts that emerge are public. This can provoke other fears: the fear of breaking up, of being misunderstood or of being attacked oneself. To a large extent these problems are reduced in hierarchical organisations. Conflicts between people can often be solved by referral to a higher authority. Hierarchy increases the social distance between people, and as a result conflicts may be divorced more easily from personal relationships. Conflicts are not usually resolved in public, and therefore fears of public ridicule are reduced.

One danger in co-operatives is that because of the personal anxiety and tension that conflict can give rise to it will be suppressed. Potentially upsetting issues will not be raised at meetings, or will be glossed over. In one co-operative meetings were not held at all for many months, perhaps because members knew they would have to decide on whether or not to take a trainee into membership, and in fact the probationary period was extended rather than holding a meeting. This can mean that real differences of opinion over the organisation and direction of the co-operative are not aired and discussed. Insistence on consensus decision-making can reinforce this process. At Suma, before they introduced majority voting, some members felt that it just was not worth raising issues because it would be impossible to get a consensus. This can lead dissidents to feel alienated and on occasion to withdraw from the decision-making process altogether. The suppression of conflict also means that newcomers are kept in the dark about the different underlying views and interests in the co-operative.

Suppressed conflict does not usually disappear and when it does break out it can be with sudden and unexpected force. Conflicts in co-operatives are often marked by emotional intensity. This may derive from the fact that the issue has been simmering away for some time, or simply from fear of public speaking. Once pent-up emotions are let loose they can be difficult to contain. Ironically, the emotion of speaking out often means that conflicts take on the personal dimension that people fear in the first place. As a result there is a danger that a cycle of suppression and then sudden release of personalised conflict is established. Indeed, a number of co-operatives have told us of their huge and furious rows. In one co-operative they were sometimes so intense that people would not be able to settle down to work for some time (Cornforth, 1981). In some ways co-operatives can act as emotional amplifiers. As one co-operator said to us: 'When things are good they are really good but when they are bad they are bloody awful.'

How can co-operatives avoid these often destructive patterns of conflict? A starting point is the recognition that conflict is legitimate, but that it is difficult to handle. Hopefully, consciousness of the difficult and widespread nature of these problems can help avoid some of the feelings of blame and failure that often accompany the outbreak of conflict. Even more importantly, co-operatives need to consider how they can develop the procedures and skills to handle conflicts more constructively.

Promoting members' interests and handling conflict constructively

As we have seen, different interests, orientations and values can lead to conflict in co-operatives. Political equality and democracy alone are not enough to ensure that members' interests are adequately protected or promoted. There is a danger that the interests of the business will come to dominate members' other collective interests. There is also the danger that the interests of individuals or minorities will be overlooked. We consider a number of specific procedures by which co-operatives can try to safeguard and promote members' interests and ensure that any conflict that results is handled both constructively and equitably. They include: facilitating conflict in meetings; grievance procedures and protecting individual rights; developing the role of trade unions in co-operatives; recruitment practices, induction and member education; and, finally, regular self-audits within co-operatives.

These procedures differ as to whether they are in common use among co-operatives. We discuss each of them in turn below, but in some cases our discussion is based on observation or on what was reported to work well, whereas in others it is our suggestion of what might help to deal with problems that we noted.

Meetings: facilitating conflict

The obvious place for conflicting views and interests to be raised and discussed is in meetings. We believe that it is essential for co-operators to learn to use their meetings in this way. Shortage of time, fear of speaking out or the belief that your views will not be supported can all lead to the suppression of conflicting views. In this chapter we have space only to outline some of the main ways in which these problems can be tackled. (The reader is referred to Randall, 1988; and Spear and Thomas, 1986, for more detailed treatment of the issues.)

One simple but important technique is the use of small groups. Large meetings can be divided into small groups to discuss important or contentious issues. Alternatively these issues can be discussed at other levels within the co-operative, for example departmental or work group meetings, before they are discussed at general meetings. In this way more people have a chance of expressing their views and sounding out opinion in a less threatening environment. In addition, the views of groups can be presented back to the general meeting so that there is less danger of issues becoming personalised.

An important role for the chair or for 'neutral' observers is to facilitate conflict. This can be done in a variety of ways. The chair may sound people out before a meeting to gauge whether there is conflicting opinion and encourage people to express their views. The chair can try to ensure that no one individual or group dominates the meeting and that all who so wish have an opportunity to speak. Those not directly involved in the conflict can try to ensure that each side understands the other, and help to bring out the underlying issues.

Co-operatives also need to exercise care in the choice of decision-making methods they employ. Consensus decision-making can, for example, lead to the suppression of conflicting views, as we saw at Suma. Either it will not be possible to reach a consensus and the issue will be dropped, or the minority will suppress its own interests in favour of the majority. When interests do conflict it may be better to resolve the issue through some form of negotiating procedure, so that a bargain can be reached, where each party makes some gains and some losses, or an agreement can be reached to take turns. Hopefully, in this way the views and interests of the minority and majority can be respected.

Where no bargain can be reached, a vote can be taken. Again steps can be taken to respect the views of a minority. One co-operative employs an interesting rule where any member can block a decision taken by vote for a cooling-off period of, in their case, seven days, after which the majority's decision goes ahead. This does give a chance for views formed in the heat of the moment to be changed, while still allowing the majority the last word.

Grievance procedures and protecting individual rights

As we saw in the last chapter, disputes concerning an individual's performance are often extremely difficult to deal with in co-operatives because of the absence of a clear authority structure. There is a danger that conflict will be suppressed because nobody wants to be seen to be acting in an authoritarian manner. In many cases where conflict does break out a vicious circle can be seen, where the criticised individuals do not feel that their contribution is valued, so they do not feel an equal part of the co-operative. They believe that the others do not trust them. The other members, unused to being employers, do not know how to cope with disagreement or disaffection, and there are no formalised procedures that could dispel some of the emotion from the situation. It is no one's job to mediate between the parties concerned.

Clearly co-operatives need to find a way of protecting individual workers' rights while at the same time protecting themselves from individuals whose performance is inadequate or too disruptive. Some co-operatives have learnt through bitter experience that it is necessary to develop formal disciplinary and grievance procedures to help resolve difficult cases. At Suma, for example, the personnel committee now deals with these matters in the first instance. A number of local CSOs have also found it necessary to develop their own written rules on grievance procedures to recommend to co-operatives. Such formal procedures may seem like an admission of failure to uphold collective ideals, but in fact they can help reduce the personal animosity that might destroy the solidarity of the co-operative.

Bernstein (1976) in his study of workplace democratisation goes further than this and suggests that other safeguards of individual rights will be necessary if genuine democracy is to be maintained. He draws parallels with political democracy and suggests that various individual rights must be guaranteed, such as freedom of speech and assembly, secret balloting, the right to appeal against disciplinary decisions, immunity of rank-and-file representatives from dismissal or transfer while in office, and written constitutions. In addition, he suggests that there must also be some independent judicial procedure to see that rules are applied fairly, and to safeguard the basic democratic rights.

The organisations that Bernstein studied are much larger than those in our sample, and his suggestions appear over-formal and elaborate for small co-operatives. However, they may well become more relevant as co-operatives grow. Some larger co-operatives have already made a step in this direction by appointing external trustees whose job is to ensure that the co-operative is run according to its constitution and co-operative principles are upheld. This is a relatively simple step that more co-operatives could adopt.

The role of trade unions

In a formal grievance procedure a worker member in dispute with the co-operative might have the right to union representation. This could mean in practice another member acting in a shop steward role or it could mean bringing in a union official from outside. This would be seen by most co-operators as a last resort, but we do know of one specific case where a member invoked the right to representation by an outside union official and found it useful.

As well as representing individual members in disputes, unions traditionally have the role of bargaining on behalf of their members collectively against management. We have argued above that in co-operatives members' interests may still conflict with the interest of the enterprise – or with managerial interpretations of their interests – so it would seem that in theory at least there is a clear place for the unions' traditional role. In practice none of the co-operatives we studied had introduced union bargaining procedures. This is perhaps not surprising given the small size of the co-operatives, the lack of any clear differentiation between workers and management and the high degree of worker involvement in decision-making. Unions are more often involved in larger co-operatives. However, experience from larger co-operatives in the UK and abroad suggests that developing an appropriate role for trade unions may not be easy. Clarke (1979) and Eccles (1981), based on their (separate) research at Kirkby Manufacturing and Engineering (KME), both warn against the dangers of union convenors or shop stewards becoming too involved in management and compromising their roles as workers' representatives. In contrast, Thornley (1983) reports that co-operators in Italy are often critical of trade unions for sticking too narrowly to their traditional role. She reports that there is dissatisfaction with trade unions for increasing conflict through aggressive negotiation, and for focussing too narrowly on pay and working conditions without considering their members' interests in commercial matters affecting the enterprise. Clearly it is a difficult balancing act for unions both to participate in management and to remain an effective opposition when they feel members' interests are threatened.

Although the role of trade unions in co-operatives in the UK is not well developed, and in some co-operatives unions are regarded as inappropriate or a waste of time, many do have high levels of union membership, as we noted in Chapter 3 in London printing co-operatives (Harris, 1985). McMonnies (1985b) reported positive attitudes among Merseyside co-operators towards unions, higher than for trade unionists in general. Although the actual mechanism of bargaining may not be brought into play in the workplace, union rates and terms agreed by industry-wide collective bargaining may well be used as a yardstick by which to judge the co-operative's progress in meeting its members' needs. For example, at Union Phoenix time spent on contracts for customers was costed at union rates and distinguished from extra time workers might put in free to help build up the co-operative. A future return to union terms and conditions of employment, including differentials, was looked forward to as the sign that the co-operative would have succeeded.

It is not just that co-operatives differ in respect of their members' attitudes to unions and the roles that they see for unions. Unions themselves differ widely in their traditions and their structure. It might be expected, for example, that general unions such as the TGWU or GMBATU would favour worker co-operatives more than craft unions that might have sectional interests in, for example, upholding skill differentials (McMonnies, 1985a). Eccles (1981) argues that the whole craft-based structure of British trade unionism makes it virtually impossible for worker co-operatives – or large co-operatives at least – to succeed, because it is likely to undermine the ideals of equality and solidarity on which co-operatives are based.

However, Tynan and Thomas (1984) argue that even in a large workplace such as KME with no well-understood model of co-operation to work towards, there can, at least initially, be enormous goodwill, commitment and willingness to work flexibly. For a limited time co-operation as a vague ideal can generate enthusiasm and participation, but then if members do not see benefits arising from co-operative working they are likely to revert to economistic and defensive attitudes. This makes it important to uphold members' material interests and not rely purely on idealism. It will certainly be easiest for a union to play a part in this if there is a single union in a co-operative, and there are very few examples of more than one union active in one co-operative workplace.

Currently most co-operatives are too small for this discussion on the role of trade unions to have much relevance. Some printing co-operatives have 'chapels' that have the same membership as the general meeting, i.e. they have small workplace union branches. The officers are different, but the same people attend two kinds of meeting – the general meeting a regular affair concerned with co-operative policy, the chapel meeting less regular, concerned with pay and conditions in the co-operative and throughout the industry.

Most co-operatives, however, are too small in union terms to have a workplace branch. In one or two well-publicised cases the TGWU has special local co-operative branches attended by members of several co-operatives. Otherwise, co-operative members attend union branches dominated by the concerns of union members in non-co-operative workplaces. Although there are likely to be few incidents involving union action, this contact with outside forces oriented towards labour can be important. Co-operators attending union branches will continue to be involved in general debates about wages and conditions, about changes in technology and working practices and about shifts in their industry at large. This should act as a stimulus to keeping going the debate about what is in members' interests, which is certainly not a matter to be settled once and for all with the formation of a co-operative. In addition co-operators can try to ensure that trade unions are responsive to their special needs.

Recruitment, induction and education
Recruitment and training practices in co-operatives can have an important impact both on the ability of members to pursue their interests and on reducing the potential for conflict. As Rothschild-Whitt (1979) has observed, recruitment is one of the most important means of ensuring social control within collectives and co-operatives. In the absence of the usual supervisory hierarchy and many of the rewards and sanctions found in bureaucratic organisations, co-operatives are more reliant on personal and moral appeals to ensure discipline. Such appeals are much more likely to be effective where the group shares the same basic values and world-view.

As a consequence recruitment practices are vitally important in co-operatives, and both selection criteria and who is involved in selection need to be carefully considered. There needs to be a careful balance in the criteria for recruitment. New recruits need to be reasonably compatible with existing members in terms of their work orientation and in sympathy with the co-operative's goals in order to minimise the risk of some of the conflicts mentioned above. But at the same time they must possess the skills necessary to do the job; otherwise the business will suffer. Those given the responsibility for recruitment will often be left to devise selection criteria, or at the very least will play an important part in interpreting the co-operative's policy in this area. As a result deciding who should be involved in recruitment is an important issue. In a way, a co-operative is allowing that person or group guardianship of its very nature as a co-operative. New recruits are potentially new members and will become the co-operative in due course. So whether all members, a sub-group, a single manager or some other combination actually makes the selection is of crucial long-term importance.

In both these respects there is a good deal of difference between how recruitment is carried out in different co-operatives. In many new alternative and job-creation co-operatives recruitment is based on friendship, family or past working relationships. The founders of The Cycle Co-op met at an unemployed workers centre. Later other family relations were employed. Wholegrain often recruited people through friendship networks, as did Recycles in its early days. Although this pattern of recruitment may go some way to ensuring compatibility between workers it can have its drawbacks, particularly in very small co-operatives where interpersonal relationships are usually very intense in any case. Friendship or family ties give no guarantee that a person will be good or efficient at their job. This led to problems at Recycles, and they had to alter their recruitment policy, laying much greater emphasis on the new workers' skills.

Nearly all the larger alternative co-operatives stressed the importance of both a minimum level of skills and a commitment to co-operative working in their recruitment practices. One larger co-operative also used the device of employing people for a trial week, so that other members could see how they got on with the new worker and assess their ability to do the job. Although this is a short period, members found it was very useful.

In collectives recruitment is usually the responsibility of the whole group or a designated sub-group of members. In dual-structure co-operatives it is more likely that recruitment is seen as a managerial responsibility. There is a danger in the latter case that recruitment will be based primarily on the co-operative's needs for skilled labour at the expense of any commitment to co-operative working or the co-operative's other goals. This applied at The Clothing Co-op with disastrous results. New recruits had no idea what the founder members expected of them in terms of solidarity as co-operative workers and little understanding or commitment to co-operative principles.

In our view it is vital then that a balance of opinion must be represented among those with the responsibility for recruitment. It should not just be a managerial prerogative. It should certainly involve those with the expertise to assess the recruits' skills and aptitude for the job, but also those who can assess their commitment to co-operative working and the co-operative's other goals. One alternative is to set up an elected personnel committee, as at Suma; another might be to have a committee, with representatives of management and members, possibly with a veto on either side.

After recruitment, a new worker needs assistance in finding out what is expected not only in terms of the job but as a potential member. Very few co-operatives take induction seriously, and those that do restrict it to learning the job, perhaps explaining job rotation and skill sharing if practised. Allowing non-members to attend meetings might be the only way the co-operative provides for them to learn about the workings and principles of the co-operative. Although this is valuable it is often a slow way to learn. As a result some larger co-operatives are now considering introducing more formal induction processes which would cover co-operative principles and how they are practised in the co-operative.

Members need training in co-operatives not only to do their jobs better but to participate in management, and to promote their own interests. Unfortunately, many co-operatives, like small businesses, either do not see its importance or are too hard pressed to devote resources to training. However, members' education is becoming more of a priority, at least in the movement at large, if not in all co-operatives. Ways of using state and other resources for employees' training are being explored, and, as we shall see in Chapter 9, many local CSOs manage to mount training programmes for new co-operators. However, if the expansion and development of existing co-operatives are to be encouraged it is important that both co-operatives and CSOs also find ways of meeting the training needs of the co-operatives' established members.

Review methods and organisational self-audit

To the extent that a conventional firm is in business to make money for its owner(s), it is reasonable that a conventional audit should be purely financial. However, particularly in the case of large corporations there has been a move to suggest they should be subject to a 'social audit'. This would detail the effects of that corporation's activities on its employees, on its neighbourhood, on the environment and so on. The idea of an 'audit' also implies independent scrutiny and publicly available results.

Thus, an audit of a co-operative could well look at how it meets the various interests and objectives of its members. Such an audit would not be purely financial, but would cover internal social objectives (individual and sectional interests), business objectives ('managerial interpretation' of the co-operative's overall interest) and external social objectives (collective interests in pursuing social or political goals outside the co-operative), as well as the workings of the co-operative as a democratic organisation.

It need not, however, necessarily be independent and public, though this is an arguable point. A co-operative consists of its members, and management either *is* the collective of all members or else is accountable to the whole membership. When a co-operative self-audit or review is carried out, it could start, for example, with a reconsideration of objectives and then incorporate personal reviews of members by each other as well as group assessments of organisational performance and some quantitative analysis of financial performance and efficiency. Although the internal benefit of such a process would be its main point, it could also be sensible to make public some version of its outcome.

Let us look briefly at how a self-audit might review the achievement of each of the three types of objective. First, the internal objectives of meeting individual and sectional interests. Probably the notion of personal reviews should be included here. They are particularly important since one of the consequences of the lack of a formal hierarchy can be uncertainty as to how well one is working or helping to achieve the co-operative's objectives. One negative consequence of the lack of supervisory hierarchy is that in a co-operative no one pats you on the back! Several ideas for personal reviews have been made by various activists, trainers and consultants to co-operatives (see e.g. Randall, 1988; Spear and Thomas, 1986). Whatever method is used, it is important to stress the positive aspects of co-operative working as well as giving a chance for negative points to emerge that might otherwise be suppressed because of 'groupthink' or the fear of conflict.

The second area for self-audit and review is that of business objectives. To some extent this is like a conventional audit. There are two big differences however. First, the measures used to judge business performance should differ from conventional ones (see Chapter 3). For example, ratios based on value added may be used, reflecting to some extent the co-operative's multiple objectives. But perhaps the main difference will be the importance attached to the co-operative members understanding the figures, to helping them to ask the right questions and have an idea of the implications of those figures for their future. This probably means that, in all but the smallest co-operatives, the function of internal financial audit, including ensuring members can understand the position implied by the figures, should fall to a different member than the person responsible for financial management. Perhaps the aid of an outsider could be called upon as well.

Thirdly, there is the question of external objectives. A regular review procedure should allow the objectives themselves to be reappraised, and perhaps shifted a little by consensus rather than by the uncoordinated actions of individuals, and also should help co-operative members see exactly how much has been achieved in those directions and at what cost.

The need for members to review their own goals, their role in the co-operative and the co-operative's objectives and policies is not one to be satisfied for good in one general review. Objectives and goals will have to change to meet new conditions. As a result self-audits need to take place regularly if they are to be effective. It is also worth remembering that the process of such a review is at least as important as its outcomes. The effective self-audit will be designed to encourage organisational learning among all members of the co-operative.

Keeping co-operative principles alive

Since Chapter 6 we have been examining whether it is possible for worker co-operatives to avoid the process of degeneration. In other words, can co-operative principles and ideals be maintained over time? This raises the question: What are the ideals and principles that co-operators are trying to maintain? In Chapter 6 we suggested that the most basic principles are: open membership for all workers; equal democratic control; limited return on capital; and the maintenance of social and educational aims. However, operationalising these concepts is not straightforward. As we have seen, there is plenty of scope for differing interpretations, for example over the extent and type of democratic control or the wider social goals co-operatives might pursue. Co-operatives have to survive in the market-place, and principles have to be balanced against the need to be viable. There is also the important issue of whether co-operative principles are an end in themselves or can be better regarded as a means to other ends. For example, in this chapter we have suggested that co-operatives can usefully be seen as a vehicle to promote their members' interests.

Because of these difficulties in putting co-operative principles into practice, it is important that co-operatives maintain a debate on what meaning co-operation has for them, and how it can be reconciled with the need for efficiency. As co-operatives change and grow, new ways will need to be found of putting principles into practice, and the continuing debate is one way of trying to ensure that this happens, and that pressures towards degeneration are resisted. As we have suggested in this chapter, some ways of ensuring this debate takes place and giving it structure are through induction and training programmes and through regular self-audits.

Maintaining co-operative ideals and principles in an environment that is largely indifferent or hostile to them is never going to be easy. One way of trying to sustain a commitment to co-operative principles is to make links with other organisations and groups that share similar values. In particular strengthening links between co-operatives and with CSOs is one important step in maintaining a movement in which co-operative principles and practice can be articulated and sustained. It is no accident that 'co-operation between co-operatives' is also one of the six basic principles of co-operation. The next chapter looks in some detail at CSOs and in particular at their role in assisting start-ups and supporting co-operatives in other ways. We should not forget, though, the enormous importance of building a movement that can be guardian of co-operative ideals as well as developing individually successful co-operatives.

9

The Role and Impact of Co-operative
Support Organisations

As described in Chapter 1, the substantial increase in the number
of worker co-operatives that has accompanied the recession has been
associated with the spread of co-operative support organisations (CSOs).
This is in line with various theoretical arguments (Cornforth, 1988b;
Horvat, 1982; Vanek, 1970, 1975) and empirical studies (Campbell
et al., 1977; Oakeshott, 1978; Thornley, 1981) which suggest that a
healthy co-operative sector is unlikely to develop, or be maintained,
unless it has its own supporting infrastructure. These arguments cover
all the difficulties of starting a co-operative in a capitalist market, and
the obstacles to its growth, from lack of external financing to the risk
of organisational degeneration. Support organisations are proposed as
a defence against some of the internal and external pressures and tensions
that co-operatives face; they can mediate between a co-operative and the
outside world, providing services and resources that are not adequately
met by the existing business infrastructure, representing the interests
of the co-operative sector and helping to build a dynamic integrated
co-operative movement. Ideally CSOs fulfil two overlapping sets of
functions, one political and the other economic.

The economic functions include: securing external finance, to
compensate for discrimination in the market and meet the special
needs of co-operatives; providing training in areas which are not covered
ultimately by the existing educational system such as co-operative
working and co-operative management; and compensating for the
alleged reluctance of individual entrepreneurs to start co-operatives.
The political functions involved might include campaigning to secure
co-operatives at least equal rights with conventional firms on taxation
and legal matters, such as registration; negotiating on behalf of
co-operatives with the state or other institutions; and working to
build a dynamic social movement.

The form that this support structure should take to perform
these functions is unclear. Vanek (1970) bases his analysis on the
Yugoslavian model and suggests that it should take the form of a
National Labour Management Agency, which would actively promote
and finance the 'self-managed' sector or economy. But few other
theorists have been so forthright. In fact, the establishment of such a

structure would require large-scale state intervention of a kind which appears unlikely in most Western countries.

In the UK a uniquely decentralised system of co-operative support has developed which relies heavily on finance from local government. This chapter examines the contributions that CSOs make towards creating successful worker co-operatives. It draws mainly upon a national survey of local and regional CSOs that we undertook in 1984 (the results of which are more fully documented in Cornforth and Lewis, 1985). Since then we have updated some of the quantitative material and carried out case studies of Brent CDA (Macfarlane, 1987b) and another local CDA as well as the Co-operatives Unit which operated within the Greater London Enterprise Board (GLEB). We also draw upon information gathered from informal contacts with a number of CSO workers and various other studies which are referenced in the text. The chapter gives an overview of the origins, organisation and work of CSOs, highlighting some of the current problems and dilemmas that they face, and considers their impact on job creation. It is argued that this support structure has various strengths and weaknesses as a means of developing a strong worker co-operative sector. The chapter ends by considering how the support structure might be further strengthened.

Background and funding

Since the oil crisis of 1974 rising unemployment levels have prompted many local authorities to develop more interventionist economic policies, particularly in regions which have been badly hit by the recession. There has been a change in strategy from property development and attempts to attract new business to more direct support and intervention in the wealth-creation process. Some councils have formed economic policies which include the promotion of co-operatives. This has been particularly common in Labour-controlled authorities, as left-wing policy has shifted away from the nationalisation of industry towards various forms of social ownership, such as worker co-operatives and community businesses. Despite the severe controls on local authority spending imposed by central government, there were approximately eighty CSOs with paid staff by June 1986. Although these were often started as voluntary organisations by local activists, the majority are now funded by local government.

The motivation of activists and policy-makers in promoting worker co-operatives varies widely from pursuing broad political goals and social change to a practical concern for local economic development. However, it is probably true to say that much of the public legitimation for forming CSOs has concerned their potential to create jobs. Macfarlane (1986) lists five possible policy objectives which may lead local authorities to support co-operative development: local economic development itself, job creation and retention, equal opportunities, political or politicising activities and community development. Given the diversity of objectives it is easy to see why CSOs have evolved in various ways according to which aims have been emphasised most by their workers, funding bodies and management committees.

CSOs have been most commonly formed at a local level with a remit that covers a local authority area, i.e. a borough, city or county. The majority of CSOs are independent organisations controlled by elected management committees. These independent CSOs are commonly called local co-operative development agencies or local CDAs for short. Some local authorities have chosen to employ co-operative development officers directly and establish their own CSOs. The first local CDA was funded in West Glamorgan in 1978. By 1986 there were 55 funded local CDAs, as well as 19 local CSOs established directly by local authorities. The early CSOs tended to be concentrated in the larger urban areas and areas suffering the worst economic decline. More recently there is a spread of smaller CSOs in the shire counties.

Regional support for co-operatives is less well established in most regions and it does not follow a common pattern. There are three well-established regional CDAs. The first was the Scottish Co-operative Development Committee (SCDC), which employed its first worker in 1977. Initially it operated primarily in the Glasgow area, but as its funding has increased it has extended its operations throughout Scotland. Northern Region CDA employed its first workers in 1982 and operates in Tyne and Wear, Northumberland and Durham. The Wales Co-operative Centre was established in 1983 and is sponsored by the Wales TUC. Originally it operated alongside a number of local CSOs but has now taken on their roles in all but a few cases.

Some other initiatives have been more closely tied to the activities of the metropolitan county councils, and formed part of the wave of municipal socialist initiatives aimed at economic regeneration of the local economy. The most important of these were in London and the West Midlands.

The London Industrial Strategy (LIS) (GLC, 1985) developed by the Labour-controlled Greater London Council (GLC) was aimed at improving job prospects for Londoners through intervention in the private sector, extension of the public sector role and the promotion of economic democracy. Assistance was targeted at large- and medium-sized firms that were locally based. It was critical of small firms for two main reasons – for being poor employers and for not providing many new jobs. However, it made three exceptions: for co-operatives because they embodied social ownership and economic democracy; for ethnic businesses; and for specific sectors that were felt to be important in maintaining traditional skills, or in restructuring the economy in a socially useful way. The GLC established an independent agency, the Greater London Enterprise Board (GLEB), as a major vehicle to implement the LIS. Within GLEB a small group of staff with responsibility for co-operatives formed a Co-operatives Unit to further develop and implement policy on co-operatives. In the period January 1983 to March 1986 GLEB managed funds of £64m. of which £36m. was available for direct investment. Approximately £5m. was invested in co-operatives and support for co-operatives. The abolition of the GLC and the subsequent cut-back in funding led to a reappraisal of policy at GLEB, and co-operatives no longer figure prominently in current strategy.

In the West Midlands the Metropolitan County Council's Economic Development Unit (EDU) originally carried out regional co-operative policy. They established a revolving loan fund – West Midlands Common Ownership Finance (WMCOF) – with allocations of £1.75m. and managed by ICOF. Because of the abolition of the Metropolitan County, WMCOF and the EDU team dealing with co-operatives were moved to the West Midlands Enterprise Board (WMEB). WMEB continued the policy supporting three independent local CDAs, with annual support of £0.25m. (1985/6 figure).

Various other initiatives at a regional level have resulted from the activities of ICOM, and from local CSOs. Activists within ICOM have tried to establish regional branches, and London ICOM is more or less independent of ICOM nationally. However, in most areas these initiatives have foundered because of lack of support or funding. Perhaps more significantly, regional networks of CSOs have formed in many parts of the country. A few have gone further and been able to obtain funding to establish joint initiatives. In London, for example, the CSOs have established London Co-operative Training (LCT) with money from the European Social Fund to provide training for co-operatives and CSOs in the London region. This is likely to become a model for initiatives elsewhere.

Much of the funding for CSOs has come from local government or from central government initiatives, such as the Urban Programme or Manpower Services Commission (MSC) schemes. The absence of a regional tier of government in most areas of the UK explains the relatively low number of regional CSOs.

Much of the funding of CSOs is either temporary or subject to annual review, which means the future of many CSOs is uncertain and vulnerable to political changes. As a result many CSOs are actively pursuing other sources of funding, such as the European Social Fund, other local authorities such as district councils and the provision of revenue-raising co-operative workspaces. A major disadvantage of this uncertainty over funding is that staff have to invest a lot of time and effort into fund-raising, which of course reduces the time they can spend assisting co-operatives. In addition, uncertainties over the life of an agency can reduce staff morale and commitment.

The majority of funding CSOs receive is for staff salaries. In 1984 the average number of staff per organisation was just over three. The largest local CSO had eight full-time posts, while eight had only one worker. A study of co-operative development in London (CAG, 1986b) recommended three full-time posts as the minimum necessary for effective development work.

Control and accountability

The support structure for co-operatives in the UK is likely to remain highly dependent on resources from national and local government for some time. One of the most important questions facing policy-makers wishing to promote co-operatives is where to locate the support that they give. In examining this question we will concentrate on the example of local government, since this remains the most likely source of finance for support organisations. However, many of the issues raised are similar for policy-makers in other bodies wishing to promote co-operatives.

Broadly speaking there are three main ways in which a local authority might channel support to co-operatives, or some combination of these. First, the local authority might employ staff itself to support co-operatives. Secondly, resources might be channelled through an autonomous agency, such as an enterprise board, as part of its broader responsibilities for economic development. Thirdly, the resources could be channelled through an independent CDA. In this section we will examine some of the advantages and disadvantages of these alternatives in terms of the control, accountability and management of these resources.

It is important that if a local authority develops a policy of supporting co-operatives then it should have officers to administer that policy. However this is different from locating all the resources for co-operative support within the local authority, for example, as part of an economic development unit (EDU). The main advantages of this latter strategy are that it potentially allows co-operative policy to be integrated with other economic initiatives; it enables development workers to call on the resources and expertise of other departments within the local authority; and it may ensure greater permanence than supporting independent initiatives that are more easily cut. In addition, it also potentially allows policy-makers greater control over the implementation of policy.

From the perspective of the local co-operative movement, this strategy of locating co-operative support entirely within the local authority has a number of disadvantages. First, it gives local co-operatives no real control over resources to support co-operatives. Secondly, development workers are not directly accountable to the co-operatives they support. Some local authority CSOs have tried to reduce these problems by encouraging the formation of an association of co-operatives to liaise with development workers. However, ultimately control still rests with the council. Thirdly, there is a danger that co-operative policy becomes diluted if it is only a small part of larger strategy dealing with economic initiatives. Fourthly, it is difficult for a local authority unit to become politically active within the co-operative movement. Fifthly, the culture and procedures of a local authority may reduce its effectiveness as a support organisation. The association with government may put people off approaching the CSO for advice. Bureaucratic procedures may mean that the service is not responsive enough. In our survey many development workers complained of the time local authorities took to process grant or loan applications. There is a danger, as we saw in the case of FDC (Chapter 4), that the support provided by a local authority becomes distorted by the available services, so that the advice given is inappropriate. Finally, it is not possible to raise additional external resources directly for an internal local authority function.

It was partly to overcome these last two disadvantages that some local authorities decided to set up autonomous enterprise boards. However, from the perspective of the co-operative movement, locating co-operative support within enterprise boards still has the first four disadvantages listed above. In addition, there is no guarantee that procedures will be streamlined enough to meet the needs of very small businesses like co-operatives. For example, GLEB took a minimum of eighty-eight days to process and release loans once they had been agreed by the board (CAG, 1986b).

Locating resources for co-operative development within an independent CDA has four main advantages to the local co-operative movement. First, assuming co-operatives are able to elect board members, it gives co-operatives the potential to influence how these resources are used. Secondly, the CDAs have the opportunity to raise finance elsewhere. Given the small size of the co-operative movement these resources are likely to be small at present but could in the longer term become more significant. Thirdly, their small size means that they can provide a fast and responsive service appropriate to small businesses. Finally, local CDAs are free to become involved in the co-operative movement. Perhaps the main disadvantage for the co-operative movement is that there is a danger that small CDAs cannot provide the range of services which might be available from larger enterprise boards or EDUs. Another potential disadvantage is that a small local CDA may be more easy to cut than a local authority service. From the policy-makers' perspective, perhaps the main disadvantage is a reduction in direct control, although clearly the local authority can retain much influence through funding agreements and representation on a CDA's board.

Our own view is that, if policy-makers want to establish a strong and independent co-operative movement, then the advantages of establishing CDAs that are controlled by and accountable to the co-operative movement outweigh the disadvantages. In fact, as we saw earlier, the majority of CSOs are established as independent CDAs.

However, establishing an independent CDA is no guarantee that support services will be accountable to the local co-operative movement or that they will be well managed. Like many voluntary organisations CDAs often experience problems in developing effective management committees (see Lord, 1986; Macfarlane, 1986, 1987b). Some CDAs have experienced problems in getting co-operators actively involved in management committees. In some instances this may be because the pressure of running their own businesses is too great; more seriously, they may find the culture and procedures of management committees alienating. There is also a danger that management committees become dominated by professionals such as the CDA workers themselves who have more knowledge of CDA work or are more experienced at such meetings. Committee members may be unfamiliar with the responsibilities and duties they are supposed to fulfil. If CDAs want representative, active and informed management committees, then time and resources will need to be devoted to involving and developing their committees. In fact, there are some signs that this is beginning to happen; for example, London Co-operative Training runs courses for management committee members.

The provision of services

In this section we examine the range of services provided by CSOs. Clearly not all CSOs carry out the full range of services described. The actual services offered by a CSO will depend on a range of factors including size, the availability of resources and local priorities. However, virtually all CSOs provide a common core of services, including promotional work, development work with co-operatives during the formation process, and training. A few CSOs have also given particular attention to promoting rescue co-operatives. As the number of co-operatives rises many CSOs are increasingly offering their services to existing co-operatives. In addition, older CSOs are tending to offer more specialised services including providing premises, marketing support and grant and loan schemes.

Promotion

Promotion is an important task for local CSOs, because the general public has a very low awareness of the co-operative option. To many people a co-operative means the shop on the corner, or possibly memories of the bad publicity about the 'Benn' rescue co-operatives. Some people may think of 'hippies' selling red beans and joss sticks, the 'brown rice and sandals brigade'. None of these images is particularly likely to tempt the average person to find out more about starting a co-operative. A local CSO has to market the whole idea of a worker co-operative as a viable way of working; a high profile must be created as quickly as possible in order to attract inquiries.

Institutions are frequently as ignorant of co-operatives and their potential as the general public. The local business community will need to be educated about co-operatives so that common myths such as 'co-operatives are non-profit-making organisations' are discounted and bank managers and accountants do not deter their clients from registering as co-operatives because the format is unfamiliar. Community groups, social workers, managers of MSC schemes, Job Centres and similar agencies all need to be aware of the existence and function of the CSO since they are in contact with many of the groups the CSO is trying to assist. An effective CSO will work continually to establish and maintain good networks with other local bodies, both formal and informal, so that potential inquirers can be referred to them from the widest possible variety of sources.

CSOs target their promotions mostly at specific groups, mainly the unemployed, but quite often at people with other disadvantages in the labour market, such as women, young people or members of ethnic minorities. This is usually in accordance with the job-creation priorities of their funders, and appears to be more effective in terms of generating inquiries than more general promotional strategies. Disadvantaged groups are likely to be receptive to any ideas that help them get jobs. However, they often lack the necessary skills and experience for starting a successful business, so CSOs have to be able to assess their skills realistically and tactfully, and be ready to provide intensive long-term support to back up their promotional work.

Developing new-start co-operatives

A major task of all CSOs, particularly in their early years, is working with groups to form new co-operatives. Just over 90 per cent of the co-operatives being formed are new starts, and for all but a few CSOs the vast majority of those they help to form are job-creation co-operatives. As a result their approaches to development work have evolved largely in this context.

Frequently, an important priority in the first stages of development work is to boost the confidence of the group approaching the CSO, since many groups lack confidence in their abilities to run a business. For example, a development worker commented that he was approached by a group of men wanting to set up a real-ale brewery. He did some rough calculations and said that they would need to raise about £10,000 capital. The men were horrified. None of them had ever had that sort of money and they could not imagine raising it or being responsible for it. The development worker never saw them again.

Development work with new-start co-operatives is often long term. It usually takes from six months to a year to get a new co-operative off the ground, and even then many CSOs like to maintain a continuing relationship with co-operatives in their area. Relative to other small business support services such as local enterprise agencies (CEI, 1985), development work by CSOs is very intensive. There are a number of possible reasons for this. First, it may be that more of the groups wanting to set up co-operatives lack basic business skills and experience than those setting up conventional businesses. Secondly, CSOs have to develop the groups' skills at working co-operatively as well as offering business advice and assistance. Thirdly, it may be that the demand for the services of local enterprise agencies is higher and that they cannot spend the time on long-term development work. During the development process groups do drop out, usually because they realise that the business they had in mind is just not feasible. A study of five CSOs estimated that between 17 and 33 per cent of groups that started development work went on actually to start a co-operative (Cornforth, 1984: 14; Cornforth and Stott 1984: 53).

How do CSOs approach development work?
Development workers commonly distinguish between two styles of development work, which they call 'top-down' and 'bottom-up' (see e.g. Mahoney and Taylor, 1981). These terms are not precisely defined. Most commonly they are used to distinguish where the initiative for forming the co-operative comes from. 'Top-down' development work means that the initiative comes from the development worker, who then tries to attract people to start the co-operative, whereas in 'bottom-up' development work the initiative comes from the potential co-operators, who then seek the help of the development worker. The terms are also used to refer to the relationship between the development worker and the co-operators. Here 'top-down' means that the development worker retains much of the initiative for forming the co-operative. He or she has a direct involvement in the plans to form the co-operative, perhaps undertaking parts of the planning for the group or negotiating resources on their behalf. By contrast, in

'bottom-up' development work the development worker is more of a facilitator and educator, and the emphasis is on the group to undertake the tasks to form the co-operative. The role of the development worker is to guide them through this process, and to help them to learn the skills that they need to do this.

In our survey, all but a few CSOs said that they would not undertake top-down development projects. There is a strong view that the commitment necessary to make a co-operative a success can be generated only if the idea for forming it comes from members of the co-operative themselves. Equally, it is argued that initiating a co-operative from outside is likely to contradict the principle that co-operatives should be democratically controlled by their members. Some development workers also believe that it is inefficient for them to be spending time generating business ideas when these can be more readily generated by members of the community from their own experiences.

However, there is evidence to suggest that in practice a purely bottom-up approach to development work may be difficult to sustain. In one CDA the workers said that in the early days they had done too much for the groups they worked with, who then became dependent on them. Macfarlane's (1987b) study of another CDA described a typical sequence for development work as follows. The group presented the agency with an idea, which the development worker developed into a fundable proposition in conjunction with potential funding bodies. The result was handed back to the group for implementation. They had been consulted throughout, but they may not have fully understood what had gone on, and the project may have changed considerably.

We observed development workers undertaking some of the tasks necessary to start co-operatives, for example preparing cash-flow forecasts for the groups that they worked with. In fact, there are a lot of pressures on development workers to undertake such tasks, for example: shortage of time; the need to establish credibility with the group they are working with; and the lack of business skills among many potential co-operators.

In our view 'top-down' and 'bottom-up' are better seen as the opposite ends of a continuum of approaches to development work rather than mutually exclusive options. The best approach to development at any time is likely to depend on the particular circumstances. For example, in an emergency it may be better for the development worker to act in a more directive manner. Also, it may be necessary for CSOs to have a greater involvement in the planning and development of the co-operative sector if it is to become stronger and more integrated. Nevertheless the overall aim of development work must remain to increase both co-operators' sense of ownership and responsibility for the success of their co-operative and the sector, and the skills necessary to achieve this end.

Developing rescue co-operatives

As we saw in Chapters 1 and 2, rescue co-operatives have figured quite prominently in the 'new wave' of co-operatives set up since the beginning of the 1970s. However, focussing on their numbers underestimates their significance in the worker co-operative sector. On average rescue co-operatives are larger than new starts and are often in more capital-intensive sectors of the economy.

A few CSOs, like Sheffield and SCDC, have deliberately tried to develop rescue and phoenix co-operatives. In most cases, unlike the 'Benn' co-operatives, they have attempted to save only the most viable parts of the previous businesses. Sheffield and SCDC have both promoted the idea to trade union leaders as a strategy for dealing with threatened business closures if more traditional methods of defence fail. In particular Sheffield has tried to develop close relations with trade unions and gives unemployed workers with traditional local skills and rescue or phoenix co-operatives very high priority. Both emphasise the importance of having early warning of a potential rescue situation. Otherwise trade unions may think of asking for help only as a last resort when the situation is hopeless.

Experience suggests that working to form rescue co-operatives presents the development worker with additional problems and constraints to those found with new starts, which affect the process of development. In contrast to new starts, rescue co-operatives have usually to be set up very quickly. They frequently involve substantial and complex negotiations with the owners of the business, or the liquidator, over the assets that the new co-operative will need, as happened at Union Phoenix (Chapter 4). External finance also has to be negotiated, and for large rescues or phoenixes this can be very substantial. Less time is available for working with the workforce to develop an understanding and appreciation of their new role in the co-operative. The larger size of many rescue co-operatives means that the development worker has to work more through workers' leaders and representatives than with the groups as a whole. As a result the development worker is much more likely to have a direct involvement in setting up a rescue co-operative than a small new start. In fact, SCDC has been prepared to 'loan' rescue co-operatives a development worker as 'acting manager' until co-operators could be trained up to take over the managerial functions or a manager could be recruited.

The greater resources that rescue co-operatives require from a CSO represent a concentration of risk in comparison to work with new-start co-operatives. This is heightened by the fact that rescue co-operatives often attract the interest of the media and public with the attendant danger of bad publicity if they fail. Some development workers are also concerned about whether it is possible to develop co-operative working in such difficult circumstances, and feel that there is a danger that rescue co-operatives will be too dependent on them for their survival. These potential problems have meant that some CSOs have been reluctant to encourage rescue co-operatives. However, to offset against this rescues can offer the potential of creating more and better jobs than many new starts. It is perhaps significant that rescues have played an important part in the growth of co-operative movements in various European countries, most notably Italy (Thornley, 1981).

It is important that both policy-makers and the co-operative move-ment try to learn from the growing experience of assisting rescue co-operatives by encouraging research and sharing practical experi-ences. This would allow other CSOs to make more informed choices about whether or not to devote resources to promoting rescue and phoenix co-operatives.

Training courses
There is a growing interest among CSOs in using training courses as part of the development process. These courses may be run by development workers, local colleges or consultants, or any combina-tion of these. Their scope and intensity vary considerably. For some CSOs they may be a more economical way of introducing the idea of co-operatives to new inquirers, or of teaching general business skills such as accountancy or marketing. For others, such as Coventry CDA, it is the central part of their development work, and each group works on the plan for their own co-operative during the course. Coventry's course was established because the workers felt that their previous style of working was resulting in some co-operatives 'becom-ing established without having done the groundwork to understand co-operation in practice and too dependent on [development] workers making management decisions about their business' (Coventry CDA, 1984: 8). Nearly all development workers stressed the advantage that bringing different groups together during the course enabled them to learn from each other and boost each other's morale and confidence. The main problem with training courses is that it can be difficult to match supply with demand. Most CSOs still see them as a complement to their normal development work, and are concerned that they should not become purely training agencies.

As development workers face increasing demands on their time they will need to look for less labour-intensive ways of approaching development work than working exclusively on a one-to-one basis with each co-operative. Training courses can provide one solution to this problem. In addition, the increasing availability of finance from sources such as the MSC and European Social Fund is likely to facilitate developments in this area.

Servicing existing co-operatives
The question of what balance of support CSOs should give to existing as opposed to new co-operatives was of concern to many development workers in 1984 and is increasingly so now. A number of factors were prompting CSOs to examine their priorities for development work. Some agencies found that their workload was increasing so that they were having to make choices about who they helped. Some were concerned that co-operatives they had helped to set up were over-dependent on them and might fail if they did not give them more support. Some felt that helping existing co-operatives to consolidate and grow was likely to create more and better jobs than helping form more new co-operatives.

Any new small business is likely to be vulnerable and may need help in its early years. However, because of pressures for job creation, or over-enthusiasm, there is a danger that co-operatives are helped into existence that are not viable or only marginally so. A number of CSOs recognised this problem and were concerned that these co-operatives would be a drain on their resources. More positively, the signs were that development workers had learnt from these mistakes and would not repeat them in future.

Potentially CSOs also have an important role servicing and developing successful co-operatives in their area. Although the majority of organisations in our 1984 survey spent most time working to create new co-operatives, many development workers emphasised the increasing importance of working with established co-operatives. It is interesting to note that a recent survey of local enterprise agencies also noted a shift in their pattern of work towards helping existing businesses (CEI, 1985). The findings from this survey suggested that involvement with existing firms might be more effective in terms of job creation than working with new starts, although no firm quantitative data were collected on this. It was also suggested that increased emphasis on existing businesses would reduce the risk of agencies helping to develop a large number of very small businesses that were only marginally viable. This consideration applies equally to CSOs. Increasingly they need to be able to help established co-operatives with the business and organisational problems of growth.

Premises

Obtaining suitable premises at a reasonable rent is a problem faced by many co-operatives and small businesses, particularly when setting up, although the intensity of the problem varies in different localities. Lord's (1986) study of twelve clients of four London CDAs suggests that some co-operatives would like more assistance in finding premises. In order to help with this problem several CSOs have developed workspace schemes for co-operatives. The largest and best known scheme is that promoted by Hackney Co-operative Developments. They leased Bradbury Street, London N16, from Hackney Borough Council and used Inner-City Partnership money to convert it into a 'co-operative street'. The two-phase development cost nearly £300,000 and now provides premises for eighteen co-operatives. Our survey suggests that the number of workspace schemes is likely to grow over the next few years, although the large amounts of capital required for conversion work are likely to restrict this growth to the larger urban areas where development grants are more readily available.

Development workers felt that putting co-operatives together in the same building or locality had a number of advantages. First, it encouraged them to help and learn from each other. Secondly, it helped sustain and reinforce a co-operative culture. Thirdly, it enabled them to share common services and made it easier for the CSO to provide advice. Finally, it helped co-operatives establish a more clearly identifiable presence in the area.

On the negative side, workspace schemes can cause problems for CSOs if they are not carefully managed. They require a lot of administrative work. In Hackney, for instance, the CDA found it had to employ a specialist property development worker. In addition, these schemes can cause role conflict for development workers who have to act as both landlord and adviser to the co-operatives they serve.

Marketing

Marketing for co-operatives has been recognised, especially by advisers, as an important issue to be addressed if a stronger worker co-operative sector is to be developed. Small businesses are notoriously weak at marketing. In co-operatives the problem may be worse if the co-operators have a negative view of marketing as the high-pressure advertising and selling of blatantly unnecessary products. They may not always agree that marketing is a problem for them.

CAG (1984) concluded that lack of marketing expertise among co-operators and CSO workers was the major problem facing many co-operatives. In our own survey, it was the third most frequently cited problem of worker co-operatives mentioned by CSO workers (Cornforth and Lewis, 1985: 14). The CAG report found that many development workers felt that they themselves lacked expertise in marketing, and also that some of the external professional advice that co-operatives had received had been inappropriate, or given in a form which made it difficult for the co-operatives to learn from the experience. Lord (1986) agreed with these conclusions.

One important response to this problem has been for the CSOs to employ specialist marketing staff. In Scotland, SCDC has set up its own 'sales division' with two full-time sales representatives, to provide new business for co-operatives in Scotland. In Wales, the Wales Co-operative Centre has a marketing trainer and with other local CSOs helped to form the Wales Co-operative Consortium which aimed to promote clothing co-operatives. In London, GLEB and the national CDA have established the Marketing Resource Centre, which also initially concentrated on advice for co-operatives in the clothing sector. Much of its effort is now devoted to running marketing courses for co-operators and CSO workers.

Local CSOs have tried various other initiatives to improve the market for co-operatives, but progress has often been difficult and slow. Some local CSOs have attempted to negotiate contract compliance with the local authority, to ensure that where possible products and services are purchased only from good local employers, such as co-operatives. However, recent legislation on competitive tendering makes this difficult. The retail and consumer co-operative movement has also been approached to see whether it could buy more from co-operatives. One problem with these initiatives is that co-operatives are frequently not of the size where they can supply the needs of these large organisations.

It is only since our survey in 1984 that marketing has emerged as an important area where co-operatives require further support. There is a need for further research to compare and evaluate the effectiveness of the various marketing initiatives that have been established since then.

Grant and loan schemes
As we saw in Chapters 3 and 4, many new co-operatives are poorly capitalised, supporting the views reported in various surveys of co-operators and co-operative development workers that raising finance is one of the most important problems facing new cooperatives (CAG 1984; Cornforth and Lewis, 1985; Wilson, 1982). Many local CSOs have been concerned to address this problem. Probably because of the widespread commitment to the common ownership model of a co-operative they have sought to do this through establishing co-operative loan funds.

In autumn 1984 approximately twenty CSOs had access to revolving loan funds and a number of other CSOs were exploring or in the process of setting up such funds. In addition, a number of local authorities had earmarked funds for loans to co-operatives. This meant that at least half the funded CSOs, and probably more, had access to special loan money for co-operatives, either through their own revolving loan funds or from regional resources such as those in the West Midlands. However, the size of the funds meant that, apart from possibly in London, the amounts of money available are really suitable for funding only very small enterprises.

In 1986 the National Network of Local CDAs received thirty replies to their survey of CSOs, and of these fourteen had revolving loan funds for co-operatives (Munro, 1987). They found that these funds had made loans worth £5,150,000 to 360 co-ops. Roughly £300,000 had been written off formally; another £1,000,000 was probably irrecoverable. Interest charged varied between 0 and 12.5 per cent and most loan funds offered flexible repayment terms depending on the sum advanced. Four funds took no security of any kind; eight used some form of debenture. With the exception of ICOF all funds had relied solely on local government for their income, and nowhere had other sources been secured for the future. The report concluded that the highest priority for discussion in the network was to develop a national strategy for co-operative finance.

The monitoring of loans can cause conflicts of interest for CSO workers and raises questions about their authority with respect to the co-operatives they serve. Development workers said that it was sometimes difficult to combine a monitoring role with their advisory function. If co-operatives thought they were being evaluated it could damage the relationships of trust and openness that they had managed to build up. This problem became particularly acute in London when GLEB expected local CSOs to monitor co-operatives with loans from GLEB (CAG, 1986b; Macfarlane, 1987b). As well as causing role conflict, this left development workers unclear what authority they had if they felt a co-operative was not performing adequately. They were concerned that advice could not be imposed if the co-operative did not want to accept it, yet they were being held responsible for these co-operatives.

It will be very important for the worker co-operative movement that the performance and operation of these loan funds are carefully evaluated and compared over the coming years, so that knowledge about how to establish and operate a system of financing for co-operatives can be developed. In particular it will be important to establish effective criteria for making loans, and to examine how the different roles of deciding on and monitoring loans, and advising co-operatives, can be carried out without creating too much role conflict for development workers.

The impact on job creation

A thorough evaluation of the performance of CSOs must examine whether they are fulfilling their objectives, which can vary considerably between organisations. Nevertheless, because job creation has been an important objective of the funders of CSOs it is both legitimate and inevitable that questions will be asked about how many jobs have been created and how much they cost, although we want to make it clear that counting co-operative jobs created with the assistance of a CSO is by itself a poor measure of organisational effectiveness. For example, even just concentrating on job creation it is also appropriate to ask what quality of jobs have been created, whether they have gone to local people, whether they have gone to unemployed or disadvantaged people who would otherwise have been supported by the state, how long the jobs are likely to last and whether the businesses will remain in the locality. It would also be sensible to remember that the development work done with groups that never actually trade, and even with some failures, can be educational and can eventually lead to these individuals gaining employment because they have improved their skills and their confidence (Macfarlane, 1986, 1987b).

We estimated the performance of CSOs in terms of job creation, using our 1984 figures. Two measures of performance were used:

1. The average number of new jobs created (with the assistance of CSOs) per person-year of effort from CSOs.
2. The support costs incurred by CSOs per new job created.

In order to calculate these measures many assumptions and simplifications have had to be made. We estimated that the average size of new co-operatives formed by CSOs was four full-time workers and that the average cost in terms of salary and overheads for each worker in a CSO was £20,000 per annum. On average each CSO worker created 2.1 new co-operatives a year. On this basis we estimate that on average each CSO worker will create 8.4 new jobs per year, at an estimated development cost of nearly £2,400 per job. It is important to note that these estimates do not take into account subsequent job gains or losses, due to the expansion, contraction or failure of the co-operatives, and that the costs do not include any other loans, grants or subsidies that the co-operatives may have received.

We noted in Chapter 2 how the failure rate of new co-operatives has gone up and then improved again in the years since 1982 when CSOs have become widespread. We attribute this to CSOs' success in promoting the idea of starting a co-operative business among all sections of the community, including those disadvantaged in various ways that would make it harder for them to succeed. Thus, although the jobs created are likely to be entirely new jobs, rather than start-ups that would have occurred anyway, they are mostly in small, marginal enterprises (as described in Chapter 3 and 4).

A rounded assessment of local CSOs and the co-operative sector can be achieved only when it is realised that many people in the co-operative movement have broader objectives than job creation: for example, objectives concerned with improving conditions of work, providing products and services to meet local social needs and developing a co-operative movement. In addition, policy-makers need to bear in mind the types of group that CSOs are working with when they attempt to assess their performance. Many groups will require intensive development work in order for a viable co-operative to be formed. It is not just a matter of two or three counselling sessions, but sustained advice and assistance over a long period of time. It is doubtful whether any other type of employment agency provides such intensive service, or has been expected to meet such varied social and economic objectives.

Strengthening the current support structure

The most noticeable characteristic of the present system of support and funding for worker co-operatives is that it is highly decentralised. This has occurred because it is local government that has been most responsive to funding co-operative development. This decentralised system of support has a number of strengths. Much development work requires regular contact between the CSO worker and the group of co-operators over a period of months or years. For small co-operatives this is most efficiently organised on a local basis where it is easy for the CSO and co-operative to keep in touch. Local CSOs can, by their sheer geographical spread, meet demand in a large number of areas and are able to be responsive to local needs. New ones are still being established and they are gradually spreading into the shire counties and the remotest corners of the UK. The success of small businesses often depends on a good understanding of the local market and business environment. Local CSOs are well placed to build up knowledge of local markets and to develop contacts with important local institutions such as banks, local authorities, trade unions and other business advisory agencies which can greatly assist the development process.

However, the system as it stands also has a number of weaknesses. First, the emphasis on 'bottom-up' development work with disadvantaged groups, coupled with the lack of financial resources, means that CSOs are primarily creating very small, labour-intensive co-operatives.

As a result the co-operative sector remains economically weak and unintegrated. Secondly, the small number and variety of co-operatives in a local area means that it is difficult to encourage joint ventures and inter-trading which could help to strengthen the co-operative sector. Thirdly, most local CSOs have the resources to provide only a general advisory service, and cannot provide the range of specialist services necessary to assist larger co-operatives, either rescues or well-established enterprises, seeking to change and develop. Finally, the loan funds that CSOs have been able to establish are suitable for funding only very small businesses.

One of the most important issues currently facing the co-operative movement is to find ways of overcoming the weaknesses of the current support structure without undermining its strengths. In order to do this, support organisations and structures need to be established or strengthened on a regional, sectoral and possibly national basis to complement the work of local CSOs. Various initiatives in recent years have begun to suggest how this might be done, although many important questions remain. What we do here is examine some of the functions that could usefully be performed by these new support organisations.

As we saw earlier, specialist loan funds for co-operatives exist in some localities and a few regions, and there is ICOF which operates nationally. Small grant schemes can be run efficiently at a local level. However, there must be some doubt whether it is efficient to administer loan funds locally, given the very small size of most funds. The establishment of loan funds on a regional basis may be a better solution. This would hopefully allow a concentration of resources and expertise to be built up. There have been moves in this direction; for example, the London Co-operative Enterprise Board now manages loan funds for some boroughs. In the longer term there is also a case for strengthening links between the various loan funds so that they can share expertise.

Training is another area where needs cannot always be adequately met at a local level. For example, there is insufficient demand to organise training for CSO workers and specialist training courses for co-operators at a local level. Various solutions have emerged to deal with these problems. At a national level a number of organisations have organised short courses for CSO workers. The most concerted effort to provide training on a regional basis has been in London, where first the GLEB Co-operatives Unit sponsored a programme of training and then various local CSOs got together to form London Co-operative Training (LCT). LCT obtained funding through the European Social Fund and now acts as focus for training initiatives in the region. It could provide a useful model for other regions.

Another important function to be carried out at regional and national level is the sharing of knowledge and information. This happens already through informal networking and more formally through regional networks of CSOs. However, it can be greatly facilitated by the establishment of regional support organisations. For example, LCT keeps a data base on training providers and experts who can help co-operatives or CSOs; London ICOM has established a data base of all worker co-operatives in the UK; and the national CDA publishes a regular directory of co-operatives and CSOs.

Specialist support for co-operatives is also probably best provided at a regional or national level. Most CSOs do not have the staff or resources to provide all the specialist help co-operatives are likely to need. Some specialist services have begun to develop, for example the Marketing Resource Centre in London, which now runs courses that are also open to people outside London. Again there is scope for similar developments in other regions. At a national level ICOM has recently established a specialist legal service for co-operatives.

Another important function which cannot be met adequately at a local level is support for the small number of larger co-operatives. It is not clear exactly how this service should be provided, though expertise and experience might develop best at a regional or possibly national level. One option would be to establish regional CSOs that specialised in working with larger co-operatives. Alternatively an organisation like LCT might organise a group of consultants who had experience of larger co-operatives.

Many questions remain about how best to develop the support structure to carry out these functions. Should support organisations be single or multi-purpose? Should they provide general support or should co-operatives in particular sectors establish their own support organisations to meet their particular needs? Where will the funding come from? Who should these support organisations be accountable to? To answer such questions presents some major challenges to the UK worker co-operative movement.

10

Building New Theory: Typology and Life-Cycles

In Chapter 1 we laid out our approach to the study of worker co-operatives in terms of a theoretical framework in four parts. First, we saw co-operatives not as completely independent entities but enmeshed in a web of *wider social and economic relations*. These give rise to both external and internal forces on a co-operative, but do not determine its performance completely. Thus the second part of our framework was to recognise both *constraint and choice*. To a limited extent, at least, then, there are a number of different possibilities for the development of particular co-operatives. We took a *dynamic approach* – the third element of our framework – and looked for a variety of patterns in the way co-operatives performed over a number of years. Finally, we recognised that *co-operators and co-operatives are not homogeneous*, so that different types could be expected to display different patterns of behaviour and development.

We used our framework to look at how well co-operatives performed in three areas: *economic performance* (Chapters 2–4); the *effect on individuals* of working in a co-operative (Chapter 5); and *social performance*, in particular whether co-operatives were able to develop and maintain democratic forms of control (Chapters 6–8). We also looked at the growth of *co-operative support* (Chapter 9).

In this chapter we recap briefly on each area in turn, to see how our approach worked and what implications our findings have for theory – both for co-operative theory and to a lesser extent for established theory from conventional disciplines. Then we go on to build on our approach and develop some concepts to aid future analysis of worker co-operatives. In particular we use concepts such as 'investment', 'resources' and 'slack' in a human as well as financial sense to build up a new typology and suggest several possible life-cycles for different types of co-operative.

Summary of findings in relation to theory

Economic performance
The most basic measures of the economic performance of co-operatives are their formation and survival rates. In Chapter 2 we saw that numbers have increased dramatically, but the formation rate has levelled off since 1984 at about 300 per year. We also noted

that the survival rate of co-operatives, having been extremely high in the 1970s, is now quite similar to that of other small new businesses. Co-operatives are concentrated in particular sub-sectors and areas, but their survival rate varies between sectors differently from how other businesses' survival rate varies.

In Chapter 3 we went on to more detailed consideration of how well those co-operatives perform that do survive. We used data from three particular sub-sectors – clothing, printing and wholefoods. In contrast to neo-classical economic theories of self-management, epitomised by the work of Vanek (1970, etc.), we see co-operatives as small firms whose economic performance and labour process are strongly influenced by external conditions in their particular labour, capital and product markets. Hence there are severe constraints on how far they can perform differently from other small firms, but these constraints are likely to be heavier in some sectors than in others. We also found it important to develop financial performance measures appropriate to co-operatives. These had to take account both of the fact that co-operatives are small businesses – hence economically productive – and of the possibility that they can be vehicles for a range of social and political goals. We used the concept of *value added* to indicate wealth created by a co-operative that it can allocate to carry out a range of objectives, including payment of good wages, reinvestment to build up the business or external social objectives. We based our overall analysis on a broad range of measures including ratios based on value added and on the concept of *return to labour*.

We followed Lichtenstein (1986) and others in being generally critical of the neo-classical basis of Vanek's approach. We disagreed with the idea of treating each co-operative firm as a black box, preferring to look inside at how individual workers react and collectively make economic decisions, and we thought it important to consider the influence of external factors such as sectoral position. We also felt that an equilibrium theory, in which it is implicit that all firms are already well established, could not be appropriate for the situation where many co-operatives are starting up or in an early development stage.

We found several different patterns of development going on in different kinds of co-operative. The underlying processes in a particular case depend on the internal and external factors mentioned above.

At start-up, co-operatives, like other small firms, are often severely under-capitalised. They may also comprise low-skill or old-skill workers and find it difficult to attract, develop or retain those with management ability. All this contributes to low labour productivity as measured by value added per head, and survival depends on low wages or long hours of unpaid overtime. In some cases this pattern continues as what has been termed 'collective exploitation', but in many other cases workers succeed in using their commitment and their effort to make enough surplus for reinvestment even when productivity is low. The term 'sweat equity' indicates that co-operatives may be able to build up reserves from retained surplus that derives from their own work, even when they had virtually no money to put in as working capital.

What little finance there was usually took the form of loans, and there are two somewhat conflicting processes that can take place with respect to these loans. The surplus gained can be used simply to repay loans, leading to a drain on the co-operative's meagre assets and continued under-capitalisation. Co-operatives may reach the point of owning their machinery, etc. outright, but be quite unable to raise further working capital. Alternatively, retained surplus can be used to lever in further loans, in this case acting like true equity! So far it looks as if co-operators have little real choice about this. Some, in certain sectors and lacking certain skills, are constrained to follow the first course and remain under-capitalised, while only those already relatively well endowed have the possibility of using retained surplus like equity. However, until further detailed research is done, it is not clear whether this position is inevitable.

If they do become better capitalised, there is the question posed by theoreticians as to whether co-operatives tend to under-invest. Typically, over the first few years of such co-operatives, productivity, as measured by value added per head, increases. Wages may also increase, though not by so much, so that the proportion of value added taken as wages falls. However, it remains consistently higher than in conventional firms; i.e. the surplus available for reinvestment in a co-operative tends to be lower than the profit in a comparable conventional firm. Again, without further detailed research this cannot be interpreted definitively. It could be that the difference is accounted for by profit-*taking* by the owners of conventional firms. However, it could also be that co-operatives on average do have less surplus to reinvest.

One should stress that this figure is an average, and includes data on new co-operatives. Also, in co-operatives that are heavily constrained in their control over the labour process it may be regarded as an achievement to trade for long periods while paying a high proportion of value added in wages despite lower levels of reinvestment than average for the industry.

There are other co-operatives that reinvest more, develop and grow. These are likely to be in sub-sectors where a less peripheral position in the economy combines with possibilities for job control and for promoting political or social goals.

However, there could be some truth in Vanek's contention about co-operatives under-investing as a result of workers' short-term economism, particularly for those co-operatives that are just trying to maintain their position in a declining sector with no particular source of renewed commitment beyond trying to save jobs. If productivity cannot be improved in such cases, co-operators may still wish to take as much as possible for themselves and leave little or no surplus for reinvestment. Why sacrifice further if the future remains cloudy?

The effect on individuals
The second area in which we studied how well co-operatives perform was their effect on the workers who make them up. How satisfied are they with working in a co-operative?

Being a member of a worker co-operative can be seen as an extreme example of industrial participation. However, the link between participation and job satisfaction is not as clear-cut as at times supposed. We cited, in Chapter 5, Curran and Stanworth (1986), Lischeron and Wall (1977) and Oliver (1986), to show that participation is not a single idea but can refer to a variety of phenomena, from taking responsibility for different aspects of one's job to representation on a company board. Not surprisingly, different people have different wishes in this direction depending in part on the opportunities available and their experiences.

We used ideas derived from exchange theory to look at the costs and benefits of co-operative working. We interpreted these in relation to individuals' personal circumstances, their wider social relationships and their opportunities or lack of opportunities in the wider labour market. We suggested four types of orientation to work: instrumental; social; moral; and control-seeking. In each case what people seek out of work is different partly because of their previous experiences, and so different people may be more or less satisfied with work in the same co-operative setting.

It is not only co-operators who are not homogeneous but also co-operatives. In Chapter 1 we suggested differentiating them according to the motivation of the founders. As time goes on, founders leave and others join. Inevitably this is likely to affect the dominant orientation of the workforce as a whole. This leads to various questions. Is there a trend towards uniformity? Are some co-operative workforces more self-selected than others? Can co-operatives succeed in offering different rewards to different people – especially, how can they offer enough to develop or keep those with managerial or entrepreneurial skills?

Two complementary kinds of process are at work here. One, hinted at in the questions above, is a shift over a period of time in the make-up of a co-operative or in what it attempts to offer its members. The other consists of changes in attitudes, expectations and orientations on the part of different co-operative members. These will occur either through changes outside the workplace (e.g. increased family commitments), or through experience of what can or cannot be achieved at the workplace. We found evidence, especially in alternative co-operatives, of some people starting with very moral orientations acquiring more instrumental needs as well; others have the reverse tendency; and a minority move to a control orientation.

For some, the benefits of co-operative working may not be apparent until they have experienced them. Others start with expectations that are too high. Just as Fox (1980) pointed out that attitudes to work are always formed by a process of accommodation to what is possible, a similar process of accommodation to what is feasible in a co-operative is necessary. However, once expectations become more realistic, real benefits have to be forthcoming to maintain commitment, and the costs, including the costs of activism and taking responsibility, must not be too great.

Clearly some co-operatives will be more effective than others in organising their structure of incentives to meet the challenge of keeping those with entrepreneurial skills, while in some way protecting the interests of all their workers. Bernstein (1976) suggests some conditions that will assist what is a process of accommodation and development on both sides. However, it is a complex and dynamic process which still requires further research. Nevertheless we hope our research has laid to rest the simplistic view that participation in co-operatives necessarily leads to greater worker satisfaction, and has shown how co-operative working tends to lead to new costs as well as benefits for those involved. Clearly though, most workers thought the benefits of co-operation outweighed the costs, although our sample is largely self-selected. In future, our research strategy could be improved by also interviewing people who leave co-operatives.

Social performance as a co-operative
Our main theoretical starting point here was the 'degeneration thesis', which we saw as taking three forms: 'constitutional' degeneration, 'organisational' degeneration and 'goal' degeneration. The first of these is relatively easy to analyse in formal legalistic terms. We developed our analysis of organisational and goal degeneration by contrasting arguments from Michels, about the inevitable superiority of bureaucracy and the tendency towards rule by élites in any organisation, with the more deterministic version of Marxist labour process theory. We followed Abrahamsson (1977) in combining these two types of argument but also in opposing them with a view that, although these forces towards degeneration are very real, there is still the possibility of resistance, and of real gains for 'workers' control'. As our empirical

evidence confirms, workplace democracy is not the inevitable 'victim' of the capitalist labour process or of oligarchic tendencies.

We looked for the possibility of workers gaining control over various aspects of work. When considering workers' relation to their own labour power there were some very real signs of workers gaining more control over job content, work organisation and conditions of work and having more autonomy at work. However, when it came to questions of finance, technology or product choice, gains were usually more limited and restricted by the same constraints that affect the co-operative as a small firm.

As Meister (1984) argues, even those co-operatives founded with the collectivist ideals of direct democracy have to come to terms with the need for management, and we took this up in Chapter 7. Meister reformulates the degeneration thesis as a life-cycle hypothesis. After a collectivist start, and a second stage bringing in professional management ideas, comes a third stage in which collectivism and managerialism conflict, and a fourth in which the managers triumph and the co-operative degenerates as a democratic organisation.

Our findings were more optimistic, although the co-operatives we studied are still relatively young. In the older ones, we certainly see evidence of the third-stage conflict. However, there is a clear possibility that the forces towards degeneration may be successfully resisted, at least in some cases. One can view this 'resistance' in two rather different ways. One is the idea of the 'maintenance' of partici-patory democratic working under certain conditions (Bernstein, 1976; Rothschild-Whitt, 1976). The other is that of opposing, positive, forces towards 'regeneration'. (In fact, both Bernstein and Rothschild-Whitt include the notion of process in their analyses. In Bernstein's case, his conditions are for maintaining a process of democratisation, rather than just maintaining democracy.)

The former involves both learning and carrying out new styles, structures and methods of management (discussed in Chapter 7) and ensuring certain procedures are maintained to safeguard democracy (Chapter 8).

The latter idea is both more difficult and more interesting, touched on only a little in Chapter 8. Where are forces for democratic regeneration to come from? They may come from within, through a number of processes: from individuals gaining positive experiences of participation, assuming with Pateman (1970) that this leads to demands for more; from activists keeping alive the ideals of co-operation and ensuring its meaning is embodied in each and every change of structure or process; and from the consequent development of a democratic culture which in turn creates the basis for individual actions. This analysis emphasises the importance of ensuring that newcomers to co-operatives understand co-operative principles and practices, and get involved. Batstone (1983) argues on the basis of evidence from French co-operatives that Meister's fourth stage might not inevitably lead to degeneration. In a representative democratic structure, even if participation has become almost entirely nominal, a crisis might allow a new generation of activists to rise and regenerate the ideals of democracy and co-operation.

Alternatively, regenerative forces may come from outside, via a lively movement. This might be through direct linkages between co-operatives or support from a local network of sympathisers, but movements also sustain themselves through informal networks that provide anything from information and advice to new workers 'via the grapevine'. We see more public manifestations in newsletters, public events and co-operative fairs. In addition, many CSO workers see themselves as movement activists. As such they have a crucial role to play in developing the spirit and practice of co-operation in these new businesses.

A movement of co-operatives is only one external source of 'regenerative forces'. Co-operation may also fit into a broader set of ideas, of workplace democracy or of alternative organisations. Also this language of degeneration, maintenance and regeneration raises the important question of how the co-operative movement sustains itself. Its ideals constantly need reaffirming and reinterpreting in the light of social, political and economic changes.

The performance of co-operative support organisations
In our study we have focussed on co-operatives themselves, so that our discussion of co-operative support organisations has mainly been in relation to co-operatives. We have seen CSOs as 'mediating' between co-operatives and the institutional environment or the market. To some extent this approach is in line with theorists such as Vanek and Horvat, as well as more practical writers such as Thornley or Oakeshott, all of whom have derived their ideas on the need for co-operative support, and the form it should take, from their analysis of co-operatives and their weaknesses.

So we could expect a variety of responses to be required for the support organisations to match the requirements of different types of co-operative at different stages. For example, we might base a support structure on Meister's first three stages (see above). This would imply that CSOs continue their successful business advice and confidence-building general development work undertaken for start-ups, and pursue management training for the second-stage development and growth of co-operatives once established. Then they would also concentrate on ways of assisting in the third-stage conflict and combating the degenerative tendencies. This might involve developing models of co-operative working and assisting with problems of individuals in co-operatives, from recruitment through discipline and pay differentials to how to reward – and control – entrepreneurialism.

We should realise, too, that different types of co-operative will have different needs. Most notably, differences in financial requirements, between sectors, and for rescues as opposed to new-start co-operatives, all point to new responses required from CSOs. Arguably, to be able to meet this variety of needs implies a change from the current situation of mainly separate, independent local CSOs to more specialised, perhaps regional or sectoral, provision.

This line of argument, analysing co-operatives' needs to develop support strategies, is taken up further in Chapter 11. However, from the point of view of how it treats CSOs, it can be criticised for being entirely normative. In future research it would be good to complement this approach with studies comparing the effects of different approaches to co-operative development. Existing theory might be enriched by reference to theory from other related fields, perhaps theories of counselling, organisation development or community development. It might also be very fruitful to focus more on the relationships between CSOs and other elements of the co-operative movement. Our four-part framework could be used directly in such a study of CSOs. One might well look at the wider social and economic relationships enmeshing CSOs. For example, how do they relate to local and central government initiatives, such as local economic development strategies and privatisation? One might try to differentiate between CSOs by, for example, examining their orientations to important issues such as co-operative principles, economic development and intervention strategies.

Concepts and ideas for the future

Our simplest theoretical conclusion is that our framework worked well. There were some inevitable limitations; for example, the time-scale of our work and the very newness of the 'new wave' prevented us from studying the full development of co-operatives over time, as our 'dynamic approach' would ideally have required. Also, we were unable to study examples of all types of co-operative in equal depth, particularly since certain types have begun to be formed only very recently. However, we feel that our framework was enough of a success for us now to go on to develop some of the ideas involved a little further. We begin to do so here in the second half of this chapter.

In the first half we divided the analysis (like Chapters 2–10 of the book itself) into a number of areas in which to judge how well co-operatives perform, and we have now summarised our findings in each area. Each of these could also be a level of analysis in which changes can originate as well as effects be seen. And the different levels interact strongly rather than staying separate. So it is not just a question of asking: Here is this phenomenon of a co-operative – does it create wealth efficiently, satisfy its members, run itself democratically, form part of a growing movement? We also want to know how these levels interact as the co-operative develops.

So, for example, when we analyse at the abstract level of finance, production, etc., not only can we measure good or bad business performance, but we can also see how business practices affect the other levels. Similarly, at the level of the individual, we both measure the costs and benefits of co-operative working and see how the way people take to working in a co-operative affects its business performance and organisational effectiveness. At the organisational level, we are interested in whether co-operatives succeed in avoiding degeneration and living up to the name of being a co-operative, and also in the effects of democratic working in terms of business efficiency or changing people's work orientations. Finally, at the level of co-operative support organisations or the co-operative movement, we can regard how and why the movement develops as a measure of success in itself, and also regard this as part of the explanation of further development at the level of individual organisations.

Towards a new typology of worker co-operatives
The typology we proposed in Chapter 1 was in terms of motivation (of the founders) and start-up circumstances. However, as time goes on, both of these factors become less important, so that a new typology which relates the different levels is likely to be of more general application.

Indeed, at various points in this book other ways of differentiating between co-operatives have been suggested or hinted at; for example: co-operatives in different sectors; co-operatives with different patterns of business performance; collectives as opposed to dual-structure co-operatives. We are not suggesting that co-operatives will remain in any particular category – indeed, much of the book has been concerned about why or how a co-operative might move from one category to another (e.g. when a collective adopts a dual structure or when there is a change of orientation within a co-operative). However, it is also clear that some of these different characteristics of co-operatives tend to group together more readily than others, with the implication that other combinations of variables are less likely to be found.

Here is our suggestion for four types, based on the evidence from our case studies. Note that although they are based mainly on two variables – economic performance and orientation (job, social and radical) – they are not meant to be put into a matrix! We are using several other variables, not just two, to describe these types, so that from a logical point of view there are many other possible types. We are suggesting that as time goes on most co-operatives continuing will be of one of these four main types. Note also that many co-operatives will not fit into these categories – the failed co-operatives, the degenerated and others that have their own distinctive patterns of development.

'Marginals' – marginal, job and socially oriented co-operatives. Examples at the moment include Happy Hands and The Cycle Co-op. They tend as units to be in particularly constrained sub-sectors and thus in very dependent positions in labour, capital and product markets. They consist of peripheral workers with low, undervalued or old skills, whose orientations to work are mainly instrumental (primarily maintaining jobs) and social. They will generally move to employ a manager or administrator, though some are so dependent on potential customers, with so little room for manoeuvre, that there are few decisions to make. Hence they may be able to maintain a very informal and thus virtually collective way of making decisions, particularly if they have the assistance of a local CSO. These co-operatives are also very much under-capitalised, though not necessarily more so than other small firms in similarly constrained sub-sectors. They work at low wages and at low labour productivities, and maintain the commitment of the workforce mainly because of social benefits, because of the lack of other job opportunities for them or because they give disadvantaged groups a sense of control over their working lives.

'Radical marginals' – marginal, politically or socially radical co-operatives. The Bean Shop and Oakleaf Books are examples. In less constrained or dependent market sub-sectors than the first type, these have a dominant moral orientation to work. The workers could be more highly skilled and could have higher labour productivity, but maintain a policy of pursuing external social or political goals (often on a minimum- or non-profit basis). Collective working is probable in such co-operatives, but not inevitable – in some cases the external goal is strong enough to allow central direction to be accepted. These co-operatives also have quite low wages, but in these cases commitment is maintained by a combination of moral orientation with labour turnover. Shared beliefs (political, religious, etc.) are particularly important, and commitment may be to the particular social goal rather than to the co-operative as such.

'Instrumentals' – *more economically successful, job-oriented co-operatives.*   The Engineering Co-op and possibly the warehouse at Wholegrain would fit in this category, though their histories are very different. These co-operatives are likely to have higher-skill, less peripheral workers, to have designated managers and, if large enough, dual structures. Their development as co-operatives may be significantly limited by the past experience and the make-up of their workforces. For example, workers in rescues will relate the benefits of co-operative working to their previous firms. Workers' orientations are likely to show a mixture more like that of a cross-section of the general working population, with some moral and control-seeking orientations, though the instrumental dominates. There will also be higher capitalisation, higher wage rates and higher labour productivity than in the marginal categories. In terms of job satisfaction, workers in such co-operatives may register gains (but only minor gains) over what they might expect in conventional employment. Their commitment may be easily lost if the rewards available do not stay high enough; this applies both to the general level of material rewards and to the opportunities for non-material rewards for those who seek control or have more moral orientations.

'Pathfinders' – *high economic performers with mixed orientations.*   We had difficulty in knowing what to call this fourth category! They are still evolving, with continuing economic and organisational self-development. In terms of the theoretical ideas discussed above, they experience conflicts similar to Meister's third stage, and embody the degeneration/regeneration struggle often with quite creative out-comes, for example in terms of developing *co-operative* management practices. We might include Suma, TPC and Recycles here, and possibly Lake. Of course, as with the other categories it is unclear whether these co-operatives constitute a stable type. It is possible this is just a stage through which certain co-operatives pass before 'degenerating'. However, we can characterise these co-operatives as we see them. They combine moral with instrumental orientations; they constantly debate idealism and pragmatism. They are usually in market sub-sectors that are not too heavily constrained; otherwise it is even more difficult for them to maintain their somewhat contradictory position, particularly without clear models of co-operative practices to draw on. They may be sustained in their challenge to conventional capitalist working and management practices by external support (formal or informal) from the co-operative or other political, social or religious movements. They are, or become, quite well capitalised and deliver reasonable productivity and wages. They will either be complex collectives or have dual structures, depending partly on size.

We can ask different questions about each of these types, along the lines of how they can maintain their position, how they might break out of constraints and move to another category or which forces are likely to prevail. This is like trying to describe different possible life-cycles for each type. However, before going on to do this, we develop some concepts that will be helpful.

Factors in developing patterns

A key to understanding the different types and processes is to look at a co-operative's development over several years from its start and to apply the concepts '*investment*', '*resources*', and '*slack*' in both a human/social and an economic sense.

First, *investment*. Business start-ups always require investment. But co-operatives may have access to different sources of investment, specifically *personal* as well as financial investment. This means commitment (working harder, being prepared to participate in running the business as well as just doing one's immediate job, etc.) and in particular 'sweat equity'.

As with investment, we see the *resources* employed in a co-operative as consisting of the human resources of the members as well as the physical resources (fixed and current assets) that can be measured financially. The *return* has to be at least sufficient to maintain the resources employed and not allow depreciation that is not provided for. This again would apply to human as well as to financial resources. Just as the co-operative business has to generate at least enough surplus to cover the cost of capital and of maintaining and replacing fixed assets, so it also has to be able to give a return on the human resources, i.e. fulfil its side of the organisation–member exchange. This means that it has to pay a reasonable wage and also provide other benefits that its worker-members require, including opportunities for control, for personal development and for seeing progress on collectively held social goals.

The concept of *slack* carries this analogy between the financial and human resources a little further. In financial terms, if there is more surplus than the minimum required for maintenance – in other words, if there is slack – there is the possibility of reinvestment, leading to business growth and development. This also means the possibility of more development of human resources, whether by improving training budgets, by allowing equal opportunities, by promoting social goals through subsidising certain groups of customers or directly via a bonus or wage rise. Lack of financial slack certainly makes it difficult to satisfy the expectations raised by the promise of 'co-operation'.

Furthermore, the concept of 'organisational slack' (Cyert and March, 1963; Lockett, 1980) indicates the situation where the organisation has more than enough to offer its members in terms of opportunities for participation, skill development, promotion of collective goals and so on. This means they, as human resources, are likely to be improved in terms of personal development, commitment, experience, skill, etc., with the additional benefit that new members will readily be attracted. Consequently, organisational slack is likely to lead to higher productivity – hence possibilities for business development as well as human development.

Note, though, one big difference between the two types of resource. In a capitalist system, at least, the opportunity cost of capital is fixed well outside a particular small firm, so that except for the possibility of 'soft' money from sympathisers or the state a co-operative has to provide the going rate of return. However, the opportunities available to labour are much more variable, depending on the area in terms of geography, skills, etc. In other words, labour is less mobile and more differentiated than capital. This means that what a co-operative has to provide to maintain – or develop – its human resources is in turn very variable from one sector or region to another.

Constraints can also be thought of as applying in both the business and human resource areas. The sort of virtuous circle hinted at above with a high degree of slack of both types is fairly unlikely to occur given constraints from financial market, labour process and members' social or family circumstances. It is more realistic to imagine co-operatives striving for at least a small amount of slack of one type or the other.

Life-cycles and choice points
Following our adherence to a 'dynamic approach', we do not expect all co-operatives to remain in their separate categories. Neither do we expect one pattern of change to be played out in all co-operatives as in Meister's four-stage life-cycle. Rather, we expect change and development at the different levels to result in a number of alternative patterns, or life-cycles, determined partly by internal and external forces and constraints and partly by the choices of the co-operators. Some of these will be stable patterns with the possibility of disruption or changes leading to failure or a new pattern. Others will be recognisable sequences of stages, though not so deterministic as Meister's. Here are some of the most likely life-cycles for the four types of co-operative described above.

Type 1: marginals. These can continue for long periods, but equally fail at any time. They are not likely to be able to retain members who develop managerial skills or who require control-type benefits. It is hard to see how such co-operatives can themselves generate any financial slack, since, once the initial willingness to put in voluntary free labour has passed, any short-term improvement is likely to be taken in well-earned extra recompense to members. If there is any surplus, it may well be used to replace loan capital with reserves held in common. Given the relatively weak trading position of such co-operatives, it is not likely that banks, etc. will be prepared to view this as like equity and allow it to lever in funds.

Thus, outside assistance will probably be essential to enable such co-operatives to attempt a 'jump' to the *instrumental* type 3. It may be possible to achieve this progressively by consolidating markets and stabilising performance whilst improving training and productivity, but it is more likely that only a 'jump' involving simultaneous changes in several areas has any chance at all. This could mean a move to a new market sub-sector, the injection of capital and the acquisition of additional skills through recruiting new members and/or a big training programme. Without substantial outside assistance, the chances of a successful 'jump' must be small.

However, in a limited way, given the constraints and the lack of other opportunities in their labour markets, such co-operatives may still be quite successful for their members. They still need to take care to maintain their democratic processes and to take selection of new members very seriously. Even to continue in a marginal state may require external assistance. However, there is a good chance for members to learn from their participative experience, to gain materially in a small way and to develop as individuals, as we have seen with Happy Hands.

Type 2: radical marginals. As with type 1, the marginals, the initial investment here is largely human investment. However, these co-operatives have a degree of organisational slack which is used not necessarily to develop the organisation but to achieve wider social goals. The maintenance of such 'alternative' organisations requires the type of conditions given by Rothschild-Whitt (1976). We also found the need for some 'return' for members' involvement in terms of visible achievement of social goals, plus minimal financial reward, as well as support from sympathetic professionals and links with a wider movement. Labour turnover and careful selection may also aid maintenance and survival by bringing in new committed people.

It is easy to see how, by the failure of outside support, by changes in the circumstances of the members or by their seeing the movement as more important than their particular small organisation, such a co-operative can 'fail' as a business after successfully achieving its outside aims during its existence. It is also possible that only people with very restricted opportunities may be attracted to fill vacancies, so that this type could turn into a type 1. However, it is often possible for such co-operatives, perhaps under the imperative of members' increased personal and domestic responsibilities, to become more instrumentally orientated and to redirect their 'slack' to develop the business and become type 4 co-operatives.

Type 3: instrumentals.   Some of these are rescues. They have a short period in which members are prepared to put in 'sweat equity', after which better wages are required to maintain commitment. In a way, the difference between this type and the marginals of type 1 may be simply one of sector, skill and opportunity, and as such parallels the difference between reasonably paid and badly paid jobs in conventional firms. However, with more financial slack there is likely to be more possibility of offering a range of rewards to a variety of members, including those with control and even moral orientations.

If the business can become reasonably successful and give its members reasonable instrumental rewards, then a co-operative of this type can remain fairly stable. We can also see some paths to failure. For example, expectations may be too high, so that when the rewards from co-operation are no more than a slight improvement, commitment drops rapidly and the co-operative is just as liable as any other small firm to fail through low productivity or poor management. There may be a clash between old work orientations and new expectations which may exacerbate the situation if rewards fail to materialise and 'the bad old ways' re-emerge. There is also the possibility of finding in this type of co-operative Vanek's suggested tendency to take profits rather than reinvest, to under-employ, and generally to act in too risk-averse a fashion. Another course of failure may occur if such a co-operative fails to take management seriously or is unable or unwilling to retain those with managerial skills.

We might postulate an alternative pathway. The positive effects of the experience of participation, which we found in some cases leading to a less instrumental orientation, might allow some organisational slack, which in turn could allow development both as a business and as a co-operative. In Chapters 7 and 8 we identified some of the conditions which are likely to be necessary to sustain a process of democratisation. These changes might take a long time. Certainly some of the altruistic founders of 'endowed' co-operatives, including Ernest Bader, expected learning to participate effectively to take a long time, and looked for a long transition to fully democratic management.

Type 4: pathfinders.   There is considerable uncertainty over where this last type will go. The examples we looked at all arose as very idealistic collectives (i.e. originally type 2 radical marginals), and developed using their own resources as summarised above. On the financial side, this implies using retained surpluses both for direct reinvestment and to bring in some outside funds. On the organisational side, it means developing participative management and representative structures to cope with growth. As for the membership, this will tend to become more differentiated. Some founders will leave, perhaps leaving the organisation too weak to continue successfully. More often, those remaining will combine with newcomers to make a go of things, maintaining ideals together and fulfilling some of their personal needs for both material and non-material rewards. Some of the ideals, such as more job creation or equal opportunities, may entail bringing in new, less highly experienced or skilled, perhaps more instrumentally oriented workers to become members in due course.

There may also be examples of this type of co-operative being set up more directly, without the long development from type 2. Certainly, some of the more ambitious new-start co-operatives supported by CSOs combine strong ideals and clear business goals in their initial plans. In our terms, they have a high degree of both human and financial investment from the start. It remains to be seen whether both types of resource can be maintained, particularly whether the human commitment and solidarity can be maintained in cases without either a long history of common struggle or a period of 'shoestring' operation.

One can certainly see the possibility of the conflict between collectivism and managerialism resulting in a decisive win for the latter, as in Meister's fourth stage. Perhaps it is only certain unusual combinations of sub-sector with lifestyle, as with wholefoods in the 1970s, that can allow enough slack for there to be doubts about this. As these sub-sectors become more competitive, these 'high performers' may find that they are under greater pressure to adopt conventional structures and management methods.

However, to date there is clear evidence for an alternative picture where both internal opportunities and rewards and the external support from the co-operative movement and elsewhere *sustain* a creative spirit of co-operation that is able to continue its challenge to conventional business and management practices. The ability of many of these co-operatives to invent practical ways of managing efficiently and working productively in a democratic context is already impressive. In economic terms they balance increases in productivity from factors such as improved commitment and flexibility against losses of efficiency from increased transaction cost and pursuing social goals. In political terms they struggle to take control of the labour process. In human/social terms they continually reinvent incentive and opportunity structures to ensure compatibility with their aims.

We do not yet have evidence on the long-term survival of these creative features. Clearly the pressures towards degeneration are strong, but as we have seen processes of regeneration as well as degeneration are possible, particularly if there is external support and some protection from unbridled market forces. Should there be a lapse, a future crisis might lead to renewed interest in, and revitalisation of, a co-operative's democratic procedures, as suggested by Batstone (1983).

11

Strengthening the Worker Co-operative Sector

The expansion of the worker co-operative sector over the last fifteen years represents a considerable achievement. Co-operatives have been able to survive and in many cases prosper. They have been able to meet new needs: creating and saving jobs; providing flexible and less alienating working conditions; and developing new democratic ways of working. The early idealism of the movement has been carried on in local CSOs, whose workers have been able to wed this with the necessary pragmatism to provide invaluable support to the new sector. However, objectively speaking the sector is still small and weak, comprised of very small firms in marginal sub-sectors of the economy. In many ways this is not surprising, since the majority of co-operatives have started from scratch and are less than five years old. Nevertheless an important challenge to the movement over the next decade must be to find ways of strengthening the sector.

This final chapter begins to take up this challenge and draws together some practical implications from our findings and analysis. We do this by examining some of the main constraints and problems that inhibit the development of the sector, and how they might be overcome. Unless effective ways of dealing with these constraints and problems can be found, the sector is likely to remain weak and marginal.

As we saw in Chapter 4, co-operatives face the usual business problems of small enterprises; for example, difficulties in raising external finance, the shortage of suitable premises at a reasonable price, the difficulty of establishing themselves in the market and low or fluctuating demand. Without detailed comparative research there is no reason to suppose that the business problems of new co-operatives are worse than those of comparable small businesses. However, it is clear that the co-operative sector faces a number of distinct challenges. First, the formation rate of co-operatives is still low because they lack appeal to the majority of entrepreneurs. Secondly, the structure of a co-operative places important constraints on how finance can be raised. Thirdly, co-operatives frequently experience problems in both developing and recruiting staff with specialist or managerial skills. Fourthly, there are the difficulties of learning how to develop new co-operative structures and working practices. Fifthly, there are various internal barriers to growth.

In addition, in common with other small businesses, each co-operative is constrained by its particular position in the economy.

We will examine each of these issues in more detail below, and consider how the co-operative movement can deal with them. Much will depend on the support available to co-operators, and we go on to discuss how the existing support structure can be strengthened to meet these challenges. We conclude by considering the future prospects of the worker co-operative movement in the UK.

Low rate of formation – the entrepreneurial problem

As we saw in Chapter 2, even with the recent growth in the worker co-operative sector, there is still a low rate of co-operative formation relative to other forms of small business. Partly this can be attributed to lack of knowledge about, or discrimination against, co-operatives. These problems have to some extent been reduced by the increase in publicity about co-operatives and the work of local CSOs, although more still needs to be done. In particular, the subject of co-operation needs to be established as part of the business education curriculum. A more immediate reason for the low formation rate is that the co-operative form of business has limited appeal to many entrepreneurs because they will have to share both the rewards and control of the enterprise (Abell, 1983; Aldrich and Stern, 1983).

An important priority for the movement then is to consider how the formation rate of worker co-operatives can be increased. One option is to attract potential entrepreneurs from other areas. Entrepreneurial activity is not just restricted to the business sector, nor is it always motivated by material rewards. It can be found in a variety of contexts: voluntary organisation, the Civil Service, education and public enterprise. A strengthening of links with other organisations and movements that share common values would help. In addition, the co-operative movement could do more to promote a positive image, including the recognition that successful businesses can be developed without compromising social goals.

In France, and particularly Italy, rescue and phoenix co-operatives have played a very important part in the recent growth of the co-operative sector (Paton et al., 1987; Thornley, 1981). A variety of factors have contributed to the success of this strategy in Italy. The trade unions have seen rescue co-operatives as an important way of creating as well as saving jobs and have supported these initiatives. Existing co-operatives have often been large and financially secure enough to take over ailing firms. In addition, the co-operative movement through its federations and secondary consortia has had the expertise to assess the feasibility of such take-overs, and access to the resources necessary to intervene successfully. Clearly the different state of development of the co-operative sector in Britain makes this strategy more difficult. However, there have been enough successful rescue co-operatives to demonstrate that there is greater potential in this strategy than has yet been realised in the UK (Thomas and Thornley, 1988). It would be in the interests of both the co-operative movement and trade unions to strengthen the links between them, and to develop strategies for dealing with rescue situations should they occur.

Privatisation could also offer new opportunities for co-operative development. Clearly this is a difficult and contentious issue. A major *raison d'etre* of the worker co-operative movement is to improve the conditions of work and control that people have over their jobs. Many in the co-operative movement oppose privatisation in principle and in any case would not want to undermine the bargaining position of trade unions. However, privatisation has occurred and is likely to continue, often with a worsening of conditions for employees. The co-operative option might offer employees a chance of retaining better conditions of employment and more control over their work. Rather than ignore the issue and stick to absolute opposition it would be better for the co-operative movement and trade unions to develop new strategies which consider under what conditions a co-operative should be proposed or supported to tender for public contracts when a particular service has been privatised.

In countries with more established co-operative sectors the CSOs themselves often take on a more entrepreneurial role, looking for new opportunities for co-operatives to expand or develop. For example, the bank at Mondragon conducts pre-feasibility studies which examine the potential of possible new product lines. It has the expertise and resources to assist and finance new entrepreneurial initiatives and to encourage spin-offs from existing co-operatives (Thomas and Logan, 1982; Weiner and Oakeshott, 1987). Also because it has the resources to establish larger co-operatives the low number of formations is less problematic. Such initiatives are likely to call for new styles of intervention by CSOs in the UK, although too much of a top-down approach from CSOs could undermine co-operators' sense of ownership and commitment to the enterprise, and conflict with the ideal of self-determination. It is very important that there be further experimentation and research on new approaches to development work.

Finance

Co-operative principles impose important constraints on how co-operatives can raise finance. The most important principles in this respect are 'limited return on capital', and 'majority control by worker-members'. This means that strictly speaking co-operative shares cannot appreciate in value and must pay a limited rate of interest, and the issue of external voting shares is restricted. Common ownership principles are even stricter: membership is restricted to workers only, and ownership is entirely collective apart from a £1 nominal share held by each member. Common ownership co-operatives have to rely entirely on loans or credit if they want to raise external finance.

The constraints on raising finance for co-operatives create two sets of problems. First, co-operatives will suffer from high gearing because of the restriction on issuing equity, which will make it difficult to raise loan finance. Secondly, a co-operative may not represent an attractive form of investment for its members, because they do not participate in the co-operative's capital growth. Thus people may be put off from forming a co-operative, or workers may be tempted to take profit in the form of higher wages or bonuses rather then reinvest.

Partly the problem of high gearing in co-operatives is technical. It depends on how gearing is measured. In our view internal loans are more analogous to 'owners' capital' than to liabilities and should be treated as such. This is why in Chapter 3 we calculated *external loans as a percentage of net assets* rather than gearing. In fact, some financial institutions do treat members' loans in this way. However, co-operatives are still heavily reliant on external loan finance. Servicing these loans can put a strain on the developing business, so that high gearing is a real as well as a technical problem. In addition, common ownerships are excluded from most sources of venture capital, which is an increasingly important means of financing the expanding small firm (Burns, 1987), because they are unable to issue equity.

Many new co-operators' problems in raising finance are simpler than this. They may have decided to form a co-operative after a period of unemployment, and consequently have little available capital to invest and few assets that could be used to secure a loan. They may lack a track record in business. They may experience problems raising a bank loan for these reasons, let alone technical questions about gearing. In addition, some development workers report that there is still some suspicion and prejudice against co-operatives among financial institutions.

Broadly speaking, two contrasting approaches have been taken to the problems of financing co-operatives. The first has been to suggest adapting the financial structure of co-operatives more in line with capitalist forms of business, in order to facilitate access to conventional sources of finance. The second has been to establish new sources of loan finance which give special attention to the particular needs of co-operatives. We briefly examine both these approaches below (see Munro, 1987, for a fuller discussion).

New structures for worker co-operatives

Various approaches to devising new structures for worker co-operatives have been suggested which, it is argued, would reduce the problems of high gearing and/or provide members with a better return on their capital. One approach is to develop co-operative constitutions that allow greater worker shareholding. This can be done without contravening co-operative principles if the shares are non-voting, do not appreciate in value but attract a variable rate of interest, and cannot be traded except back to the co-operative when a member leaves. In other words, the shares are similar to a long-term loan. However, neither a company limited by guarantee nor a co-operative registered under the Industrial and Provident Societies Act (IPSA) can issue preference shares (Munro, 1987: 39). The national CDA and the Scottish Co-operative Development Committee have established a model for a co-operative limited by shares under the Companies Act which enables preference shares to be issued to members or outside investors. There is a concern over whether co-operative principles can be safeguarded properly within this structure, since the members could vote to create ordinary shares for sale to outsiders.

Another approach has been to find ways of enabling co-operators to participate in the capital growth of their co-operative while retaining their funds for use by the co-operative. An amendment to the 1978 Finance Act passed in 1986 enables co-operatives registered under the IPSA to claim corporation tax relief on an employee profit-sharing scheme. A co-operative can transfer a proportion of pre-tax profits to an employee trust to purchase shares in the co-operative on behalf of employees. The shares are transferred to individuals after five years and can be redeemed when they leave the co-operative as a tax-free lump sum. Another method of building up member benefits while retaining the use of some of the capital by the co-operative would be to establish a self-administered pension scheme. Up to 50 per cent of a fund may be invested in such a way as to assist the co-operative, as long as the capital receives a commercial return.

The Mondragon co-operatives provide the model for another way of addressing the problem. In Mondragon each worker has to invest a sum in his or her co-operative on joining. This sum is held in a capital account for the worker until they leave the enterprise. The sum attracts interest. In addition, a proportion of the co-operative's surplus each year is added to each account, or if the co-operative makes a loss then a proportion of the loss is subtracted. As long as the return on the capital account from profit is not based on the amount of capital in the account then the principle of limited return on capital is preserved. These capital accounts are a way of raising long-term finance from members and retaining more of the surplus for reinvestment. Whether or not such an option would reduce the gearing of a co-operative would depend on how financial institutions treated these capital accounts. However, since the capital in the accounts can be withdrawn only when the worker leaves the enterprise there is a good case for not treating all the money in these accounts as a short-term liability. The idea of members' capital accounts has been strongly advocated by Ellerman (1984, 1988) and Oakeshott (1978), who see them as an important means not only of raising capital but also of increasing workers' motivation and commitment to the enterprise.

Both the employee trust and the Mondragon system of capital accounts can be criticised on two grounds. First, they represent a concentration of risks for workers, who stand to lose both their jobs and substantial sums of capital if their co-operative fails. The second objection is that the co-operative will face problems if a high proportion of workers leave the business and withdraw their capital together.

More radical solutions for dealing with the problem of shortages of external loan finance and high gearing have been proposed, which depart from the principle of having only worker-members and allow some form of external voting shares in the enterprise. The national CDA has developed model rules under the IPSA which allow external members of a co-operative as long as they are approved by the committee of management of the co-operative. A possible drawback of these rules is that they may not provide an adequate safeguard against external shareholders eventually being able to out-vote worker-members and take the co-operative over. External shareholding of this sort should be considered only if there are also constitutional safeguards, at least ensuring workers have a majority on any committee of management and that constitutional changes have to be agreed by a majority of worker-members.

The issue of non-voting preference shares or members' shares under the IPSA still conforms to co-operative principles in that they allow only a limited return on capital. However, this suggests that only those sympathetic to co-operatives are likely to invest in this way, and they are unlikely to attract much new capital to the co-operative sector. Nevertheless they do provide a vehicle for sympathetic investors to put finance into a co-operative and to have a say in how their investment is managed, without adversely affecting a co-operative's gearing ratio.

The national CDA has also developed a scheme to try to attract risk capital for worker co-operatives. In this scheme the new enterprise is not a worker co-operative, because it can issue external shares which do not have a limited return; however, it is intended that the enterprise will become a worker co-operative. The workers' shareholding is held by an equity participation co-operative (EPC). The EPC has a co-operative constitution and its purpose is the acquisition and management of shares and the representation of members' interests in the new enterprise –

which is a conventional company. The company would also issue shares to other external investors. It is envisaged that over time the EPC would acquire shares on behalf of the workforce so that eventually the company would be majority or 100 per cent controlled by the EPC and become in effect a worker co-operative.

The drawback of this scheme is that there is no guarantee that the EPC will acquire enough shares for the company to become a worker co-operative. However, the scheme does have advantages over many employee share ownership schemes, in that it allows workers to use their shareholdings collectively to have a say in how the company is run.

The ability to devise new structures for co-operatives is constrained by existing legislation. A review of relevant legal provisions is an important priority, and should include looking at a number of ideas for making raising capital easier for worker co-operatives. Ellerman (1988) suggests that a special 'table' should be appended to the Companies Act to facilitate the formation of Mondragon-style co-operatives. Munro (1987) suggests that a new Co-operative Law should be enacted similar to the Companies Act. This would define a third form of capital 'halfway' between debt and equity. It would not carry voting rights and be redeemable at the co-operative's discretion. It would be entitled to some degree of performance-related dividend or capital growth, but within prescribed limits.

Various initiatives to develop new financial structures for co-operatives are very recent and have been either not tried in the UK at all or tried only in isolated cases. Further experiments in this area need to be supported and carefully researched before the real value of these initiatives can be evaluated. This is a high priority for future research.

So far proposals to extend internal and external shareholding in co-operatives have not gained much support in the co-operative movement. The fear is that they would undermine workers' control and the principle of limited return on capital. Also ICOM model rules are seen as the clearest and most readily available means of establishing a co-operative constitution and these do not permit shareholding to be extended. Instead most effort has been devoted to establishing new sources of loan finance for co-operatives.

Loan finance

As we saw in Chapter 9, most of the money for new loan funds has come from local government, although a few funds have managed to attract money from other sources. These funds have been particularly useful in assisting co-operatives during the start-up phase, and their spread should be encouraged. However, the amount of capital available is relatively small, and is unlikely to be able to meet the requirements of co-operatives as they grow. An important priority for the future must be to find ways of increasing the funds available for loaning to co-operatives. There are several options, but their potential has only just begun to be explored.

For the individual co-operative, informal loans from members and supporters are an important source of finance. Various devices have recently been used to formalise this process and so facilitate raising finance in this way. A few co-operatives have issued debentures which they hope will be taken up by their supporters. These debentures are secured against the assets of the co-operative, pay a fixed rate of interest and are repayable at the end of a specified period of time. ICOM has also developed a form of 'loan note' for co-operatives which acts more like a share than does a debenture. It is intended to supply the co-operative with capital which does not have to be repaid until the co-operative can afford it. The loan note may be redeemed at any time at the discretion of the co-operative at par value or using some agreed formula. Interest is paid only when profits are sufficient, at a variable rate worked out by another agreed formula with an upper ceiling. The loans are unsecured and rank behind all other creditors except the co-operative members. Again they are a financially unrewarding form of investment and are likely to be taken up only by sympathisers.

Various loan funds have also experimented with new ways of raising capital. The Scottish Co-operative Development Committee has launched the Scottish Venture Capital Fund, raising capital in the form of £10,000 debentures secured against the assets of the fund. This fund raised £250,000 in 1987 (Munro, 1987: 37). The debentures are in two classes, both redeemable after ten years. One pays 6 per cent interest per annum and is redeemable at par; the other pays no interest but is redeemable at a premium based on any surplus left in the fund after ten years. ICOF has established a separate company, ICOF plc, to raise money through the issue of non-voting preference shares in multiples of £250. They pay a maximum of 6 per cent interest and are redeemable in ten years. So far ICOF looks like meeting its target of £500,000. These initiatives demonstrate that more capital can be made available from sympathetic investors. However, given that the rate of return is likely to be much less than can be obtained elsewhere, there may be a fairly low ceiling on the amount that can be raised in this way.

Another option would be to establish some form of deposit-taking institution or bank that invests in co-operatives. The successful Mondragon group of co-operatives have their own bank. As well as providing banking services for the co-operatives it acts as a savings bank for the local community, and has been able to use the savings of the community to invest in local co-operatives. In theory such a model could be followed in the UK. However, in practice, the legal restrictions on deposit-taking institutions and banks make this very difficult. ICOF, for example, failed in its attempt to secure deposit-taking status. While we recognise the importance of investor protection, we believe that it is time for a review of the legal barriers which make it difficult to establish deposit-taking institutions which invest in co-operatives.

The most obvious source of further capital for investment in co-operatives is the state. The Labour Party has proposed establishing a national Co-operative Investment Bank with initial money coming from the state. It is unlikely that such a proposal will find favour with a Conservative government that is generally opposed to what it sees as state subsidy for business. However, a case can be made for the establishment of a state investment fund for co-operatives. There is a contradiction between co-operative principles which subordinate capital to members' interests, and the 'rights' and returns capital is able to demand in the open market. As a result co-operatives will always be at a disadvantage compared to private companies in raising capital. Government support should not be seen as a subsidy for enterprises that are unable to survive by themselves, but as a means of redressing the discrimination inherent in the present system.

Investing in co-operatives has other advantages over government investments and subsidies for private companies. Because co-operatives are locally controlled by their workforces they are likely to be committed to the area in which they are located. Also there are safeguards in common ownership constitutions that prevent members from closing down their enterprise for personal gain.

While the campaign for greater state financing of the co-operative sector is vitally important, for co-operators to pursue this strategy exclusively would be a great mistake, given the inevitable political uncertainties and the problems that over-dependence on the state can cause. Quite simply, all the various means of increasing the availability of loan finance described above need to be pursued with vigour.

Management

It is commonly acknowledged that many small businesses suffer from a shortage of management skills. Very few small business owners have received any formal management training. In particular, weaknesses in financial management and marketing strategy and techniques are common. Before trading, and with no basic appreciation of management techniques, many do not see the relevance of management training and advice. Once they start trading and experience problems, it is difficult to take time off for training.

Many worker co-operatives share these typical problems, although the origins and orientation of different co-operatives affect how these problems manifest themselves and their extent. The ideology behind some radical or idealistic co-operatives has led them to deny the legitimacy of management and to undervalue management skills. However, once management functions are seen to be necessary the members of these co-operatives have often been quick to acquire the new skills. Management functions are frequently shared quite widely between members in these co-operatives, giving them greater strength and flexibility.

In job-creation co-operatives those involved often have no previous experience of running or managing a business. Rescue and phoenix co-operatives can face similar problems, when managerial staff from the failing enterprise are able to obtain work elsewhere. The problem may be exacerbated by the fact that rescue and phoenix co-operatives often have to be established very quickly. As a consequence there is little time for workers' leaders to acquire management skills.

Some co-operatives have tried to resolve the problem by recruiting managers or specialists externally, but this has often proved difficult for a number of reasons. First, the wages that they can offer, at least initially, are low because the business is not yet established, in a marginal sector or under-financed. Secondly, most small businesses require people with general management skills. Many of the people most likely to have these skills are running their own businesses anyway, and the financial incentives are greater for such individuals to establish their own businesses. Thirdly, a co-operative has no guarantee of the loyalty of a manager. There have been a number of examples where a manager has tried to take over a co-operative or, as we saw in the case of The Clothing Co-op, has used the experience to go on and establish their own business with detrimental consequences for the co-operative.

Successful and expanding co-operatives are also not without problems in recruiting managerial and/or specialist staff. First, the co-operative sector is so small that a labour market for 'co-operative managers' has not yet developed. As a result potential staff will not usually have experience of co-operative working. Second, many co-operatives because of their size and commitment to low wage differentials do not offer the same incentives as private firms.

There are no simple solutions to increasing management skills within the sector. However, a successful strategy is more likely to evolve if it tackles the problem at different levels and from a variety of angles.

A simple but important message for co-operators is that, whatever their reasons for forming a co-operative, management functions need to be performed well if the enterprise is to be successful economically or socially. From a business perspective, financial management, marketing and planning skills are crucial. Although not always practical, it may be better to develop these skills, either through training courses or working in a similar business, before embarking on a co-operative venture. Once established, co-operatives need to build training and management development into their organisation. In addition, they need to learn how to make good use of informal contacts and professional advisers.

If co-operatives do decide to recruit staff with management skills externally they must exercise extreme caution. As far as possible they must try to assess that the manager is genuinely committed to the co-operative. If there is any doubt it may be worth drawing up a contract which prevents the manager leaving to form a rival business in the same vicinity. If the co-operative has a commitment to no or low wage differentials it may need to balance this goal with the need to pay the wage levels that will attract skilled personnel.

CSOs have a vital role to play in developing skill levels within the sector. Perhaps most importantly the aim of development work must be to increase the capacity of a co-operative to deal with problems themselves in the long term. The emphasis must be towards helping co-operators analyse and understand the problems they face, and teaching the skills and techniques they need to deal with them. Such a strategy is labour intensive, and usually demands an input over many months.

As a complement to intensive development work, CSOs need to ensure that there is appropriate formal training provision for co-operatives in their area, either through putting on courses themselves or by organising courses with local colleges. CSOs are also in a good position to facilitate links between co-operatives and sympathetic professional advisers in the area, and to encourage co-operators and co-operatives to make use of both training facilities and advice services.

At a national level a priority for the co-operative movement should be to get co-operation established within the curriculum for business education and training in general, and to ensure that co-operatives have the same access to training schemes and resources as other businesses.

Co-operative working

Like all organisations, co-operatives face the challenge of devising suitable structures and working practices as they grow and change. In co-operatives this problem is accentuated because many people do not have experience of working co-operatively; in particular, there is little experience of designing appropriate structures and procedures for larger co-operatives.

The problems emerge in different ways. In co-operatives with a commitment to collective management the challenge may be how to develop more differentiated structures as the co-operative grows. In rescue and conversion co-operatives the problem may be democratising existing structures. A range of factors including size, technology and the origins of the co-operative will influence the appropriate solution, so that no one formula is suitable for all co-operatives. However, there are a number of general guidelines that co-operatives can follow in their attempt to be both efficient and democratic (see Chapters 6–8).

Whatever structure is adopted it is important that the authority of groups and individuals is clearly and explicitly defined, so that members understand the democratic structure, and those with positions of authority can be held accountable for their actions. In the absence of clear structure there is a danger that a co-operative will become dominated by an informal élite.

If democracy is to be effective and self-sustaining it is important that it is introduced at all levels within the co-operative. As we saw in Chapter 5, people are often more concerned to have more control over their own work than over the organisation as a whole. Participation at lower organisational levels is also an opportunity for all workers to learn how to participate effectively.

As far as possible functional responsibilities should be decentralised and groups self-organising, so that power is spread throughout the organisation. This is an important check on the emergence of a powerful central élite. However, in decentralised structures care needs to be taken that adequate procedures are established to co-ordinate activities.

If individuals are to take part effectively in democratic processes they must have access to the information necessary to make decisions. They must also be free to speak their minds without fear of reprisal. Co-operatives need to make specific provision for upholding the basic democratic rights of 'freedom of information' and 'freedom of speech' (Bernstein, 1976).

As in any democracy, conflict needs to be recognised as a legitimate and inevitable part of life in a co-operative. Procedures for dealing constructively with conflict at all organisational levels need to be devised. Insistence on consensus for all decisions is likely to suppress conflict. Majority decision-making is one alternative but can mean that the interests of minorities get ignored. Where there are important disagreements a negotiated solution may be better, so that both sides achieve some gains.

Conflicts and disputes concerning individuals are often difficult to deal with because of the close relationships and informal working practices common in co-operatives. It is advisable to establish formal disciplinary and grievance procedures. In addition, there should be procedures for regularly reviewing each member's development and performance within the co-operative. Hopefully, this will enable problems to be identified and dealt with before they become too serious. There is also a role for trade unions in co-operatives to protect the interests of individual members and of all members as workers, for example ensuring health and safety standards and good terms and conditions of employment.

If differences between members in a co-operative become too large there is a danger that a destructive cycle of conflict can develop. The potential for this to happen can be reduced through careful selection procedures. Members should be selected for their ability to do the job, their commitment to the values and goals of the co-operative and compatibility with other members. A trial period before a new worker is accepted as a full member is advisable.

A co-operative is its members. If co-operative ideals and principles are to be maintained the members must share a commitment to them. Careful selection, although important, is unlikely to be enough in itself to guarantee this commitment. The way principles are put into practice will vary between co-operatives. It is important then that there are induction processes within co-operatives to introduce new members to co-operative working, and that co-operative practices are kept under periodic review. In addition, it is more likely that co-operative principles will be sustained if a co-operative has links with other individuals, groups and organisations that share similar values (Rothschild-Whitt, 1976).

It is important for all businesses regularly to review their goals and activities in the light of changes internally and in their environment, and to develop and implement plans to meet changed circumstances. There is a danger in all small businesses that longer-term planning becomes overlooked under the pressure of day-to-day events. In a co-operative the responsibility for planning is usually best delegated to a small team. However, every effort should be made to get inputs into the process from all areas of the co-operative, at the various stages in the planning process. This should increase both the acceptability and quality of decisions made, and ensure that the membership as a whole can have a say in crucial decisons affecting the future of their co-operative.

An important component of planning is a regular evaluation of the performance of the co-operative. This should go beyond examining just business performance to include the co-operative's social goals, through some form of social audit. Unless both economic and social priorities are reviewed together there is a danger that one set of goals will come to dominate the other, with the result that the co-operative will either fail as a business or degenerate. The challenge facing all co-operatives is to achieve a workable balance between social and business objectives.

Internal limits to growth

If co-operatives are successful in meeting these challenges they still may face a number of limiting factors which seriously constrain their growth. First, being able to have a say in the overall governance of the enterprise becomes more difficult as the enterprise grows. In addition, the informal and friendly style of the smaller enterprise is inevitably lost. As a result many co-operatives are reluctant to grow too large. For those co-operatives committed to collective working, the size limit can be very low, perhaps as few as eight or ten workers. Even in co-operatives with representative forms of democracy there may still be limits on size (Abell, 1977; 1983). After a strike in the largest of the Mondragon co-operatives in Spain they have tried to keep the size of new co-operatives down to a limit of 500 workers. Secondly, there may not be the same economic incentives to grow as for private businesses, because co-operative shares are not linked to the value of the enterprise and cannot be traded. Thirdly, the financial and legal structure of co-operatives may limit their ability to grow or take over other firms. As we have seen, co-operatives cannot issue external shares to fund growth or to finance a take-over. Equally there may be organisational difficulties in taking over a firm whose members are not committed to working co-operatively (McMonnies, 1984).

If co-operatives want to achieve economies of scale, or the advantages that come from horizontal and vertical integration, then they must pursue other strategies for growth. In Mondragon this has been achieved through the central bank which has actively encouraged the formation of an inter-linked system of co-operatives (Cornforth, 1987; Weiner & Oakeshott, 1987). In Italy co-operatives in similar industrial sectors and regions have established consortia to enable them to engage in joint purchasing and bid for contracts jointly. In addition, the consortia are able to provide expertise and resources that no individual co-operative could have access to by itself (Earle, 1986; Thornley, 1981). It is important that co-operatives in the UK begin to explore these new patterns for growth. Equally it should be a priority for CSOs to consider how a more integrated system of co-operatives can be developed rather than a collection of isolated co-operatives (Jordan, 1986). It is sometimes argued that co-operatives will have to give up some of their autonomy if they establish joint initiatives. However, without joint initiatives co-operatives are likely to remain in marginal subsectors of the economy at the mercy of market forces or dominated by large companies. The price of autonomy may be control over very little.

The place of co-operatives in the economy

Co-operatives have to survive within the economy in which they are located be it capitalist or socialist. In the West today co-operatives are being formed at a time when capital is highly concentrated, and decisions over how this capital is allocated are dominated by large corporations, government and financial institutions. This is perhaps particularly true of Britain, whose small firms sector is relatively small compared with many other Western countries. Small firms tend to be restricted to sectors dominated by large firms, or those which serve fragmented, highly competitive markets (see Chapter 3). In either case their control over market conditions is quite limited. The chances of breaking out of the small firms sector through growth are low. Even those firms that do grow are likely to be taken over by large firms.

As we have seen, much can be done to expand the role of co-operatives in the small firms sector. However, if policy-makers wish co-operatives to gain a more significant position in any industrial sector then more radical action will be required. In Italy and France this has been achieved in the construction industry where some degree of market protection has been provided for co-operatives by the government. This does not imply that co-operatives have to be subsidised. In France government legislation ensures that a quota of public building work is temporarily reserved for co-operatives at the average price for the job (Thornley, 1981: 146). One of the most significant actions government could take to improve the position of worker co-operatives (or small firms in general) would be to improve their access to the market through some form of quota system.

Co-operatives and their advisers can also take some action to try to avoid establishing businesses in the most dependent or least profitable areas. There are often quite wide variations of profitability within sectors. For example, in the clothing industry profit margins are often better for firms in sub-sectors producing high-quality or specialist garments. In addition, small firms may be able to find new market niches that have not been exploited. Careful analysis of different markets and how they are changing should guide the choice of business for new co-operatives, not forgetting the possibilities for developing business ideas from links with different social movements.

Co-operative support

We have argued throughout this book that the business infrastructure in which worker co-operatives have to work today is often not suitable to meet all their needs, and may even be hostile towards them. We see CSOs as an important means to help co-operatives and the co-operative sector overcome the problems and constraints on development outlined earlier in this chapter. In broad terms CSOs have three main functions. First, they mediate between co-operatives and the wider environment to try to ensure that the existing business, educational and government infrastructure better meets the needs of co-operatives. For example, they try to ensure adequate training for co-operatives, and that co-operatives are treated fairly in government legislation. Secondly, CSOs provide services to co-operatives that are not adequately met otherwise. So far most effort in the UK has been focussed in this area, giving advice and assistance to new and existing co-operatives, providing model rules and promoting the idea of co-operation. The third function is to establish new infrastructure specifically for co-operatives. Perhaps the most important example of this has been the development of co-operative loan funds.

Support for worker co-operatives is organised primarily at the national and local levels in the UK. At the national level the support structure is rather weak and fragmented. ICOM is the main member organisation for common ownership co-operatives. It is heavily reliant on member subscriptions and fees for its finances, which, while the co-operative sector is small but growing, means that it is under-financed. The national CDA is government-funded, and its board is appointed by government. It is not accountable to the co-operative movement, and its brief is wider than worker co-operatives. Local CDAs have formed themselves into a network to try to ensure that they also have a national voice. However, there are few resources to support the network. Clearly such fragmentation and lack of resources weaken the ability of the worker co-operative movement to negotiate with government and other organisations at a national level.

An important priority for the worker co-operative movement must be to strengthen its organisation at a national level. There is a strong case for government grant aid to ICOM until its membership base is large enough to make it self-financing. The national network of local CDAs could become integrated with ICOM, which would help to provide be+ter local–national linkages. If the national CDA is to be more influentiai within the co-operative movement then it may need to become more accountable to the movement.

The majority of support for worker co-operatives has been organised at a local level. As we have seen, these local CSOs have had an important impact on the development of worker co-operatives in their areas. Because of working with disadvantaged groups and the need to develop skills among new co-operators, their co-operative development work has been quite intensive and long term. On average CSOs have helped to create two new co-operatives per staff member per year as well as providing advice and assistance to existing co-operatives. In addition, they have done much to improve the local climate and infrastructure for co-operatives, which is likely to have important long-term benefits.

However, the system of support does have its limitations. In particular, the emphasis on 'bottom-up' development work with disadvantaged groups, coupled with the lack of financial resources, means that CSOs are primarily creating small, independent, labour-intensive co-operatives in marginal sectors of the economy.

In order to overcome these weaknesses additional support for co-operatives needs to be organised, possibly on a regional or national basis. This could concentrate on promoting larger co-operatives, providing specialist back-up and training for local CSOs and co-operatives, facilitating joint ventures between co-operatives, helping co-ordinate co-operative support and helping to ensure that there is adequate finance available for co-operatives.

Important questions remain about how support for co-operatives can be best financed and organised. At the moment finance comes primarily from local and national government. Until the co-operative sector grows in size and co-operatives become better established as businesses, government is likely to remain the main source of finance. This raises the question whether support for co-operatives should be located within government organisations or independently.

As we have seen, practice varies at a local level. Some CSOs have been established as part of local government, although the majority are independent CDAs accountable to elected management committees. It is important that within local and central government there should be staff with the responsibility for overseeing policies relating to co-operatives in order to ensure smooth liaison with other departments. However, if the majority of support for co-operatives were located within local and national government departments there would be a danger that they would impose their own priorities on the co-operative sector, which might not be those of the co-operative movement. There would also be a danger that the co-operative sector would become too dependent on the state. For these reasons we believe that independent support organisations should continue to be funded and more established. Clearly while public money is involved they should also remain accountable. This can be achieved through representation on the management committees of CSOs, and through periodic reviews of performance. However, given that democratic accountability is central to co-operative principles, CSOs should be at least equally accountable to the co-operatives and groups that they serve.

Analysis of the Italian co-operative movement, where worker co-operatives are well established, suggests that in the long term the UK co-operative movement should be aiming to establish a plurality of support for co-operatives. In particular, it should aim to establish its own independent support structures, through strong membership organisations such as ICOM, to represent and campaign for the movement, and through secondary co-operatives like the consortia to further the economic interests of particular groups of co-operatives. It may be appropriate to view current state support as a transitional stage in this strategy.

Prospects

The growth of worker co-operatives in the UK has been cyclical, with periodic bursts of formation followed by long periods with no new co-operatives. This pattern is in contrast to several European countries where the worker co-operative sectors have had a more sustained pattern of growth, until in some localities and industrial sectors they have become a significant force. This raises the question: Is the recent growth of the worker co-operatives sector in the UK a temporary phenomenon or can it be sustained in the future?

The periods of co-operative formation have been stimulated by dislocations in the social and economic fabric of society. As we have seen, several interrelated factors have influenced the current growth in new co-operatives, particularly the development of the alternative movement and the increase in political support for job creation resulting from high unemployment. For at least the foreseeable future, unemployment is likely to remain very high, so this important impetus for co-operative development will remain. However, this alone will not guarantee the emergence of a strong worker co-operative sector.

We believe a strong and thriving worker co-operative sector is likely to develop only if action is taken to tackle the problems and constraints outlined in this chapter. In the short term a crucial factor will be whether the movement can obtain more resources from the state, both to strengthen the support structure for co-operatives, particularly at regional and national levels, and for investment in co-operatives. In the longer term the co-operative movement must aim to develop a plurality of support for co-operatives. In particular it is vital that support organisations should encourage the formation of an integrated system of co-operatives which can help strengthen the sector economically and reinforce and sustain co-operative ideology.

For individual co-operatives, perhaps the most fundamental dilemma is finding the appropriate balance between the idealism needed to keep co-operative principles alive and the pragmatism needed to survive as a business. The challenge over the next decade will be to develop new relationships, structures and procedures both within and between co-operatives that enable them to grow and meet new commercial opportunities without undermining democratic control. As we have seen, there are some guidelines that can be followed, but frequently co-operatives will be charting new waters. Success will depend crucially on the ability to experiment, to keep an open mind and to learn from mistakes as well as from successes.

We hope that this book will contribute to this process.

References

Abell, P. (1977) 'Notes towards a definition of democratic organisation'. Paper for the Second World Conference on Participation and Self-Management, Paris.

Abell, P. (1983) 'The viability of industrial producer co-operation', in C. Crouch and F. Heller (eds), *International Yearbook of Organizational Democracy*. London: Wiley.

Abrahamsson, B. (1977) *Bureaucracy or Participation: The Logic of Organisation*. Beverly Hills, Calif., and London: Sage.

Alchian, A.A. and Demsetz, H. (1972) 'Production, information costs, and economic organisation', *American Economic Review*, 62: 777–95.

Aldrich, H. and Stern, R. (1983) 'Resource mobilization and the creation of US producers' co-operatives', *Economic and Industrial Democracy*, 4 (3): 371–406.

Averitt, R.T. (1968) *The Dual Economy*. New York: Norton.

Bachrach, P. and Baratz, M. (1963) 'Decisions and non-decisions: an analytical framework', *American Political Science Review*, 57: 641–51.

Bate, P. and Carter, N. (1986) 'The future for producers' co-operatives', *Industrial Relations Journal*, Spring: 57–70.

Batstone, E. (1983) 'Organization and orientation: a life cycle model of French co-operatives', *Economic and Industrial Democracy*, 4 (2): 139–61.

Bennett, J. (1984) *Producer Co-operatives: a Case for Market Protection*, Discussion Paper 11, Centre for Research in Industrial Democracy and Participation, University of Glasgow.

Bernstein P. (1976) *Workplace Democratization: Its Internal Dynamics*. New Jersey: Transaction Books; 1980 edn.

Birch, D. (1979) *The Job Generation Process*. Cambridge, Mass.: MIT Program on Neighborhood and Regional Change.

Birchall, J. (1987) *Save our Shop: The Fall and Rise of the Small Co-operative Store*. Manchester: Holyoake Books.

Blum, F. (1968) *Work and Community*. London: Routledge & Kegan Paul.

Bonner, A. (1961) *British Co-operation: The History, Principles and Organisation of the British Co-operative Movement*. Manchester: Co-operative Union.

Bradley, K. and Gelb, A. (1983) *Worker Capitalism: The New Industrial Relations*. London: Heinemann.

Braverman, H. (1974) *Labor and Monopoly Capital*. New York: Monthly Review Books.

Bray, J. and Falk, N. (1974) *Towards a Worker Managed Economy*. Fabian Tract 430. London: Fabian Society.

Brown, M. and Hoskins, D. (1986) 'Distributed leadership and skilled performance as successful organization in social movements', *Human Relations*, 39 (1): 65–79.

Burchall, S., Clubb, C. and Hopwood, A. (1985) 'Accounting in its social context: towards a history of value added', *Accounting, Organisations and Society*, 10: 381–413.

Burns, P. (1987) 'Financing the growing firm', in *Proceedings of the Tenth National Small Firms Policy and Research Conference*. Cranfield: Cranfield School of Management.

Cable, J. and Fitzroy, F. (1980) 'Co-operation and productivity: some evidence from West German experience', *Economic Analysis and Workers Management*, XIV: 163–80.

CAG (1984) *Marketing in Worker Co-operatives in the UK*. Co-operative Advisory Group, 272–276 Pentonville Road, London N1.

CAG (1986a) *The London Wholefood Sector: An Analysis and Support Strategy*. London: Co-operative Advisory Group.

CAG (1986b) *Greater London Council's Co-operative Development Policies 1981–86: An Evaluation*. London: Co-operative Advisory Group.

Campbell, A., Keen, C., Norman, G. and Oakeshott, R. (1977) *Worker-Owners: The Mondragon Achievement*. London: Anglo-German Foundation.

CDA (1980) *Co-ops: A Directory of Industrial and Service Co-operatives*. London: Co-operative Development Agency.

CDA (1982) *Co-ops: A Directory of Industrial and Service Co-operatives*. London: Co-operative Development Agency.

CDA (1984) *The New Co-operatives: A Directory and Resource Guide*. London: Co-operative Development Agency.

CDA (1986) *The National Directory of Co-operatives and Community Businesses*. London: Co-operative Development Agency.

CEI (1985) *The Impact of Local Enterprise Agencies in Great Britain*. London: Centre for Employment Initiatives.

Clark, D. and Guben, M. (1983) *Future Bread: How Retail Workers Ransomed Their Jobs and Lives*. Philadelphia: O and O Investment Fund.

Clark, P. and Wilson J. (1961) 'Incentive systems: a theory of organizations', *Administrative Science Quarterly*, 6: 129–66.

Clarke, T. (1979) 'The market constraints to self-management: the experience of a British workers' co-operative', in H.C. Jain (ed.), *Workers' Participation: Success and Problems*. New York: Praeger.

Coates, K. (ed.) (1976a) *The New Worker Co-operatives*. Nottingham: Spokesman Books.

Coates, K. (1976b) 'Some questions and some arguments', in K. Coates (ed.), *The New Worker Co-operatives*. Nottingham: Spokesman Books.

Cockburn, C. (1983) *Brothers*. London: Pluto Press.

Cole, G.D.H. (1925) *Life of Robert Owen*. London: Macmillan.

Cole, G.D.H. (1944) *A Century of Co-operation*. London: Allen & Unwin.

Commisso, E.H. (1979) *Workers' Control under Plan and Market: Implications of Yugoslavian Self-Management*. New Haven, Conn: Yale University Press.

Cornforth, C. (1981) *The Garment Co-operative*. Milton Keynes: Co-operatives Research Unit, Open University.

Cornforth, C. (1983) 'Some factors affecting the success or failure of worker co-operatives: a review of empirical research in the UK', *Economic and Industrial Democracy*, 14 (2): 163–90.

Cornforth, C. (1984) 'The role of local co-operative development agencies in promoting worker co-operatives', *Annals of Public and Co-operative Economy*, 3: 253–79.

Cornforth, C. (1987) 'Can entrepreneurship be institutionalized?', in *Proceedings of the Tenth National Small Firms Policy and Research Conference*. Cranfield: Cranfield School of Management.

Cornforth, C. (1988a) 'Lake School of English', in A. Thomas and J. Thornley (eds), *Co-ops to the Rescue*. London: ICOM Co-Publications.

Cornforth, C. (1988b) 'Worker co-operatives: temporary phenomenon or growing trend', in C. Lammers and G. Szell (eds), *Handbook of Participation in Organizations*. Oxford: Oxford University Press.

Cornforth, C. and Lewis, J. (1985) *The Role and Impact of Local Co-operative Support Organisations*. Milton Keynes: Co-operatives Research Unit, Open University.

Cornforth, C. and Stott, M. (1984) *A Co-operative Approach to Local Economic Development*. Milton Keynes: Co-operatives Research Unit, Open University.

Cornforth, C. and Thomas, A. (1980) 'A model of decision-making for worker co-operatives', in *Proceedings of the Fifth Co-operative Seminar*. Oxford: Plunkett Foundation of Co-operative Studies.

Coventry CDA (1984) *Coventry CDA 1983 Report*. Coventry Co-operative Development Agency, Unit 15, The Arches Industrial Estate, Coventry.

Curran, J. (1986) *Bolton Fifteen Years On: A Review and Analysis of Small Business Research in Britain 1971–1986*. London: Small Business Research Trust.

Curran, J. and Stanworth, J. (1986) 'A new look at job satisfaction in the small firm', in J. Curran, J. Stanworth and D. Watkins (eds), *The Survival of the Small Firm* Vol. 2: *Employment, Growth, Technology and Politics*. Aldershot: Gower.

Cyert, R. and March, J. (1963) *A Behavioural Theory of the Firm*. Englewood Cliffs, NJ: Prentice-Hall.

Defourney, J. (1982) *The Problem of Self-Financing in Workers' Co-operatives: A Survey*. Working paper. Liège: CIRIEC, University of Liège.

DTI (Department of Trade and Industry) (1987a) 'Lifespan of businesses registered for VAT, *British Business*, 3 April: 28–9.

DTI (1987b) 'Increase of 500 a week in businesses registered for VAT. Registrations and deregistrations for VAT: UK 1980–86', *British Business*, 31 July: 30–1.

Earle, J. (1986) *The Italian Co-operative Movement: A Portrait of the Lega Nazionale delle Co-operative e Mutue*. London: Allen & Unwin.

Eccles, T. (1981) *Under New Management*. London: Pan.

Ellerman, D. (1984) 'Workers' co-operatives: the question of legal structure', in R. Jackall and H. Levin (eds), *Worker Co-operatives in America*. Berkeley, Calif.: University of California Press.

Ellerman, D. (1988) 'Worker ownerships legislation in America', in E. Bayley and E. Parnell (eds), *Yearbook of Co-operative Enterprise*. Oxford: Plunkett Foundation of Co-operative Studies.

Etzioni A. (1961) *A Comparative Analysis of Complex Organisations*. New York: Free Press.

Evans, P. and Bartoleme, F. (1980) *Must Success Cost so Much?* London: Grant McIntyre.

Fairclough, M. (1986) 'Conditional degeneration and producer co-operatives: a reappraisal of the socialist tradition', in *Proceedings of the National Conference for Research on Worker Co-operatives*. Milton Keynes: Co-operatives Research Unit, Open University.

Fanning, C. and McCarthy T. (1986) 'A survey of economic hypotheses concerning the non-viability of labour-directed firms in capitalist economies', in S. Jansson and A.B. Hellmark (eds), *Labor-Owned Firms and Workers' Co-operatives*. Aldershot: Gower.

Fox, A. (1980) 'The meaning of work', in G. Esland and G. Salaman (eds), *The Politics of Work and Occupations*. Milton Keynes: Open University Press.

Freeman J. (1972) 'The tyranny of structurelessness', *Berkeley Journal of Sociology*, 17: 151–64.

Friedman, A. (1977) *Industry and Labour*. London: Macmillan.

Furubotn, E.G. and Pejovich, S. (1970) 'Property rights and the behaviour of the firm in a socialist state: the example of Yugoslavia', *Zeitschrift fur Nationalokonomie*, 30: 431–54.

Gallagher, C.C. and Stewart, H. (1986) 'Jobs and the business life-cycle in the UK', *Applied Economics*, 18: 875–900.

Ganguly P. (1983) 'Lifespan analysis of businesses in the UK 1973–82', *British Business*, 12 August: 837–45.

Ganguly, P. and Bannock, G. (1985) *UK Small Business Statistics and International Comparisons*. London: Harper Row/Small Business Research Trust.

GLC (1985) *London Industrial Strategy*. London: Greater London Council.

GLEB (1984) *A Strategy for Co-operation: Worker Co-ops in London*. London: Greater London Enterprise Board.

Goldthorpe, J., Lockwood, D., Bechhofer, F. and Platt, J. (1968) *The Affluent Worker: Industrial Attitudes and Behaviour*. Cambridge: Cambridge University Press.

Harris, M. (1985) 'Unionised self-management in London printing co-operatives'. MA thesis, Department of Industrial Relations, London School of Economics.

Hird, C. (1983) *Challenging the Figures*. London: Pluto Press.

Holyoake, G.J. (1906) *The History of Co-operation*, Vol. II. London: Fisher Unwin.

Homans, G. (1950) *The Human Group*. New York: Harcourt, Brace & World.

Horvat, B. (1982) *The Political Economy of Socialism: A Marxist Social Theory*. Oxford: Martin Robertson.

ICOM Training (1987) 'Futon company case study', in *Managing Change or Changing Management*. Leeds: Industrial Common Ownership Movement.

IPP (1987) *No Single Model: Participation, Organisation and Democracy in Larger Co-ops*. ICOM Pilot Programme Training Experience. Leeds: Industrial Common Ownership Movement.

Jay, P. (1980) 'The workers' co-operative economy', in A. Clayre (ed.), *The Political Economy of Co-operation and Participation*. Oxford: Oxford University Press.

Jefferis, K. and Thomas, A. (1987) 'Measuring the performance of worker co-operatives', in T. Hopper and D. Cooper (eds), *Critical Accounts*. London: Macmillan.

Jensen, M.C. and Meckling, W.H. (1979) 'Rights and production functions: an application? Labour managed firms and co-determination', *Journal of Business*, 52(4): 469–506.

Jones, B. (1894) *Co-operative Production*. Oxford: Clarendon Press.

Jones, D.C. (1975) 'British producer co-operatives and the views of the Webbs on participation and the ability to survive', *Annals of Public and Co-operative Economy*, 46: 23–44.

Jones, D.C. (1976) 'British producer co-operatives', in K. Coates (ed.), *The New Worker Co-operatives*. Nottingham: Spokesman Books.

Jones, D.C. (1982) 'British producer co-operatives, 1948–1968: productivity and organizational structure', in D.C. Jones and J. Svejnar (eds), *Participatory and Self-Managed Firms*. Lexington, Mass.: Lexington Books.

Jordan, J. (1986) 'A system of interdependent firms as a development strategy', in S. Jansson and A.B. Hellmark (eds), *Labor-Owned Firms and Workers' Co-operatives*. Aldershot: Gower.

Kimberley, J.R. and Miles R.H. (eds), (1980) *The Organizational Life Cycle.* San Francisco, Calif.: Jossey-Bass.

Kirkham, M. (1973) 'Industrial producer co-operation in Britain: three case studies', MA thesis, University of Sheffield.

Landry, C., Morley, D., Southwood, R. and Wright, P. (1985) *What a Way to Run A Railroad: An Analysis of Radical Failure.* London: Comedia.

Lichtenstein, P.M. (1986) 'The concept of the firm in the economic theory of alternative organisations: appraisal and reformulation', in S. Jansson and A.B. Hellmark (eds), *Labor-Owned Firms and Workers' Co-operatives.* Aldershot: Gower.

Lindenfeld, F. (1982) 'Worker co-operatives: remedy for plant closings?', in F. Lindenfeld and J. Rothschild-Whitt (eds), *Workplace Democracy and Social Change.* Boston, Mass.: Porter Sargent.

Lischeron, J. and Wall T. (1977) *Worker Participation: A Critique of the Literature and Some Fresh Evidence.* London: McGraw-Hill.

Lockett, M. (1980) 'Workers' co-operatives as an alternative organisational form: incorporation or transformation?', in G. Salaman (ed.), *International Yearbook of Organisation Studies.* London: Routledge & Kegan Paul.

Lord, S. (1986) 'Local co-operative development in London'. MBA thesis, Polytechnic of Central London.

Lukes, S. (1974) *Power: A Radical Approach.* London: Macmillan.

Macfarlarne, R. (1986) *Councils Support Co-ops.* CLES Report No. 2. Manchester: Centre for Local Economic Strategies.

Macfarlane, R. (1987a) *Collective Management under Growth: A Case Study of Suma Wholefoods.* Milton Keynes: Co-operatives Research Unit, Open University.

Macfarlarne, R. (1987b) *Politics, Race and Co-operative Development.* Milton Keynes: Co-operatives Research Unit, Open University.

Mahoney, N. and Taylor A. (1981) 'Help to worker co-operatives in Wandsworth', *Co-op Development News,* 7.

Mandel, E. (1975) 'Self-management dangers and possibilities', *International,* 2/3: 3–9.

Mansbridge, J. (1980) *Beyond Adversary Democracy.* Chicago: University of Chicago Press.

Marris, T. (1984) 'Worker co-operatives', *Accountants Digest,* 162.

Marx, K. (1966) *Capital.* Moscow: Progress Publishers.

McMonnies, D. (1984) *Trade Unions and Co-ops?: The Scott Bader Synthetic Resins Saga.* Occasional paper. Department of Political Theory and Institutions, University of Liverpool.

McMonnies, D. (1985a) *Trade Union Attitudes towards Worker Co-operatives: District Officers and Shop Stewards.* Occasional paper. Department of Political Theory and Institutions, University of Liverpool.

McMonnies, D. (1985b) *Co-op Workers' Attitudes Towards Trade Unions: A Merseyside Case Study.* Occasional paper. Department of Political Theory and Institutions, University of Liverpool.

McMonnies, D. (1985c) *Fine Fare Closures: USDAW and Worker Co-operatives.* Occasional paper. Department of Political Theory and Institutions, University of Liverpool.

Meade, J. (1972) 'The theory of labour managed firms and profit sharing', *Economic Journal,* 82, March: 402–28.

Meister, A. (1974) *La Participation dans les Associations.* Paris: Editions Ouvrières.

Meister, A. (1984) *Participation, Associations, Development and Change.* New Brunswick, NJ: Transaction Books.

Michels, R. (1949) *Political Parties: A Sociological Study of Oligarchical Tendencies of Modern Democracy*. New York: Free Press.

Milford, P. (1986) 'Worker co-operatives and consumer co-operatives: can they be combined?', in S. Jansson and A.B. Hellmark (eds), *Labor-Owned Firms and Workers' Co-operatives*. Aldershot: Gower.

Mintzberg, H. (1973) *The Nature of Managerial Work*. New York: Harper & Row.

Munro, C. (1987) 'The financing of worker co-operatives: a comparison with conventional businesses and evaluation of proposed mechanisms for investment'. MBA thesis, Polytechnic of Central London.

Mygind, N. (1986) 'From the Illyrian firm to the reality of self management', in S. Jansson and A.B. Hellmark (eds), *Labor-Owned Firms and Workers' Co-operatives*. Aldershot: Gower.

Nichols, T. (ed.) (1980) *Capital and Labour: Studies in the Capitalist Labour Process*. London: Athlone Press.

Oakeshott, R. (1978) *The Case for Workers' Co-ops*. London: Routledge & Kegan Paul.

Oliver, N. (1984) 'An examination of organizational commitment in six workers' co-operatives in Scotland', *Human Relations*, 37 (1): 29–46.

Oliver, N. (1986) 'Commitment in producer co-operatives: a perspective from the social psychology of organisations'. PhD thesis, Open University, Milton Keynes.

Oliver, N. (1987) *The Evolution of Recycles Ltd. 1977–1983*. Milton Keynes: Co-operatives Research Unit, Open University.

O'Mahoney, D. (1979) 'Labour-management and the Irish economy', *Journal of Irish Business and Administrative Research*, 1 (1): 16–41.

PA Management Consultants (1985) *Worker Co-operatives: Past, Present and Future*. Manchester: PA Management Consultants/Co-operative Bank.

Pateman, C. (1970) *Participation and Democratic Theory*. Cambridge: Cambridge University Press.

Paton, R. (1978a) *Fairblow Dynamics*. Milton Keynes: Co-operatives Research Unit, Open University.

Paton, R. (1978b) *Some Problems of Co-operative Organisation*. Milton Keynes: Co-operatives Research Unit, Open University.

Paton, R. et al (1987) *Analysis of the Experiences of and Problems Encountered by Worker Takeovers of Companies in Difficulty or Bankrupt*. Report to the Commission of the European Communities (Study No. 85/4).

Plumpton, B. (1988) *Oakleaf: The Story of a Radical Bookshop*. Milton Keynes: Co-operatives Research Unit, Open University.

Pollard, S. (1960) 'Nineteenth-century co-operation: from community building to shopkeeping', in A. Briggs and J. Saville (eds), *Essays in Labour History in Memory of G.D.H. Cole*. London: Macmillan.

Rainnie, A. (1984) 'Combined and uneven development in the clothing industry', *Capital and Class*, 22: 141–56.

Rainnie, A. (1985a) 'Small firms, big problems: the political economy of small businesses', *Capital and Class*, 25: 140–68.

Rainnie, A. (1985b) 'Is small beautiful? Industrial relations in small clothing firms', *Sociology*, 19 (2): 213–24.

Randall, R. (1988) *Better Meetings*. Milton Keynes: Community Education, Open University.

Robinson, M. (1988) 'Computer assisted meetings: modelling and mirroring in organisational systems', *EURINFO 88 – First European Conference on Information Technology for Organisational Systems*, Athens, May.

Robinson, M. and Paton, R. (1983) *Worker Information Systems and the Development of Large Co-operatives*. Working paper. Co-operatives Research Unit, Open University, Milton Keynes.

Rothschild-Whitt, J. (1976) 'Conditions facilitating participatory democratic organisation', *Sociological Inquiry*, 46: 75–86.

Rothschild-Whitt, J. (1979) 'The collectivist organisation: an alternative to rational bureaucratic models', *American Sociological Review*, 44: 509–27.

Russell, R. (1985) *Sharing Ownership in the Workplace*. Albany, NY: State University of New York Press.

Scott, M. (1982) 'Mythology and misplaced pessimism: the real failure record of new small businesses', in D. Watkins, J. Stanworth and A. Westrip (eds), *Stimulating Small Firms*. Aldershot: Gower.

Shirom, A. (1972) 'The industrial relations system of industrial co-operatives in the United States: 1890-1985', *Labour History*, Fall: 533–51.

Shutt, J. and Whittington R. (1987) 'Fragmentation strategies and the rise of small units: cases from the North West', *Regional Studies*, 21 (1): 13-23.

Spear, R. and Thomas, A. (eds) (1986) *P944 – Co-operative Working*. Milton Keynes: Community Education, Open University.

Stephen, F. (1984) *The Economic Analysis of Producers' Co-operatives*. London: Macmillan.

Stewart, H. and Gallagher, C.C. (1985) 'Business death and firm size in the UK', *International Small Business Journal*, 4 (1).

Storey, D.J. and Johnson, S. (1986) 'Job generation in Britain: a review of recent studies', *International Small Business Journal*, 4 (4): 29–54.

Storey, D.J., Keasey, K., Watson, R. and Wynarczyk, P. (1987) *The Performance of Small Firms*. London: Croom Helm.

Taylor, A. (1981) *Democratic Planning through Workers' Control*. London: Socialist Environment and Resources Association.

Taylor, A. (1983) *Worker Co-operatives: How Local Authorities Can Help*. London: ICOM Co-Publications.

Thibaut, J. and Kelley, H. (1959) *The Social Psychology of Groups*. New York: Wiley.

Thomas, A. (1988a) 'A Union Phoenix', in A. Thomas and J. Thornley (eds), *Co-ops to the Rescue*. London: ICOM Co-Publications.

Thomas, A. (1988b) 'An ordinary small supermarket', in A. Thomas and J. Thornley (eds), *Co-ops to the Rescue*. London: ICOM Co-Publications.

Thomas, A. and Thornley, J. (1988) *Co-ops to the Rescue*. London: ICOM Co-Publications.

Thomas, H. and Logan, C. (1982) *Mondragon: An Economic Analysis*. London: George Allen & Unwin.

Thornley, J. (1981) *Workers' Co-operatives: Jobs and Dreams*. London: Heinemann.

Thornley, J. (1983) 'Workers' co-operatives and trade unions: the Italian experience', *Economic and Industrial Democracy*, 4: 321–44.

Tomlinson, J. (1981) 'British politics and co-operatives', *Capital and Class*, 12: 58–65.

Tynan, E. (1980a) *Sunderlandia*. Milton Keynes: Co-operatives Research Unit, Open University.

Tynan, E. (1980b) *Unit 58*. Milton Keynes: Co-operatives Research Unit, Open University.

Tynan, E. (1984) 'Little women', in R. Paton et al. (eds), *Organisations: Cases, Issues and Concepts*. London: Harper & Row.

Tynan, E. and Thomas, A. (1981) *Careers of Activists in Workers' Co-operatives.* Working paper. Co-operatives Research Unit, Open University, Milton Keynes.

Tynan, E. and Thomas, A. (1984) *KME: Working in a Large Co-operative.* Milton Keynes: Co-operatives Research Unit, Open University.

Uglow, J. (1985) 'Unicorn: co-operative or mythical Beast?'. Unpublished study, Ruskin College, Oxford. Edited version to be published in A. Thomas and J. Thornley (eds), *Co-ops to the Rescue.* London: ICOM Co-Publications.

Vanek, J. (1970) *The General Theory of Labour-Managed Market Economies.* Ithaca, NY: Cornell University Press.

Vanek, J. (1971) *The Basic Theory of Financing of Participatory Firms.* Working paper 27. Department of Economics, Cornell University, Ithaca, NY. Reprinted in Vanek (1975).

Vanek, J. (ed.) (1975) *Self-Management: Economic Liberation of Man.* Harmondsworth: Penguin.

Wajcman, J. (1983) *Women in Control.* Milton Keynes: Open University Press.

Walsh, K. et al (1981) 'Power and advantage in organisations', *Organisation Studies*, 2 (2): 131–52.

Ward, B. (1958) 'The firm in Illyria: market syndicalism', *American Economic Review*, 48: 566–89.

Webb, S. and Webb, B. (1914) 'Co-operative production and profit sharing', *New Statesman* (special supplement).

Webb, S. and Webb, B. (1920) *A Constitution for the Socialist Commonwealth of Great Britain.* London: Longmans.

Webb, S. and Webb, B. (1921) *Consumers' Co-operative Movement.* Published by the authors.

Weber, M. (1968) *Economy and Society*, I, II, III, eds Gunther Roth and Claus Wittich. New York: Bedminster Press.

Weiner, H. with Oakeshott, R. (1987) *Worker Owners: Mondragon Revisited.* London: Anglo-German Foundation.

Wilson, N. (1982) 'Economic aspects of worker co-operatives in Britain: recent developments and some evidence', in *Proceedings of the Seventh Co-operative Seminar.* Oxford: Plunkett Foundation for Co-operative Studies.

WMCC (1983) *The Clothing Sector in the West Midlands: Structure, Policies and Problems.* Preliminary Report No. 3. Economic Development Unit, West Midlands County Council.

Woolham, J. (1987) *Wholegrain Foods and The Bean Shop.* Milton Keynes: Co-operatives Research Unit, Open University.

Young, M. and Rigge, M. (1983) *Revolution from Within: Co-operatives and Co-operation in British Industry.* London: Weidenfield & Nicolson.

Index

Abell, P. 17
Abrahamsson, B. 197
accountability
    of industry 1
    of management 143, 147–8, 150, 152-3, 170, 221
    of support organisations 20, 179, 226
agenda setting 149–50, 151
aims
    differences in 8
    educational 3, 7, 172
    political 158, 194
    social 3, 7, 105, 108, 112, 125, 132, 145, 158, 172
    see also objectives
'alternative' co-operatives 21, 25, 59, 76, 91, 197
    benefits 99, 101–3, 109–10
    conflicts of interest 158, 169
    job content 129–30, 131
    and management 134, 138, 140
    motivation for 9
    product choice 125
    recruitment policies 168–9
    technology choice 126
    wages 124
Amazon Press 57
    as shoestring start-up 68
assets, net 45–6, 213
    clothing industry 50, 52, 54, 64
    printing industry 55–7
    wholefood co-operatives 61–2
attitudes to co-operatives
    centre parties 1, 4–5
    left-wing 1, 3–4, 16, 18–20, 122, 174–5, 218
    right-wing 1, 4, 218
audit 170–1, 222
AUEW 84
Averitt, R.T. 44

Bader, Ernest 17, 207
Bate, P. and Carter, N. 17
Batstone, E. 7, 135, 154, 198, 209
Bean Shop, The 74, 76, 100
    conflicts of interest 158
    management issues 138
    membership 121
    as radical marginal 69, 202

wages 124
benefits, of co-operative work 97–103, 107-10, 128–9, 156, 196–7, 204
    and control 101–3, 140, 205
    instrumental 98–9
    interrelationships of 103
    morai 100–1, 102, 108
    social 99–100, 108, 202
'Benn' co-operatives 18, 20, 25, 30, 180, 183
Benn, Tony 18
Bernstein, P. 151, 165, 197–8
Birch, D. 30
Bonner, A. 11
book retailing
    co-operatives in 18, 26, 38, 72–3, 76
    product choice 125
    see also Oakleaf Books
Braverman, H. 116
Brent CDA 174
Brown, Jim 136
Bryon, William 11
building co-operatives, survival rates 36, 38
Burchall, S. *et al.* 46

Cable, J. and Fitzroy, F. 90
CAG 59, 186–7
capital accounts, members' 214–15
capital, return on 46–7
    limited 3, 5, 172, 212–15
capitalism, challenge from co-operatives 4
case studies 7, 21, 68–92
catering, co-operatives in 26, 38, 74–6
Christian Socialism 13–14
Clarke, Kenneth 4
Clarke, P. and Wilson, J. 98, 99–100
Clarke, T. 166
cleaning, co-operatives in 26
Clothing Co-op, The 69, 87, 90–1, 98–9, 102
    conflict of interests 86, 159, 169
    job content 129
    management issues 149, 152, 219
    supervision 129
clothing manufacture
    CMT firms 26, 49, 51–2, 54, 64–6, 73–4, 76, 86
    co-operatives in 19, 26, 38, 187

costs 104
  job content 129
  performance 48–54, 64–6, 90, 194
  supervision 129
  survival rates 36, 48, 73–4
  small firms in 45, 224
  technology in 126
co-operation, with other co-operatives 3, 172, 191, 220, 222–3
co-operative
  capitalised 68–71, 83–8, 89–90, 92
  complex, and management 142–6, 152, 154, 203
  definition 3
  as dynamic 7, 193, 200, 205
  as non-homogeneous 8–10, 193, 196
  origins 1, 10–17, 29
  radical 9–10
  simple, and management 138–42
  strengthening 210–27
co-operative development agencies (CDAs) 19, 29, 73, 74–6, 83–4, 87, 92, 175, 178–82, 225–6
Co-operative Development Agency (CDA) 19–21, 187, 192, 214–15, 225
Co-operative Productive Federation (CPF) 15
co-operative support organisations (CSOs) 6, 9, 19–21, 28, 43, 148, 172, 173–4, 199–200, 210, 227
  background 174–6
  control and accountability 177–9
  developing new-starts 180–1, 212
  development work 36, 181–3, 220, 223, 224–6
  and existing co-operatives 185
  funding 176–7, 225–6
  grant and loan schemes 178, 187–89, 191
  and job creation 180, 185, 189–90
  marketing 186–7
  obtaining premises 186
  promotion of co-operatives 5, 180
  and rescue co-operatives 183–4
  strengthening of 190–2
  and survival rates 35–7, 39
  training courses 184–5, 191–2, 220, 224–5
Co-operative Union 14

Co-operative Wholesale Society 15, 16–17
co-partnerships, co-operative 16–17, 20, 25, 45, 48–52, 64
Cockburn, C. 56
Commisso, E.H. 117
commitment
  and equity participation 42
  political 58–9, 65, 72–3, 76, 90, 98, 100–1
  worker 84, 100, 108, 110-11, 113, 128, 161, 169, 222
    as asset 90, 93–5
Companies Act (1988) 3, 216
'competence' gap 152
conflict, industrial 1, 4–5
conflict, of interests 5, 106, 144–5, 157–63, 188, 208, 221–2
  dynamics of conflict 162–3
  facilitating conflict 163–4
  grievance procedures 164–5
  over objectives 158–9
  personality clashes 159–60
  recruitment and training 168–70
  in work orientation 160–1
Conservative Party, policies towards co-operatives 20
constraints 6–7, 19, 44, 58, 88–92, 111, 112, 116–17, 194, 205
  see also dependency; financing
consumer co-operatives 10, 14–16, 117–18
content of job, control over 73, 129–32, 198
control, democratic 14, 20, 90, 95–6, 133, 172, 197–8, 212
  and benefits of co-operative working 101–3, 110–11, 221
  constraints on 6–7, 110, 115–20
  as defining feature 3–4
  loss of, *see* 'degeneration'
  as motivation for co-operatives 10
  see also investment, control over; management; product choice; technology, control of; wages, control over
conversion co-operatives 29, 58, 71, 78, 151, 152, 154, 220
costs, transaction 140, 154, 208

costs, of co-operative working 99, 101, 103–10, 128, 196
  instrumental 104–5, 140–1
  intrinsic 104
  and problems of activists 22, 106–7, 148, 197
  social and control 105–6
Coventry CDA 184
credit control, need for 84
culture, alternative 17–19, 59, 109–10, 140, 227
Curran, J. 26
Curran, J. and Stanworth, J. 95, 196
Cycle Co-op, The 74, 77
  as marginal 69, 203
  recruitment policies 168

data, collection 7, 21–2, 30–7, 48, 174
debentures 80, 83, 188, 217
decision-making 105, 106–8, 122–7, 138–39, 162
  control of agenda 151–2
  majority 141, 145, 161, 162, 221
  methods 140–4, 164
  see also management
'degeneration'
  of early co-operatives 13, 16
  of modern co-operatives 7, 101, 112–20, 203, 209
    combined perspective on 119–20
    constitutional 113, 114–15, 132, 154, 197
    goal 113–14, 115
      avoiding 122–7, 154, 159, 171–2, 197
    Marxist theories of 115–17
    organisational 114–15, 117–19, 133, 135, 143, 154, 197–200
      avoiding 127–32
Demintry (Democratic Integration of Industry) 17
democracy, representative 134–5, 223
democratisation of co-operatives 135, 148–52, 165
dependency, as constraint on co-operatives 64, 66, 87, 89, 117, 124, 202, 224
development work
  bottom-up 181–2, 190
  top-down 13, 148, 181–2, 212

differentials, pay 99, 123–4, 133, 219–20
discipline
  control over 128–9, 136–7, 160, 221
    possible lack of 77, 90, 91, 105–6, 117–18
distribution of co-operatives 26–8, 36, 38–9, 48, 194
dividend, early payments of 12–13
'dual structure' co-operatives 135, 148, 151, 154, 155, 169, 203
Dun & Bradstreet organisation 30–1

Eccles, T. 166, 167
Economic Development Unit (EDU) 176
efficiency 41–3, 45–7, 64, 113, 130, 146, 154, 172
  clothing industry 50–2
  and members' interests 156
  wholefood co-operatives 60–2, 64
élites, domination by 118, 127, 133, 135, 137, 140–3, 145, 197, 221
Ellerman, D. 215–16
employment
  conditions, control over 72, 127–8, 212
  creation of 1, 4, 25, 108, 180, 185, 189–90, 208
employment, part-time 73, 98, 127
'endowed' co-operatives 8–9, 25, 29, 95, 207
  and management 148
Engineering Co-op 69, 83–4, 98, 99, 102
  as instrumental co-operative 203
  management issues 49–51
engineering co-operatives 26, 38, 84–5, 87, 90
  job content 129
enterprise agencies 35–6, 39, 178, 181, 185
Enterprise Allowances 35–6, 39, 85
entrepreneurship, possible lack of 17, 91, 109, 137, 196–7, 200, 211–12
equilibrium approach 43, 194
equity participation 42, 66, 89, 215–16
Etzioni, A. 98, 100, 111
European Social Fund 85, 176, 185, 191
exchange theory 95–6, 98, 103, 111, 196
exploitation collective 68, 194–5
extent of co-operatives 24–30

Fabian Society 16, 113
Fabric Design Co-operative (FDC) 69, .
    75, 77
failure rates 30–9, 117–18, 189–90, 205–7
Finance Act (1986) 214
financing of co-operatives 28, 41–4,
    64–6, 76–81, 83–7, 88–9, 92, 183,
    187–89, 200
        clothing industry 50, 52, 53–4,
        64–5, 66, 86
        constraints on 19, 64–6, 120, 210,
        212–15
        printing industry 55–8, 65
        under-capitalisation 18, 88, 187,
        194–5, 202, 225–6
        wholefood co-operatives 60–4
        see also grants, external; invest-
        ment; loans, external
food, co-operatives for 10
    see also wholefoods, co-operatives in
footwear, co-operatives in 48, 52, 64
formation rate 25, 29, 193, 210, 211–12
Fox, A. 197
France, co-operatives in 1, 211, 224
Freeman, J. 140–1
furnishings, co-operatives in 48

Gallagher, C.C. and Stewart, H. 31
Ganguly, P. 30–1
gearing, high 47, 52, 65, 88, 213–15
gender, conflict over 161
        Goldthorpe, J. *et al.* 98
government, local
    and CSOs 174, 177–9, 188, 190, 216, 226
Grand National Consolidated Trade
    Union 11–12
Grand National Moral Union of Useful
    and Productive Classes 11
grants, external 72, 75, 187–89, 191
Greater London Enterprise Board 21,
    174, 176, 178, 187, 188, 191
    Co-operatives Unit 174, 176, 191
grievance procedures 164–5, 221
growth 1, 26, 30–2, 35–9, 65, 92, 174,
    210–11, 227
        limits to 222–3

Hackney Co-operative Developments
    186
Happy Hands clothing co-operative

employment conditions 127
    job content 129
    management issues 138
    as marginal 69, 202, 206
    membership 121
    performance 53–4
    product choice 124
    as shoestring start-up 68, 73–4, 76
hierarchy, in co-operatives 106, 113–14,
    131, 134–5, 140–2
Honeysuckle, wholefood co-operative
    62–3
Horvat, B. 200
hours of work, flexible 127–8

idealism 103, 108, 110, 113
induction, of new worker 169–70, 222
Industrial Common Ownership Act
    (1976) 18, 21, 30
Industrial Common Ownership Finance
    (ICOF) 18, 73–4, 77–8, 82, 84, 176,
    191, 217–18
Industrial Common Ownership Move-
    ment (ICOM) 17–18, 20–1, 30, 176,
    192, 217, 225–6
        London 32, 176, 192
        model rules 18, 20–1, 60, 78, 115,
        121, 216
industrial conflict 1, 4–5
Industrial and Provident Societies Act
    (1852) 3, 14, 114, 214–15
information, management 77, 80, 84,
    113, 138, 151, 152–3, 221
'instrumentals' 203, 206, 207
interests, members' 5, 154–72
    individual/collective 156, 163
    and management 155–6
    minority 156, 163, 164, 221
    promotion of 163–71
    see also conflict, of interests
International Co-operative Alliance 3
investment
        control over 14–15, 122–3
        social 204
        see also surplus, reinvestment of
Italy, co-operatives in 1, 184, 211–12,
    223–4, 226

Jefferis, K. and Thomas, A. 46
job satisfaction 93–6, 98, 196–7, 203

job-creation co-operatives
 and benefits of co-operative working 99, 102, 110
 clothing industry 49
 conflicts of interest 160
 and management 138, 219
 motivation for 9, 15
 recruitment policies 168
 start-up 25, 76, 98
 support for 19, 180–1, 227
 wages 124
Jones, D.C. 5, 7, 118

key worker system 131
King, William 11
Kirkby Manufacturing and Engineering
 (KME) 166–7
Kirkham, M. 118

La Fontaine 69, 75–6, 77
labour
 division of 114, 129–32, 134, 140
 return to 46–7, 93, 194
Labour Party, policies towards co-
 operatives 18, 19–21, 174, 218
labour process theory 44, 114, 116, 155,
 197–8, 208
Lake School of English 69, 80–1, 82–3
 benefits of co-operative working
  99–102, 109
 investment 123
 job content 131, 136
 management issues 81, 138, 139,
  153, 203
 membership 121
 working costs 105, 109
Landry, C. *et al.* 141
leadership 146–8
legislation 216, 224–5
Lichtenstein, P.M. 43, 194
life-cycles, projected 205–6
liquidity
 clothing industry 50, 52, 54
 printing industry 55–6, 58
 wholefood co-operatives 61–2
Lischeron, J. and Wall, T. 94–5, 110, 196
Lithosphere co-operative 57, 58, 71
loans
 external 65–6, 68, 77, 82, 85, 87,
  88–9, 187–89, 191, 195, 225

clothing industry 50, 52, 54, 66
 printing industry 55–8
 proposals for 213–18
 wholefood co-operatives 61–2
 internal 42, 54, 213-14, 217
 revolving 188
local government
 and CSOs 174, 177–79, 188, 190,
  216, 226
location 72
London Co-operative Enterprise Board
 (LCEB) 81, 82, 192
London Co-operative Training (LCT)
 176, 179, 191–2
London Industrial Strategy (LIS) 21,
 175–6
Lord, S. 186, 187

Macfarlane, R. 68, 174–5, 182
McMonnies, D. 166
management
 for change 136, 137–8, 146–8
 complex collectives 142–6, 152,
  154, 203
 co-operative 5, 134–54, 155, 161,
  198, 203, 208, 219–20
  theories of 134–5
 financial 77, 79–80, 84, 218–19
 leadership and initiative 106, 110,
  137–8, 146–8
 maintenance 136–7, 138–46
 need for skills 78, 82–4, 87, 91–2,
  137, 194, 196, 207, 210, 218–19
 new role of 151, 152–3, 169
 simple collectives 138–42
 and supervision 128
managers, external 87, 91, 219–20
Mandel, E. 116
Mansbridge, J. 162
manufacturing, co-operatives in 26, 35,
 38
marginals
 commercial 58, 64–5, 68–9, 70,
  71–7, 89–92, 205–6
 radical 202, 206–7
market entry, ease of 28, 52, 54–6, 224
marketing
 skills 77, 81, 82, 91, 218–19
 support for 186–7
Marketing Resource Centre 187, 192

Marris, T. 46
Marx, Karl 113
maternity allowances 128
Meade, J. 5
media, co-operatives in 26
meetings, general
    and conflict 163–4
    and management issues 144–5,
        149–50, 152–3
Meister, A. 7, 113, 118, 135, 198–9,
    203, 205, 208
membership
    external 215
    open 3, 115, 120–2, 172, 213
    see also interests, members'
Michels, R. 114, 118–19, 134, 139, 140,
    155–6, 197
Milford, P. 15
minorities, ethnic 75–6
Mondragon group 1, 5, 212, 214–16,
    217, 223
motivation
    for founding co-operatives 8–10,
        29, 75, 92, 148, 174, 196
    to co-operative work 43, 100
multi-skilling of workers 129–30
Munro, C. 216
Mygind, N. 7

National Building Guild 16–17
National Labour Management Agency
    173–4
National Network of Local Co-operative
    Development Agencies (NNLCDA)
    21, 188, 225
Neale, E.V. 14, 15
neo-classical economics
    and performance of co-operatives
        40–4, 194
    on self-management 4, 5, 7
'new wave' co-operatives 8, 11, 17–21,
    24–5, 183
'new-start, philanthropic' co-operatives
    9, 13
Nichols, T. 44, 116
Northern Region CDA 175
Northern Wholefood Collectives, Feder-
    ation of (FNWC) 78

Oakeshott, R. 5, 199, 215

Oakleaf Books 72–3, 76, 90
    conflicts of interest 158
    job content 131, 136–7
    management issues 138, 139
    product choice 125, 126
    as radical marginal 69, 202
objectives
    business 158–59, 170–1, 222
    political 202
    social 158–9, 170, 190, 194, 202,
        204, 206, 208, 222, 272
    see also aims, social
oligarchy, theory of 7, 118–19, 143, 155,
    197–8
Oliver, N. 95, 98, 196
opportunities, equal 56, 58, 156, 161,
    204, 208
orientation 96–7, 108, 112, 129, 150,
    196–7
    conflicting 160–1, 207
    control-seeking 97, 106, 110, 197,
        203, 207
    instrumental 43, 97–9, 103, 110–11,
        144, 197, 202–3, 207, 208
    moral 97–8, 100–1, 106, 110–11,
        197, 202–3, 207
    social 97, 100, 110, 202
Owen, Robert 7, 10–12, 13, 114
ownership
    common 3, 5, 17–19, 120, 156, 187
    individual 5

PA Management Consultants 89, 90–1
participation, worker 93–5, 118, 196–9,
    221
Pateman, C. 198
paternity allowances 128
'pathfinder' co-operatives 203, 207–8
Paton, R. 151
performance 30, 68, 70, 94, 193–6, 202,
    222
    clothing industry 48–54
    economic theories 40–7
    social 93–111, 197–9
        and organisation 112–33, 222
    variation in 52–4
personality clashes 159–60
personnel committees 169
'phoenix' co-operatives 9, 21, 29–30, 38,
    110, 219

as capitalised co-operatives 83
clothing industry 54, 65
development of 19, 183–4, 211
printing industry 58
self-developing 80
survival rates 36, 39
planning, long-term 222
Plumpton, B. 136–7
Pollard, S. 12
Potter, Beatrice 16
    see also Webb, Beatrice and Sydney
premises, obtaining 186, 210
Print Co-op, The (TPC) 57, 68, 69, 81,
    82, 92, 203
    benefits of co-operative working
        100, 101
    conflicts of interest 158
    costs of co-operative working 105
    job content 131
printing industry
    co-operatives in 18, 28, 48
        access to technology 81, 126,
            131
        costs 104
        performance 54–8, 64, 65–6, 90,
            194
        survival rates 38, 48
    small firms in 45, 54
privatisation, and formation of co-
    operatives 20–1, 212
producer co-operatives 14–17, 35, 38,
    114, 117–18
product choice, control over 124–6, 198
production control 91
productivity 1, 47, 64, 68, 84, 94, 194–6,
    203
    clothing industry 49, 50–1, 54, 65,
        71
    printing industry 55–8, 65
    and self-management 4–5
    wholefood co-operatives 62, 65
profit-sharing 14, 15–16
profitability, as measure of efficiency
    45–7, 52, 76
promotion, of co-operatives 180
publishing, co-operatives in 48

Rainnie, A. 45, 48–9
recruitment practices, and conflict of
    interests 168–9

Recycles 69, 77–8, 82, 92
    conflicts of interest 158
    employment conditions 128
    management issues 138, 139, 140–1,
        203
    membership 121
    product choice 125–6
    recruitment policies 168–9
Red Dragon Stores 69, 85–6, 87, 102
    employment conditions 128
    job content 129
    product choice 125
    supervision 128
    wages 123
'redemptionist societies' 12
'regeneration' 7, 135, 143, 154, 198, 203,
    209
regions, support for co-operatives 175–6
relationships, wider 6
'rescue' co-operatives 9, 14, 20, 21, 25,
    29–30, 38, 68–71, 180, 200
    benefits of 98–9, 102–3, 110, 203
    as capitalised co-operatives 83,
        86–8, 89, 90, 92
    clothing industry 15, 49, 87
    conflicts of interest 160
    costs of 105
    development of 19, 183–4, 211–12,
        220
    job content 129
    and management 134, 148, 154, 219
    product choice 124–5
    survival rates 36, 39
    wages 123–4
research, earlier 5–6
resource allocation, control over 122–3
resources, return on 204–5, 208
retailing, co-operatives in 11, 26, 60–4,
    85–6
    clothing 48–9
    costs 104
    survival rates, 35, 38
review, personal 170–1, 221
rights, individual 164–5
Rochdale Co-operative Manufacturing
    Society 13
Rochdale Equitable Pioneers' Society
    12–13
rotation, job 81, 82, 101, 103, 129–32,
    133, 140, 144, 146

and management 136, 138–9, 143, 154
Rothschild-Whitt, J. 72, 168, 198, 206

satisfaction, job 93–6, 98, 196–7, 203
Scott Bader Commonwealth 6, 8, 17, 25, 29
Scott, M. 30
Scottish Co-operative Development Committee (SCDC) 77–8, 82, 175, 183, 187, 214, 217
Scottish Venture Capital Fund 217
sector, industrial 89–90, 95, 194, 200
selection, criteria for 107, 168, 222
self-audit 159, 170–1
self-developers, co-operatives 68–9, 70, 77–83, 89–92
self-interest, economic 96, 115
self-management, economic theory of 5, 7, 194
services, co-operatives in 19, 26–7
shareholding
    external 3, 13, 16, 20, 215, 223
        and control 14–15, 114–15, 132, 213, 216
    worker 214–16
'shoestring' co-operatives 68–82, 90, 92, 208
Shutt, J. and Whittington, R. 44
size 19, 26, 30, 38, 95, 189, 223
slack, concept of 204–5, 206–7
small businesses
    co-operatives as 44–5, 223–4
    co-operatives compared with 26, 33–8, 43, 68, 194, 210–11
socialism, guild 16–17
Spain, co-operatives in, *see* Mondragon group
specialisation 131–2
    increase in 81–2, 133, 138–39, 140, 145–6, 154
start-up, co-operative 68–71, 194
state, investment in co-operatives 174, 218, 224, 226, 227
Stephen, F. 43
stock control, need for 77, 80, 82, 91
stores, co-operative 11, 12, 14
Storey, D.J. *et al.* 38
stress, of management 107, 109
structurelessness 140–2

structures, new, proposed 214–16, 227
Suma Wholefoods, 60, 62–4, 68, 100
    benefits of co-operative working 100–2
    conflicts of interest 158, 162, 164–5
    costs of co-operative working 105
    employment conditions 128
    investment 123
    job rotation 130
    management issues 138, 141, 142–3, 145–6, 152–3
    membership 121
    product choice 125
    recruitment practices 169
    as self-developing co-operative 69, 78–80, 82–3, 203
    supervision 128
    technology choice 126
    wages 124
supervision, control over 90, 128–9, 136–7, 138
support, *see* so-operative support organisations (CSOs)
surplus
    equitable distribution of 3, 12, 213
    reinvestment of 51, 65–6, 74, 77, 89, 122–3, 194–6, 204–8, 214
        early co-operatives 14–15
        and individual incomes 41–3
        printing industry 56
        wholefoods 54, 64, 79, 123
survival rate 30–9, 48, 118, 193–4
'sweat equity' 64–5, 68, 72, 77, 83, 132, 161, 195, 204, 207

Taylor, A. 29
technology, control of 126, 198
technology, new, in printing industry 54, 131
textile industry 48–9
TGWU (Transport and General Workers' Union) 167
Thornley, J. 4, 5, 166, 199
Tomlinson, J. 4, 116–17
trade unions
    in clothing industry 49
    and development of co-operatives 183, 211–12, 221
    and early co-operative movement 11–12, 14, 15–17

in printing industry 56
reduction of power 5
role in conflict 165–8
training
    and conflict of interests 168
    management 151, 219–20
    services 91, 101, 184–5, 191–2
    workers 169–70, 176, 204
trust, employee 214–15
trustees, external 165
turnover
    staff 78, 81, 144, 206
    stock 72, 79
Tynan, E. and Thomas, A. 96, 101, 107, 150, 167
typologies, of co-operative 7–10, 29, 201–3

Union Phoenix 69, 84–5, 177
    conflict of interests 166–7
    product choice 125
    wages 124
Union of Shop, Distributive and Allied Workers (USDAW) 60, 85, 87

value added
    clothing industry 50–2, 54
    as measure of efficiency 46–7, 64, 83, 123, 171, 194–5
    printing industry 55–8
    wholefood co-operatives 60–4
Vanek, Jaroslav 5, 40–3, 46, 51, 64–6, 88, 127, 173, 194–7, 199, 207

wages
    book retailing 72
    catering co-operatives 76
    clothing co-operatives 50–1, 53–4, 65, 68, 71, 73–4, 76, 86
    control over 42, 123–4
    engineering 85
    and instrumental benefits 98–9
    printing industry 55–8, 65, 68, 81, 105
    shoestring co-operatives 71, 73–4, 76, 79, 81, 82–3
    wholefood co-operatives 60–2, 64, 65, 79, 105

Wales Co-operative Centre 21, 84, 175, 187
Wales Co-operative Consortium 187
Ward, B. 5, 40–1
wealth creation, measurement 45–8
Webb, Beatrice and Sydney 7, 16, 91, 113, 117–18
Welsh Development Agency 84–5
West Indian Catering Co-operative (WICC) 69, 74–5, 76, 90, 101–2
    working costs 105, 109
West Midlands Common Ownership Finance (WMCOF) 176
West Midlands Enterprise Board (WMEB) 176
wholefoods, co-operatives in 18, 26, 38, 48, 98
    benefits of working in 100
    performance 45, 59–64, 65–6, 82, 90, 194
    product choice 125
    survival rates 35, 48, 74, 76
Wholegrain Foods 62–3, 68, 80, 82, 100
    conflicts of interest 69, 151, 158–60
    as instrumental co-operative 203
    investment 123
    job content 130–1
    management issues 142, 143–5, 147
    membership 121
    product choice 125
    recruitment policies 168
    wages 124
wholesaling, co-operatives in 48, 60–2, 64, 65
Wilshaw Rainwear clothing co-operative, performance 53–4, 87
WMCC 49, 52
women, access to printing technology 81, 126
Worker Co-operative Database, London ICOM 32
workers, skills 90
    see also multi-skilling
workers' control movement 9–10
working hours 73, 98
workshops, co-operative 13–14

Yugoslavia, co-operatives in 40